SCHOOLS
ON TRIAL

SCHOOLS ON TRIAL

How Freedom and
Creativity Can Fix Our
Educational Malpractice

NIKHIL GOYAL

Doubleday

New York   London   Toronto   Sydney   Auckland

www.doubleday.com

DOUBLEDAY and the portrayal of an anchor with a dolphin are
registered trademarks of Penguin Random House LLC.

Book design by Maria Carella
Jacket design by Emily Mahon

Library of Congress Cataloging-in-Publication Data
Names: Goyal, Nikhil, author.
Title: Schools on trial : how freedom and creativity can fix our
    educational malpractice / by Nikhil Goyal.
Description: New York : Doubleday, an Imprint of Penguin Random
    House, [2016]
Identifiers: LCCN 2015023598 ISBN 9780385540124 (hardcover)
    ISBN 9780385540131 (ebook)
Subjects: LCSH: Alternative education—United States. School
    improvement Programs—United States. School environment.
Classification: LCC LC46.4 .G69 2016 DDC 371.04—dc23 LC record
    available at http://lccn.loc.gov/2015023598

MANUFACTURED IN THE UNITED STATES OF AMERICA

10   9   8   7   6   5   4   3   2   1

First Edition

For Mom and Dad

How could youths better learn to live than by at once
trying the experiment of living?

—Henry David Thoreau

CONTENTS

Introduction

On most mornings, millions of young people depart from their homes and travel by cars and yellow buses to drab-looking, claustrophobic buildings. Here, they will be ware-housed for the next six to seven hours. Some are greeted by metal detectors and police officers, others by principals and teachers. In the hallways, security cameras keep tabs on them. Every forty minutes, they are shepherded from room to room at the sound of a bell. They sit in desks in rows with twenty to thirty other people of similar age, social class, and often race. They are drilled in facts and inculcated with specific attitudes and behaviors. They are motivated to par-ticipate in this game by numbers, letters, prizes, awards, and approval of various authority figures. If they get out of their seat, talk out of turn, or misbehave, they risk being drugged to induce passivity. Their day is preplanned for them. In a world of increasing complexity, there is little critical think-ing expected of them. To succeed, orders and rules must be followed. The fortunate ones have recess. During lunch, many have little choice but to consume unhealthy, unappetizing food. At the end of the day, they return home bone tired. There, they are forced to complete a few more hours of free labor, known as homework. They follow the almost exact same routine five days a week, 180 days a year, for thirteen years, until they are set free or begin another game called college with its own set of absurd rules.[1]

This is what is known as school for most children. If a sensible race of aliens paid a visit to our planet, they would think we are crazy. It still amazes me how most people don't find it particularly odd that you have this small subset of the population—people from ages five to eighteen—who are locked up in buildings for seven hours a day, while most of the rest of us are living and learning in the world.

During a visit to an alternative, progressive school, I remember someone once asking me, "So when did you realize this whole compulsory school system was bullshit?" There wasn't one specific moment or event that triggered my awakening. It was more of a gradual change in beliefs over some time.

In the summer of 2010, my family and I moved from Hicksville, New York, to Woodbury, a couple of towns over on Long Island. I transferred from the Bethpage to the Syosset schools, one of the highest-ranking and wealthiest school districts in the country. That fall, I enrolled as a sophomore at Syosset High School. There are more than two thousand students in the school. Almost three-quarters are white, about one-quarter is Asian, and just 4 percent are black and Latino.

Every school morning at 6:30 a.m., my alarm clock began to blare. After I mustered enough courage to crawl out of bed, I dragged myself into the bathroom to get ready, wolfed down my breakfast, and caught the bus. I usually plopped into a seat in the back and nursed my sleep-deprived self by dozing off for the next twenty minutes or so. Once I arrived at school, my way-too-energetic principal greeted me at the door. Then the social ostracism began. Each clique of each grade generally gathered in a different part of the building: the football players and cheerleaders near the science wing, some of the nerds in the student lobby trying to squeeze every last second of studying in before the bell. I trudged to my first-period class, like thousands of my fellow inmates—I mean students—while fluorescent lights beamed down on my half-closed eyelids.

For the next seven hours, it was as if I were on a conveyor belt. At each station (class), my head got filled with content. Every forty minutes I was told to stop what I was doing, get up, and find the next classroom that I would be imprisoned in, with a few minutes of rest in between if I was lucky. By the end of the nine-period exertion, I was mentally and physically drained.

Take a look at my sophomore year schedule:

7:39–8:19	Period 1: Physical Education/Investment Decision Making (on alternate days)
8:24–9:07	Period 2: Math Theory Honors
9:12–9:52	Period 3: Chemistry Honors
9:57–10:37	Period 4: Chemistry Lab/Science Research
10:42–11:22	Period 5: English 10 Honors
11:27–12:07	Period 6: Orchestra
12:12–12:52	Period 7: Advanced Placement European History
12:57–1:37	Period 8: Lunch
1:41–2:21	Period 9: Spanish 3 Honors

In the entirety of a seven-hour day, I had one forty-minute lunch break and five-minute "breaks" between periods, which were spent bolting to my next class. With the way the building was laid out, classrooms were often very far apart from one another.

In high school, I played the game. I got mostly A's and a few B's to set myself up in case I eventually wanted to have a shot at getting accepted into a prestigious college. And so I tolerated the endless drudgery of my classes. Unpleasant memories of my chemistry class, in particular, are still fresh in my mind. Our teacher would just lecture at us for most of the period, and we, the students, were supposed to copy down notes mindlessly. There was little interaction or engagement. And the exams were heavily recall based. Honestly, I couldn't tell you what I learned in that class, because I have forgotten it all. When we did laboratory exercises, it felt like a mockery. The labs were scripted. We were told to follow the precise directions given to us. We were penalized if we didn't get the "correct answer." The whole charade went against the most fundamental tenets of science: experimentation and failure.

In my English classes, we often received a reading assignment to complete that evening, and the next day, we were quizzed on the material. Five-question quizzes with each question worth twenty points. Some of the questions revolved around very trivial details: What was a character wearing? What time of day was it? It's almost as if my teachers were involved in a plot to help us develop a fervent hatred for reading. When I was younger, I would spend my days absorbed in novels and short stories, and I sometimes came up with my own. Being forced to read these books and be subjected to these meaningless tests are why I don't enjoy reading fiction today. I love reading nonfiction books about current affairs, however. Not coincidentally, I can't recall reading more than two or three nonfiction books in class throughout my thirteen years of schooling.

During writing assignments, I would get irritated when my teachers took points off my essays for the crime of not having the "proper five-paragraph format"—a lockstep approach to composition. After high school, I had no choice but to unlearn the silly rules and inflexible structures I was taught if I was ever going to become a skilled writer.

IN ADDITION TO the boredom and monotony of school, there was a hidden and unacknowledged mental health crisis that few teachers or administrators seemed to be aware of. Within a short time at the school, I couldn't help but notice what a wretched state my classmates were in.

I decided to conduct a little experiment. One morning, after I arrived at school, I stopped and observed hundreds of students walking into the building. I inspected their faces and postures. There wasn't a jubilant face to be found. (Well, duh. What human being would look forward to being caged in this hellhole for the next seven hours?) It appeared that some of them had gotten their only sleep on the ride to school (one study has found that nearly all American high school students are sleep deprived).[2] Others were hunched over, stressed out, buried in a textbook, or traumatized by what the day would bring them, from tests to peer pressure to bullying. Almost all of them would rather be somewhere else. And this was an elite public high school.

Syosset High School is much like many other prestigious, wealthy public high schools. A dog-eat-dog culture prevails, and a student's health, well-being, and happiness are tossed to the side. For the students who anticipate acceptance to an elite college (and that was a good chunk of the student body), consistently earning high marks, taking as many Advanced Placement (AP) courses as possible, and landing leadership positions in extracurricular activities was of great import. Some students did not schedule a lunch period so that they could squeeze in another AP class. But once the long grind of college applications came to a close in the middle of senior year, so did the students' effort to learn and excel. Because colleges wouldn't be closely examining their second-semester grades, they did as little work as possible in order to just scrape by in their classes.

I can't put it any better than education expert Alfie Kohn in his book *Feel-Bad Education*: "In some suburban schools, the curriculum is chock-full of rigorous Advanced Placement courses and the parking lot glitters with pricey SUVs, but one doesn't have to look hard to find students who are starving themselves, cutting themselves, or medicating themselves, as well as students who are taking out their frustrations on those who sit lower on the social food chain."[3]

I quickly picked up on the drug and alcohol culture entrenched in the high school. In the parking lot, students were habitually smoking cigarettes and marijuana in the morning before heading to first period. Students were also popping prescription drugs, such as Adderall and Ritalin, like mints to help them better concentrate in class and on tests. The pills were even sold on school grounds. (Talk about youth entrepreneurship.) There was one incident where a student was arrested for illegal possession of Xanax in school. On the weekends, underage drinking was common.

I admit that I had it much better than most children growing up in America. My school was well funded. I wasn't being taught by newly minted privileged college graduates who were looking for a "life-changing experience" before cashing in on a position in banking, consulting, or law. I had real, professionally trained teachers. I had access to librarians, nurses, and athletic trainers. There were more than adequate sports and extracurricular clubs. Indeed, the only tolerable and enjoyable parts of school for me were seeing my friends, running on the cross country and track teams, and competing in speech and debate.

But year after year, Syosset schools have been graduating classes of young people who are apathetic about humanity, conformists in their thinking, and hesitant to challenge the conventional wisdom. Students don't deserve the lion's share of blame—it isn't their fault that they were raised in a sanitized, privileged bubble of a community, shielded from poverty, mass incarceration, the war on drugs, police brutality, and environmental hazards.

When I raised my complaints about the school to my classmates, some agreed wholeheartedly, while others felt downright threatened by them: What right did I have, as a student, to question the holy education system? You are supposed to do as you are told. My classmates were "doing school," as Stanford Graduate School of Education senior lecturer Denise Pope has described it, where they were simply "going through the correct motions"—getting good grades solely to be admitted into a top college.[4] Meanwhile, they were passive, obedient, petrified of risk taking, and unable to entertain any doubts about their schooling. They were perfect sheep under the spell of a herd mentality.

At my school, guidance counselors routinely shoved students into AP courses, even if they were not prepared or had no interest in the subject. At Syosset, students forfeit graduation credit for an AP course if they fail to sit for the May exam. This was designed to shore up the student's college application, but more importantly to boost the school's position on the infamous *Newsweek* rankings of the "best" high schools in the country. In 2014, Syosset High School was ranked eighty-fourth nationally and sixteenth in the state of New York. What's outrageous is that the community's property values are directly influenced by such rankings, so there is economic pressure put on school officials to maintain or lift the school's position. None of this has anything to do with actual learning.

A HALF CENTURY ago, University of California, Berkeley, free speech student activist Mario Savio stood on the steps of Sproul Hall and delivered his most famous speech: "There's a time when the operation of the machine becomes so odious, makes you so sick at heart, that you can't take part. You can't even passively take part. And you've got to put your bodies upon the gears and upon the wheels, upon the levers, upon all the apparatus, and you've got to make it stop. And you've got to indicate to the people who run it, to the people who own it, that unless you're free, the machine will be prevented from working at all."

During my sophomore year, I decided I wasn't going to be a lackey to the school machine any longer. I wasn't going to be like the rest of my classmates. I wasn't going to sit quietly and do nothing while injustices were unfolding before my eyes each day. I began thinking to myself that there must be a better way to educate children—a way that didn't entail killing a part of yourself to succeed, to paraphrase the Indian philosopher Jiddu Krishnamurti.[5]

I started poring over countless books, articles, journals, and interviews on education reform. I reached out to teachers, students, parents, policymakers, and experts to glean their insights on the issue. I even skipped school to attend and speak at conferences and events. As someone who has been an autodidact—a self-directed learner—since I was very young, I followed Mark Twain's famous dictum: "I have never let my schooling interfere with my education."

In January 2013, I graduated from Syosset High School, six months early. I couldn't wait to be paroled. But don't ever call me a product of Syosset schools. I'm a bug in the system, a defect, a student who went terribly astray of the herd. I was supposed to complete my schooling without raising questions. I was supposed to knuckle under to authority. I was supposed to stay out of trouble. I've tried to become someone the founders of the American compulsory school system didn't ever want our schools to create—a freethinking human being.

Since my graduation, I've learned so much, traveled to amazing places, and met some remarkable people—I could never have dreamed of doing all this had I been in school for seven hours a day. When the month of September 2013 rolled around, it was the first time in thirteen years that I wasn't returning to school.

I had never felt more free and in control of my life.

ONE REASON I wanted to write this book was that I became very disenchanted with how the mainstream media reports on education issues. What they've done is frame the discussion in a polarizing fashion: Are you for or against charter schools, testing, Common Core standards, and teachers unions—pitting one side against the other. That completely neglects the more important issue: the anti-democratic and cruel nature of contemporary schooling itself. It's the elephant in the room that very few bother to address head-on.

In my view, any education journalist serious about the subject should first learn the actual history of schooling in this country, experience authentic learning environments, speak to actual young people, students, and teachers, and visit some alternative models of education before writing about the subject. With certain exceptions, few have. I did what most education writers embarrassingly fail to do: I listened to the kids. I went directly to the people most affected by the education system. And because of my youth, I was able to connect with them on a level that someone older might not have been able to. Over the past three years, I've been traveling around the country and spending time in all types of schools and learning communities. The experiences opened my eyes to the astonishing potential of what a sea change in education might look like. I've traveled from Chicago to the Mission District of San Francisco to the neighborhoods of Brooklyn. I've had the tremendous honor of meeting and speaking with scores of brilliant young people, teachers, parents, and administrators. They have given me optimism that change is in the chutes.

You probably will not have heard of most of the schools profiled in this book. Because they don't fall on the narrow spectrum of conventional education "reform," they have become invisible. Some observers consider these schools to be radical. Actually, what they're doing is normal. The students in these schools are learning in the same way human beings learned for thousands of years before compulsory schooling was invented—through play and self-directed learning. What traditional schools are doing is radical. Their students are learning (or trying or failing to learn) in environments that squelch talents and abilities and operate in a fashion opposed to the way the brain actually works.

My hope is that after reading, you will feel more outraged with the status quo than when you began and inspired to take action.

The ultimate goal of this book is to shine light on the most extraordinary models of learning around the nation, offer stories of people who have bypassed formal institutions in favor of self-education, present evidence that schools are exhausting the gifts of creativity, curiosity, and zeal that we all come into the world with, and make the case for why there should be no difference between living and learning.

In the first part of the book, I examine the problems with formal schooling, the history of public education in America, and the corporate education reform movement. Then, I profile the Brightworks school, a cutting-edge progressive school in San Francisco, and show why human beings are natural learners and the importance of play and unstructured learning in our lives. Next, I analyze the free school movement from the fabled Summerhill School in England in the early twentieth century to some present-day schools like Sudbury schools, Brooklyn Free School, and Philly Free School. I touch upon some of the unconventional elements of these schools, like democratic meetings, the judicial process, and absence of grades, tests, and required classes. Later, I look to the maker movement, which is tapping into the power of learning by doing and is one of the most powerful crusades in education today. Next, I examine avant-garde models of higher education, critique the vogue for online courses, and offer lessons from autodidacts who have not been dependent on formal institutions for education. And finally, I make the case for why cities and communities can be catalysts for bringing about a learning revolution.

Some of the core questions that will be addressed throughout the book are: What are the origins of American schools? Why are schools breeding grounds for bullying and violence? How did the concept of unstructured, unsupervised play as a mode of learning disappear? How can parents raise a self-directed learner? What types of schools produce happy, curious, fulfilled, and passionate adults? Conversely, what types of adults are our traditional schools actually producing? How can we revive our cities and communities so that they are places of engagement, collaboration, and problem solving?

For some of you, this book could be a bumpy ride. You might be taken off guard while reading some of the chapters. You might disagree passionately with my beliefs. But that's the point. I want to make you feel uncomfortable. I want to challenge you. I want to help you reconsider your opinions and become skeptical about everything you once thought you knew about schooling, education, and learning.

I don't expect my writing to change the system. But what I do hope is that you will begin questioning some of your assumptions. If you are a parent, perhaps next time your child comes home from school stressed about tests to the point of tears, feeling like a failure, emotionally damaged from shame, bullying, or harassment from students or teachers, telling you about how much he or she hates learning, or just begging not to go back tomorrow, you won't think he or she is lazy or crazy. You will listen and take their opinions and thoughts seriously.

In this book, I draw upon the work of pioneering thinkers, including John Holt, Jonathan Kozol, Maria Montessori, Alexander Sutherland Neill, Ivan Illich, John Taylor Gatto, Peter Gray, George Dennison, Paul Goodman, and many others. Some of the proposals and ideas advanced in this book are not particularly new. During the free school movement of the 1960s and '70s, they were widely endorsed, hashed out, and even implemented. The arguments presented are backed up by years of research and reporting. I don't have a hidden agenda. I try to be as direct and as forth-right as possible.

As author and mental health counselor Laurie A. Couture argues in her book *Instead of Medicating and Punishing,* "Historically, children have been and are still the most oppressed, exploited and victimized group of human beings on the planet. Children remain the most voiceless and the most discriminated against group of people in our culture. While every adult group in the United States has won basic human rights, protections and freedoms, children remain the only group of human beings without the same rights to equality, respect, protection from bodily harm and free-dom of speech."[6] The perpetual education wars make this issue seem more complicated than it is. In reality, it boils down to understanding that children deserve to be treated like human beings, like any other member of society. That they should not be inappropriately controlled, managed, and measured but given freedom and treated with dignity and respect. That isn't too much to ask.

We have become obsessed with making tweaks and small dents to the system when what we genuinely need is a total overhaul, a transformation, a goddamn revolution. It's time to break free from the shackles of our oppressive school system.

CHAPTER 1

The Radical Notion That Children Are People

To put it bluntly, conventional schooling is one of the most oppressive and antidemocratic institutions of modern times and, in the words of educator John Holt, "a crime against the human mind and spirit."[1] The system is the primary cause of students' unhappiness, boredom, apathy in learning, and diminishing levels of curiosity. The system is harmful. The system is culpable. However, what happens in nearly every instance is that instead of castigating the perpetrator of this crime, we—society—chide the victims. We blame the students for "refusing to be educated." We blame the millions of dropouts. We blame the misfits who weren't able to or refused to conform to the standards of conventional schooling. We blame the kids who goof off during class, the kids who don't shut up and sit down, the kids who don't pay attention, the kids who don't study enough, the kids who don't perform well on tests, the kids who don't finish their homework, and the kids who cut class or school altogether. This is demeaning and unacceptable when it is the institution of schooling that produces such attitudes and behaviors. In the

United States, according to the Department of Education, about 90 percent of students from prekindergarten through twelfth grade attend public schools. There are fifty million students at just under one hundred thousand schools.[2] It is a vast and failing system.

Some may interpret this as an attack on teachers. It's not. It's a critique of the education system, not the teaching profession or individual teachers or classrooms. In any case, as we'll see, educators have been terribly brutalized and failed by corporate education policies. We need to support teachers and their unions.

Every school day, on average, nearly seven thousand American students drop out of school. That tallies up to 1.2 million dropouts each year.[3] But here's the kicker: while many young people drop out due to family needs and the lack of parental engagement, a Civic Enterprises report titled "The Silent Epidemic: Perspectives of High School Dropouts" pointed to other factors. After interviewing hundreds of high school dropouts in twenty-five towns and cities with schools with high dropout rates, 81 percent said they would have probably not left school if their classes were more relevant to real life. Additionally, 88 percent of the dropouts actually had passing grades, with 62 percent earning C's and above.[4] As educator John Taylor Gatto once declared, "What does it say to us that a million and a quarter young people a year don't want to be in classrooms, don't want to be there so much they're willing to endure scorn, insult, and constant discrimination as the price of escape?"[5] These dropouts are sending an unequivocal message that their schools are failing them.

In 1909, Chicago factory inspector Helen Todd asked 500 children aged fourteen to sixteen who were working in twenty factories the question, "If your father had a good job and you didn't have to work, which would you rather do—go to school or work in a factory?" A staggering 412 out of 500 favored the latter. Some of the reasons offered: "Because you get paid for what you do in a factory." "The boss he never hits yer, er slaps yer face, er pulls yer ears, er makes yer stay in at recess." "What ye learn in school ain't no good." One fourteen-year-old girl, who toiled in a factory where they lacquered canes, enduring the foul odor of turpentine in an attic and debilitating heat from the cement furnace, responded to Todd by saying, "School is de fiercest t'ing youse kin come up against. Factories ain't no cinch, but schools is worst."[6]

In the 1980s, educator John I. Goodlad offered the question, "Why are our schools not places of joy?" A 2003 report by the U.S. Department of Health and Human Services on the health and well-being of American teenagers compared their counterparts in other countries and found that four out of five fifteen-year-old American students "like school only a little, not very much, or not at all." They were also some of the least likely students in the world to "feel that they participate in making rules at school" and "feel that their classmates are kind and helpful." This, unsurprisingly, has tragic effects. The report concludes, "Not only are students who feel unconnected [to school] more likely to abuse substances, engage in violence, and become pregnant, but they may be less likely to acquire developmental assets and to experience opportunities to demonstrate competence through increasing autonomy appropriate to their developmental stage."[7]

What's more, children are arguably more unhappy and dissatisfied in school than in any other place. In a 2003 study conducted by psychologists Mihaly Csikszentmihalyi and Jeremy Hunter, more than eight hundred students from thirty-three elementary and secondary schools in twelve communities wore programmable wristwatches that signaled eight times a day for a week. Once students heard the signal, they had to complete a form with questions about what they were doing, whom they were with, and their feelings and conditions at the moment. What the psychologists found was that some of the lowest happiness scores were associated with school activities, while the highest scores were associated with being with friends and leisure activities.[8] Other research from Purdue University professor Donald Felker reports that "the very nature of school is detrimental in its effect on children's self-image."[9] Most children enter kindergarten with lots of self-worth, but many exit their senior year of high school with almost none of that self-esteem left. And then there's the Gallup poll that shows that the more years a child attends school, the less engaged that child becomes. Engagement is defined by Gallup as "the involvement in and enthusiasm for school." They call this sharp drop in engagement a "school cliff."[10]

Dare I admit that some students actually enjoy school? Of course. But they're in the tiny minority. And many of them prefer going to school solely because they get to see their friends. There are also many students who suffer from Stockholm syndrome, a phenomenon in which a hostage shows an emotional bond or sympathy toward his or her captor. It's often the case, in my experience, that the students who are academically competitive, in several Advanced Placement courses, or have the highest grades are the staunchest defenders of this inhumane system. They're essentially saying, "We prefer being controlled. We prefer having our rights violated."

One afternoon, I was watching the great film *The Shawshank Redemption,* and a particular scene caught my eye. Andy Dufresne, one of the inmates, began blaring the "Letter Duet" from Mozart's *The Marriage of Figaro* on the record player over the loudspeaker at the Shawshank State Prison. At once, everyone in the prison, guards and inmates alike, stopped dead in his tracks and did nothing but stare at the loudspeakers and listen with full attention to the opera music for a few minutes until some guards managed to shut it off. Red, one of Andy's friends at the prison, said, "It was like some beautiful bird flapped into our drab little cage and made those walls dissolve away, and for the briefest of moments, every last man at Shawshank felt free."

This image reminded me of what happened every Friday during high school. Between periods, my school's student government would blast pop music over the loudspeakers. It was intended to cheer up the students and make their day a little better. Like in the film, it was really meant to make them forget for a few minutes that they are confined in a place where they feel miserable and bored most of the time and have very few freedoms and rights and no control over what they are doing or what happens to them.

In both prisons and schools, you are cut off from the rest of society, stripped of your basic freedoms and rights, like free speech and free press, told what to do all day, and surveilled dragnet style. In general, both designs are strikingly similar. One of the few differences between schools and prisons is that in school you're booked and then set free at the same times each day.

Psychologist Robert Epstein, with his colleague psychologist Diane Dumas, asked teenagers, U.S. Marines on active duty, noninstitutionalized adults, and incarcerated felons to fill out a checklist of restrictions that applied to them. The results were staggering. They found that "teens are indeed subjected to more than ten times as many restrictions as are mainstream adults and to twice as many restrictions as are incarcerated felons and active-duty U.S. Marines."[11]

Much of the hell children go through in school would not be tolerated by any adult. The irony is that adults continue to subject children to the conditions and rituals they once despised when they were in school. In most schools, students cannot chew gum. They cannot wear hats in the building. They cannot use their cell phones or other electronic devices. They cannot use the bathroom without permission and a hall pass. They cannot wear clothing that is considered disruptive or inappropriate—they must obey a sexist dress code. They can't go anywhere in the school without being surveilled and monitored by cameras, security guards, and, increasingly, behavior-tracking apps and technologies. And in some urban schools, they cannot enter without first being screened by a metal detector.

Beyond the foolish and restrictive rules students have to abide by, there's also the intrusion into their privacy, violation of their civil liberties, corporal punishment (legal in nineteen states), forced confinement, age segregation, required classes and tests, and a burdensome amount of homework.

By sitting in desks in rows, following orders, competing for grades, and being punished for talking out of turn, students are learning the "hidden curriculum"—the unspoken values, behaviors, and attitudes instilled in students in school. Neil Postman and Charles Weingartner, in their wonderful book *Teaching as a Subversive Activity,* offered many of the curriculum's tenets:

- Passive acceptance is a more desirable response to ideas than active criticism.
- Discovering knowledge is beyond the power of students, and is, in any case, none of their business.
- Recall is the highest form of intellectual achievement,

and the collection of unrelated "facts" is the goal of education.

• The voice of authority is to be trusted and valued more than independent judgment.

• One's own ideas and those of one's classmates are inconsequential.

• Feelings are irrelevant in education.

• There is always a single, unambiguous Right Answer to a question.

• English is not History and History is not Science and Science is not Art and Art is not Music, and Art and Music are minor subjects and English, History, and Science major subjects, and a subject is something you "take" and, when you have taken it, you have "had" it, and if you have "had" it, you are immune and need not take it again. (The Vaccination Theory of Education?)[12]

SCHOOLS HAVE ALSO committed systemic human rights abuses. The following are some of the articles in the Geneva Conventions, the rules concerning the treatment of captured or wounded soldiers in war:

Article 13: Prisoners of war must at all times be humanely treated. . . . Likewise, prisoners of war must at all times be protected, particularly against acts of violence or intimidation and against insults and public curiosity.

Article 17: No physical or mental torture, nor any other form of coercion, may be inflicted on prisoners of war to secure from them information of any kind whatever. Prisoners of war who refuse to answer may not be threatened, insulted, or exposed to unpleasant or disadvantageous treatment of any kind.

Article 53: Prisoners of war must be allowed, in the middle of the day's work, a rest of not less than one hour.

Article 99: No moral or physical coercion may be exerted on a prisoner of war in order to induce him to admit himself guilty of the act of which he is accused.

No prisoner of war may be convicted without having had an opportunity to present his defence and the assistance of a qualified advocate or counsel.[13]

At least one, but more likely all, of these are violated in some shape or form in public schools every day: bullying and harassment by teachers and administrators, corporal punishment, limited or no time for recess or breaks, threats of suspension, expulsion, or punishment, and violation of due process rights. As filmmaker Cevin Soling put it in a talk at the Harvard Graduate School of Education, "If children could have declared themselves enemy combatants, public schools would be guilty of war crimes."[14]

The malign effects schooling has on students are often permanent and yet not visible on the surface. Simply put, school is harmful to their health and well-being. In the packet for kindergarten parent orientation, most schools should add a visible disclaimer: If you send your child to a traditional school, there are extremely high odds that he or she, by his or her high school graduation, will become depressed, stressed, suicidal, unethical, shamed, disrespected, and physically and verbally abused; have low self-esteem; suffer from an eating disorder; get hooked on a prescription drug; be bullied; become emotionally deprived, less curious, creative, and happy; internalize that they are worthless, stupid, and a failure; and/or come to detest learning. Is that a risk you are willing to take?

Rampant bullying is one of the most pernicious symptoms of this system. The following story of a victim of bullying may sound more extreme than others, but it is not an exception. Countless children face similar realities every single day. And these harrowing bullying stories will not stop making the rounds until we dismantle our toxic school environments.

THEY CALLED HIM "gay," "four eyes," "chubby," and "the loner."[15] They would take his notebook and draw profane images on it. They taunted him during lunchtime, when he was the most vulnerable, because he milled around by himself. They forced him to fork over his lunch money. In late 2008, Sam arrived in middle school in the San Francisco Bay Area to perpetual bullying and suffering. He was a sixth grader. He had recently moved from a nearby city. He didn't have any friends, which designated him as "fresh meat" for the bullies.

Sam was mostly picked on by those whom he deems "the gangster kids"—the ones who always misbehaved and wanted to cause trouble. One particular incident etched in his memory was when he was shoved to the ground and gum got stuck in his hair. His mother had to pick him up from school and clean off the muck. Another time he was in art class sitting next to a smug, pompous girl who despised him solely because he was known as "the weird kid" in school. She then intentionally gave him a paper cut. He remembers her saying, "Good, I'm glad you have a paper cut!" "It still boils my blood to this day," he says. A seemingly minor incident, it became a symbol of the bullying he suffered over the years.

Since Sam has Asperger's syndrome, he has always been more socially isolated. He doesn't like to approach and chat up people he doesn't know personally. In the classroom, which is tailored for extroverts, he has had an aversion toward group assignments.

Overall, the school did next to nothing to help with his transition to the new school, nor did they try to stop the physical and verbal harassment he dealt with regularly.

Norwegian researcher Dan Olweus has offered one of the most widely accepted definitions for bullying: "A student is being bullied or victimized when he or she is exposed, repeatedly and over time, to negative actions on the part of one or more other students."[16] In schools, this bullying can be from peers, teachers, administrators, or staff members.

The National Association of School Psychologists regards "bullying [as] the most common form of violence in our society."[17] Data from the federal government estimates that up to thirteen million American children are bullied each year, or nearly a third of all school-aged children.[18] With the ubiquity of social networking sites and texting, bullying can now extend into after-school hours. As journalist Emily Bazelon notes in her book, *Sticks and Stones,* "The depersonalized features of technology can exacerbate the cruelty, but its roots are in the real world rather than the virtual one."[19]

In the aftermath of the 1999 Columbine High School shootings, politicians rushed to pass anti-bullying laws. A report by the U.S. Department of Education found that between 1999 and 2010, "there were more than 120 bills enacted by state legislatures nationally that have either intro-duced or amended education or criminal statutes to address bullying and related behaviors in schools."[20] Every state has adopted anti-bullying legislation. As well-intentioned as these policies may be, they are ineffective and inappropriate. By many measures, they have done significantly more harm than good. Seokjin Jeong, a University of Texas at Arlington criminologist, and Byung Hyun Lee, a Michigan State University doctoral student in criminology, analyzed data from a study called Health Behavior in School-Aged Children 2005/2006 Survey, which included 7,001 children between the ages of twelve to eighteen in 195 schools. The pair of researchers found that students who attend schools with anti-bullying programs may be more likely to be vic-tims of bullying than students who go to schools without such programs. The programs can even offer bullies some new techniques on how to bully more effectively.[21]

Anti-bullying programs are based on the assumption that there is something intrinsically wrong with children and that their inclination to bully others is something that demands reforming by adults; if we somehow just teach them to be kinder to one another and to stop being bystand-ers when witnessing someone else being bullied, we'll solve the bullying issue in school. That couldn't be more wrong. Until the school environment is radically transformed, every anti-bullying initiative will fall flat. Virtually everyone who has commented on bullying in schools has committed a grave error by failing to draw the link between the design of schools—age segregation, prison-like atmosphere, authori-tarian governing structure, and deprivation of freedom and rights—to the acts of aggression. Our schools are veritable petri dishes for bullying behavior.

Later, we will see that bullying is nearly nonexistent in

schools where children have healthy and meaningful relationships with peers and teachers, are given an opportunity to participate in the governing body, and are allowed to exercise their right to express themselves freely. As Gever Tulley, founder of the Brightworks school in San Francisco, told me, "It's hard to bully someone you know so well."[22]

IF YOU WERE to place Sam on the social food chain of his middle school, he would be on the dead end. As journalist Alina Tugend put it in a piece for *The New York Times,* "Surveys estimate that about 20 percent of students in any school are highly liked, about 50 percent are average—having some friends, but not necessarily a lot—and the rest are considered neglected or rejected students. These are either ignored or actively disliked."[23] In almost every school, there are multiple cliques: the jocks, punks, preps, nerds, goths, stoners, band geeks, and outcasts, with some aspects or another of the infamous 2004 film *Mean Girls* brought to life. In order to be popular, you need some combination of good looks, athletic ability, and brand-name apparel. Students who don't measure up or conform are inevitably ostracized.

Researchers have discovered that as a student ascends the pecking order of school, his or her behavior often becomes more aggressive toward other kids. University of California, Davis, sociologists Robert Faris and Diane Felmlee, using data from the Context of Adolescent Substance Use study, analyzed the results from surveys taken by 3,722 eighth-, ninth-, and tenth-grade students at nineteen public schools in three counties in North Carolina. The students were asked to provide the names of up to five classmates they bullied and up to five who bullied them. They also had to characterize acts of aggression into one of three categories: physical attacks, direct verbal harassment, or indirect aggression. Ultimately, Faris and Felmlee conclude that the social hierarchy is critical in understanding bullying in school. At the 98th percentile of popularity, aggression hits its peak. The kids in the top 2 percent of the hierarchy are the least aggressive. There is no need for them to assert their status, since they are so well liked.[24]

Why is bullying so common in traditional schools? The first reason is the autocratic governing structure that shuts out the voices of the *incarcerated*. "Bullying," wrote Peter Gray, Boston College research professor of psychology, in his book *Free to Learn,* "occurs in all institutions where people who have no political power and are ruled in top-down fashion are required by law or economic necessity to remain in that setting. It occurs regularly, for example, in adult as well as juvenile prisons. Those who are bullied can't escape, and they have no legislative or judicial power to confront the bullies."[25] Most schools are run like totalitarian regimes. Up to roughly 94 percent of a school's population consists of students, with the rest teachers, administrators, guidance counselors, and staff.[26] So what you have is 6 percent of the population making decisions on behalf of the 94 percent without their consent. If that's not considered anti-democratic, I'm not sure what would be.

On top of which, most student governments or councils are a farce. They are simply forms of propaganda and deception designed to give the false impression that the administration listens to its students. As Dennis Littky, cofounder and codirector of Big Picture Learning, sardonically observed in a piece for *Horace,* the journal of the Coalition of Essential Schools, "Voting for homecoming queen does not prepare students for democracy."[27] In response to being powerless, students construct their own power structures in the form of cliques—structures to wield control over those who are "inferior" and don't fit in.

Second, school environments discourage the fostering of deep relationships and a larger sense of belonging. Out of the thirteen years most of us spend in school, we can usually only recount a handful of teachers we were genuinely attached to. Rarely do students and teachers have a reciprocal, nurturing relationship and get to know one another at a personal level. Instead, students are lost in a sea of anonymity with thousands of others, and over time, many end up accumulating pent-up anger, fear, and aggression, with nobody to turn to for help. Sociologist Robert Faris told *New York* magazine that whenever you have a "giant box of strangers" crammed together, such bullying incidents ensue.[28]

SAM ONCE HAD some lofty fantasies about creating an empire to take over the world, enslave his bullies and other classmates, and subjugate them in brutal conditions. "Oh, so you picked on me, what are you doing now? I run an oppressive regime. You can't do anything about it." At the time, he was trying to keep his mind off of school by studying dictatorships throughout history, like North Korea, the Soviet Union, and Nazi Germany. He admitted to me that "those were some wacky delusions."

As sixth grade rolled on and the bullying wouldn't let up for even a single day, Sam began feeling worthless and like he had nothing to live for. "I bottled up my emotions because I was scared to speak about it," he recalled. "I often ate less and didn't care what I was eating and felt as if the entire world was against me and that my destiny was to be damned and be sad forever." His grades plunged.

Because he didn't want to encounter his bullies, he faked

illnesses and often came home early from school. He skipped so many days that he received a warning from the school that if he continued to be truant, the police would make a visit to his home.

Sometime into the school year, he started drawing pictures of himself being killed and thought to himself, *Man, life is nothing but a pile of shit*. He also googled "how to kill yourself quickly and painlessly." On a few occasions, he got a kitchen knife and considered stabbing it through his stomach, but he fortunately wasn't able to go through with it.

According to the Centers for Disease Control and Prevention (CDC), suicide is the third leading cause of death for people between the ages of ten and twenty-four. Roughly 4,600 young people take their own lives each year.[29] In addition, the CDC's 2011 Youth Risk Behavior Surveillance survey revealed that about one in twelve high school students has attempted suicide and one in six has seriously considered it.[30]

Why are young people killing themselves in droves? Drug, alcohol, physical and sexual abuse, family dysfunction, depression, and academic pressure are the main causes. And school has a large part to play in this.

An October 2011 paper titled "Back to School Blues: Seasonality of Youth Suicide and the Academic Calendar" provides some insight. Benjamin Hansen, assistant professor of economics at the University of Oregon, and Matthew Lang, assistant professor of economics at Williams College of Business, Xavier University, were scrutinizing the effects of extending the length of the school year and came across some startling data on youth suicides. There was a sharp downswing in the number of youth suicides during the summer months of June, July, and August, which are also the months of summer vacation for schoolchildren. They also found that the nonsummer month with the lowest number of suicides is December, when students spend a week or more on break.

Perhaps this unusual shift could be explained by weather, unemployment, or seasonal affective disorder (SAD), Hansen and Lang hypothesized, but none of those theories panned out. Eventually, they studied the suicide rate for nineteen-year-olds, who are usually not enrolled in high school, during the summer, and concluded, "The fact that 15 to 18 year old suicide rates decrease in the summer, but the 19 year old suicide [rate] does not, suggests that the high school calendar is playing a prominent role in youth suicide." They further argued that the stress and pressure young people experience in school may trigger suicide.[31]

Bullying in school adds another dimension. While bullying alone rarely leads to suicide, it is often one of the main contributors. Researchers at the Yale School of Medicine combed through thirty-seven studies conducted on the link between bullying and suicide among children and adolescents in thirteen countries. Of the fifteen studies that specifically looked at the risks of suicidal thoughts in bullying victims, three showed no correlation and twelve showed that victims were 1.4 to 5.6 times more at risk of considering suicide.[32]

What few realize is that due to the compulsory attendance requirement, students who are suffering because of issues related to school are effectively trapped. Day after day, they are lawfully forced to return to the very places where they are derided by others and feel miserable unless they move to a new school (which is no guarantee the same problems won't arise), have access to a progressive school, or are able to be homeschooled.

Fortunately, Sam did not become another statistic.

When he was eleven, in the summer before seventh grade, his parents became aware that his condition had deteriorated to a dangerous level and took him to see a therapist, who spoke to him about bullying, controlling his anger, and coping strategies. He told me that the sessions helped him ward off his suicidal thoughts. Then finally, after two years of round-the-clock bullying, Sam's time in school improved slightly in the eighth grade. He grew taller. He gained some respect, made a few friends, received support from teachers, and didn't get ridiculed nearly as much as before.

CONTINUING HIS PROGRESS, ninth grade was Sam's best year in school. He had "good teachers and engaging enough material," which helped him land among the top-performing students in his class, having earned a 3.8 grade point average. But his grades took a turn for the worse the following year, because his classes were very boring. He began berating himself for his lackluster 2.8 grade point average. Twice, once in the fall and spring, the school held a school-wide assembly where students would leave class and come to the gymnasium during fourth period. As congratulatory music roared in the background, the names of the students with the highest grades would appear on the projector screen. Sam remembered that in the ninth grade he used to be on that list. "I felt on top of the world," he said. Now with his name nowhere in sight, he felt ashamed that he wasn't there anymore. He told himself: *I'm not smart enough. I can't get these high grades.*

After doing some research online about standardized testing and the far more innovative Finnish education system, it finally hit him: *I am pretty smart. The school is dumb for thinking I am dumb.* This led him to begin questioning his schooling: *Why don't we have any rights? Why is school like a prison? Why aren't we given a choice about attending school or what classes to take?*

On August 1, 2013, Sam typed "school sucks" into Google and stumbled upon an anti-schooling site called School Survival. "I've been much different ever since," he said. The site debunks the myths of compulsory schooling and offers forums, articles, and books to support "students who can't stand being forced to go to school."

"I remember going on School Survival and spending the rest of August browsing that site and reading threads and articles. I remember reading about how school is much more based on rigorous memorization, the increasing standardized testing and workload, the bullshit zero tolerance policies and how schools essentially were prisons, and also reading from other people's experiences with teachers and their schools. It shaped my view on school and life radically." There was a community eager to listen to him. He says that it felt "liberating."

In school, he said, "I'm a lot less passionate [about] work and testing than I once was. I stopped accepting the 'it's for your own good' bullcrap. I started taking notice of what teachers said and their actions, but also of the students and the entire school itself. I remember becoming somewhat more rebellious . . . I developed somewhat of a 'take no shit' attitude. If I believe I can justifiably question a teacher, I will."

Outside of school, Sam has not lost an iota of curiosity or zeal for learning. Ever since he was younger, he has had an obsession with history and geography. Twice, he won first place in his middle school's National Geographic Bee. He studied maps, watched countless history documentaries, browsed Wikipedia, and read books. One night he stayed up late to watch a documentary about North Korea. It was midnight, and he knew that he was going to wake up feeling exhausted, but he decided to do it anyway. He says that as long as he doesn't have more than two tardies a week, he should be all right. That's another quibble Sam has about school: the sleep schedule it forces him to conform to. "School starts around 8 a.m.," he said. "I have to wake up at 7 a.m. It's actually really tough. You feel unmotivated, sleepy. Your eyes are weary. It feels terrible." In another conversation, he told me, "My natural sleep [bedtime] schedule is around 12 a.m. to 1 a.m. I only get 6–7 hours of sleep, so I feel really tired and by fourth period I'm feeling drowsy."

A few weeks before we first spoke, he was studying the Cornish language and how it is being revived. "Language has been always something I've been so interested in, especially the evolution of language, where languages are spoken." Sam also enjoys writing stories. One day, he hopes to have a novel published. Inspired by "the growing authoritarian nature of schools," one idea that has lingered in his head is penning a novel about "a dystopian United States in which the worst students, gradewise and behaviorwise, have to go to these prison schools where they are not allowed to get out of these schools unless it is break and they are subjected to absolute authoritarianism . . . They have to get up at certain times. They have to go to sleep at certain times. And they are verbally abused."

He imagined, "What if schools really began operating almost exactly like a prison? What if we had public schools [that] you had to spend most of your life in? That dystopian [idea] appealed to me."

. . .

NOT LONG BEFORE Sam and I first spoke, which was in early 2014, he had suffered a mental breakdown. It was a Monday afternoon and he was in class at the time. All at once, several disturbing thoughts flooded his mind. He was getting flashbacks of both positive and painful memories from his past along with delusions that he believes signified fear and conflict. "To be more accurate," he said, "in my head, I feel as if all these conflicting thoughts and emotions are going to war against each other."

Holding back tears for two whole class periods, Sam recalled that during the breakdown, "I felt as if my soul died, or was at least dying then. I felt that there was nothing worth living in life, that all I was going to do was trot the earth and wait for something that never arrives, or just wonder what I'll do. I feel as if there's almost no one outside my family [whom] I can get any kind of motivation or comfort [from], or actually cares about me. That specific thought came through my mind: *Does anyone give a shit about me, anyway?*" He opted not to go to the school office and call home, which he now regrets. Once he arrived home, Sam started wailing uncontrollably. His sister offered to go on a walk with him in the park, which ultimately made him feel better.

Sam told me that the breakdown was caused by several events. First, his relationship with his brother has never been steady, but it had been particularly terrible recently. "I don't think my brother has ever understood my preferred introversion, or the social anxiety I developed in middle school," he said. "He always wanted me to be like him." Second, for weeks leading up to the breakdown, he had been experiencing many conflicts and uncertainties in his head. *Should I drop out of school? What does the future hold for me? What job will I end up with?* Third, he was agonizing over his grades with finals testing on the horizon. Fourth, he had felt very lonesome for weeks. And last, he was getting worn out by "the authoritarianism of school." It's important to note that the breakdown happened shortly after he returned to school from winter break—"after being given two weeks of freedom of thought and control over my body." Add up all these ingredients and they combined into a dangerous mix that led to his breakdown.

Contrary to popular belief, many who have borne the brunt of bullying in their childhood and teenage years never fully recover. Their unhealed scars get carried well into adulthood. I've spoken with quite a few adults who shudder at the memory of traumatic bullying events to this day.

Using the data from the Great Smoky Mountains Study, researchers analyzed the effects of bullying on 1,420 children aged nine, eleven, and thirteen from eleven counties in North Carolina who had bullied or been victims of bullying. Their health was assessed several times between the ages of nine and sixteen and in young adulthood using structured interviews. The study had some unsettling findings.[33] As summarized by *The New York Times,* "Researchers found that victims of bullying in childhood were 4.3 times more likely to have an anxiety disorder as adults, compared to those with no history of bullying or being bullied. Bullies who were also victims were particularly troubled: they were 14.5 times more likely to develop panic disorder as adults, compared to those who did not experience bullying, and 4.8 times more likely to experience depression."[34] In short, bullying can result in serious psychological damage that may never be fully healed.

Sam told me, "I'm still scared to talk to people at school to this day because of that torment. The fear of being rejected, the fear of being hated irrationally. I can't say I've fully recovered from middle school."

.   .   .

FOR SOME TIME, Sam had been strongly considering dropping out of school. In the spring of 2014, during his junior
year of high school, he sat for the California High School
Proficiency Examination, which is the legal equivalent of a
high school diploma. He passed the English language arts
section but failed the mathematics section. He didn't retake
the exam, because the fee was out of his financial reach. So
Sam planned to get through his final year of compulsory
schooling with as little pain, stress, unhappiness, and boredom as possible. And he did. He said his senior year went
"surprisingly smooth." A month before graduating, he told
me with glee in his voice, "I'm about to be a free man. I can
feel it. I cannot wait to celebrate." That fall, he enrolled at a
local community college and is interested in studying sociol-
ogy, psychology, and music production. After two years, he
plans to transfer to a university.

"I shouldn't be forced to do something meaningless,
especially if I'm going to be scolded if I don't do it," Sam
insisted in one of our early conversations. "I have my own
priorities. I have my own interests. I am a human being."

CHAPTER 2

The Disturbing Origins of
Compulsory Schooling

"The American people will appear to be the most enlightened community in the world," observed French political scientist Alexis de Tocqueville in his 1835 masterpiece *Democracy in America*. Describing the average American, he wrote, "He wears the dress, and he speaks the language of cities; he is acquainted with the past, curious of the future, and ready for argument upon the present; he is, in short, a highly civilized being, who consents, for a time, to inhabit the backwoods, and who penetrates into the wilds of the New World with the Bible, an axe, and a file of newspapers."[1]

Citizens in that period of American history were submerged in the affairs of politics and civics, especially through town meetings in the New England colonies. Tocqueville was captivated by the amount of political participation, writing, "No sooner do you set foot upon the American soil, than you are stunned by a kind of tumult; a confused clamour is heard on every side; and a thousand simultaneous voices demand the immediate satisfaction of their social wants. Everything is in motion around you; here, the people

of one quarter of a town are met to decide upon the building
of a church; there, the election of a representative is going on;
a little further, the delegates of a district are posting to the
town in order to consult upon some local improvements; or
in another place the labourers of a village quit their ploughs
to deliberate upon the project of a road or a public school."[2]

In 1727, Benjamin Franklin created the Junto club, to
"promote useful knowledge in the colonies."[3] In his autobiography, he explained, "We met on Friday evenings. The
rules that I drew up required that every member, in his turn,
should produce one or more queries on any point of Morals,
Politics, or Natural Philosophy, to be discuss'd by the company; and once in three months produce and read an essay
of his own writing, on any subject he pleased. Our debates
were to be under the direction of a president, and to be conducted in the sincere spirit of inquiry after truth."[4]

During the eighteenth and nineteenth centuries, America
(specifically the white people) had one of the most educated
populations in the world. Educating children in the colonial
era and many decades after independence was a community
undertaking. Churches, libraries, community centers, museums, dame schools (informal day cares), and families all
pitched in to assist. Many girls, who were denied access to
school, learned to read and write at home. There were only
a few public schools, reserved for the sons of elite and affluent families. As Stanford professor David Labaree explains
in his book *Someone Has to Fail,* "Colonial America had no
system of education. Instead it offered a loose collection of
informal ways to provide basic literacy and numeracy skills
to most of the population and to supply advanced learning
to a few . . . Most students received some form of education
during this period, and most of these did not attend anything resembling a school."[5]

Americans were literary aficionados, occupied by books, newspapers, and pamphlets. American historian Daniel Boorstin has written that reading was "the product and the producer of a busy, mobile, public society."[6] In 1853, Swedish visitor Per Siljeström wrote, "In no country in the world is the taste for reading so diffused among the people as in America."[7] By 1837, Noah Webster's *The American Spelling Book,* which was first published in three parts from 1783 to 1785, had sold more than fifteen million copies.[8] The U.S. Census in 1840 showed a population of about seventeen million people.

The average American today would struggle with reading most of the books that entertained his counterparts back then. The vocabulary is too challenging. Educator John Taylor Gatto wrote in *Dumbing Us Down,* "Pick up a fifth grade textbook in math or rhetoric from 1850 and you'll see that the texts were pitched then on what would today be considered college level."[9]

As a result, the literacy rates of white Americans were extremely high. In 1800, *The Columbian Phoenix and Boston Review* stated, "No country on the face of the earth can boast of a larger proportion of inhabitants, versed in the rudiments of science, or fewer, who are not able to read and write their names, than the United States of America."[10] In 1812, French immigrant Pierre Samuel du Pont de Nemours wrote in his book *National Education in the United States of America,* "Most young Americans, therefore, can read, write, and cipher. Not more than four in a thousand are unable to write legibly—even neatly; while in Spain, Portugal, Italy, only a sixth of the population can read; in Germany, even in France, not more than a third; in Poland, about two men in a hundred, and in Russia not one in two hundred."[11]

Historian Harvey J. Graff reports in his book *The Legacies of Literacy* that the 1840 U.S. Census collected data on the literacy rates of free adults in each state. Here are some of the rates (in percentages): Connecticut: 99.7, New Hampshire: 99.4, Massachusetts: 99, Maine: 99, Vermont: 98, Michigan: 98, Rhode Island: 97, New Jersey: 96, New York: 96, Pennsylvania: 95, Ohio: 94, Louisiana: 94, Mississippi: 88, Delaware: 82, Virginia: 81, South Carolina: 81, Georgia: 80, North Carolina: 72.[12] A literacy test was not administered, so admittedly this data was self-reported by participants in the census. As for enslaved African Americans, their illiteracy rates were extremely high, because in most southern states, it was illegal for slaves to learn to read or write, and it was also illegal for individuals to teach them how.

In modern times, according to the 2003 National Assessment of Adult Literacy, 14.5 percent of adults in the United States were lacking "basic prose literacy skills."[13]

It would be far-fetched to make the assertion that compulsory schooling has led to the decrease of literacy rates, as the skein of cause and effect would be too complex to unravel. But what we can conclude is that it is not necessary to mandate formal schooling in order to spawn a literate society.

IRONICALLY, HORACE MANN, founder of the American public school system, serves as a conspicuous example of a successful product of the community-and-family education system.

The son of a poor farmer, Mann grew up in Franklin, Massachusetts, during the early nineteenth century. According to *Appletons' Cyclopædia of American Biography,* he was "forced to procure by his own exertions the means of obtaining an education. He earned his school books when a child by braiding straw, and his severe and frugal life taught him habits of self-reliance and independence."[14] From age ten to twenty, Mann had no more than a few weeks of formal schooling each year, so he self-educated himself by reading books.[15] His sister Lydia once told him, "Every day of your life when you were with your parents and sister, at least, you were *at school* and learning that which has been the foundation of your present learning."[16]

In 1816, he was offered admission to Brown University. There, he excelled in debate and graduated in three years. Finishing first in his class, Mann's valedictorian oration was titled "The Gradual Advancement of the Human Species in Dignity and Happiness." It demonstrated his fondness for social justice, offering an inkling of the work he would do for the rest of his life.

While teaching Latin and Greek at Brown, he decided to pursue law and enrolled at the Litchfield Law School in Connecticut in 1821. He was later admitted to the bar.

After a few years, he entered politics, serving in the Massachusetts House of Representatives and later winning a seat in the state senate. In 1836, he became the president of the senate and established the Massachusetts Board of Education, the first one of its kind in the nation. The appointees to the board were some of the most powerful people in the state.

Mann left the Senate in 1837 and was appointed the first secretary to the board, granting him powers that could shape both the Massachusetts and the nation's education systems. During his term, he was the chief campaigner for the common school movement. Common schools were publicly funded schools controlled by the government.

In the summer of 1843, Mann took a leave of absence from the board to visit European schools, including Prussia's, and report his findings. Since the beginning of the century, a roster of American intellectuals and officials had been inspecting Prussian schools, awed by their efficiency, standardization, and breeding of hardworking and obedient citizens. On the day of his departure, Mann married Mary Peabody, a member of one of the prominent families in New England. The couple combined their honeymoon with Mann's European school tour.[17]

PRUSSIA'S CRUSHING DEFEAT by French emperor Napoleon Bonaparte in the Battle of Jena in 1806 left the nation in shambles. In the aftermath, Prussian leaders acknowledged that extreme reforms were required. A year later, German philosopher Johann Gottlieb Fichte delivered a series of roaring addresses to the nation, including one that offered a blueprint for a state-funded, compulsory, and universal schooling system:

> Then, in order to define more clearly the new education which I propose, I should reply that that very recognition of, and reliance upon, free will in the pupil is the first mistake of the old system and the clear confession of its impotence and futility . . . On the other hand, the new education must consist essentially in this, that it completely destroys the freedom of will in the soil which it undertakes to cultivate, and produces on the contrary strict necessity in the decisions of the will, the opposite being impossible. Such a will can henceforth be relied on with confidence and certainty . . . If you want to

influence him at all, you must do more than merely talk to him; you must fashion him, and fashion him in such a way that he simply cannot will otherwise than what you wish him to will.[18]

The underlying thought was that by producing a citizenry who would obey and submit without question to the government, Prussia and its economy and army would be transformed for the better. King Frederick William III of Prussia threw down the gauntlet and put Fichte's suggestions into effect by 1819. The system was split into three tiers. The elite children of society (0.5 percent) went to schools where they were taught "how to manage materials, men, and situations —to be problem solvers," as Gatto wrote in *The Underground History of American Education*. The next tier of children, roughly 5.5 to 7.5 percent of society, were destined to be politicians, doctors, engineers, and lawyers. They were sent to *Realschulen*, where they were taught how to think, albeit in a distorted fashion. The remaining 92 to 94 percent of children went to *Volksschulen*, an eight-year period of compulsory schooling, where they learned "obedience, cooperation and correct attitudes, along with rudiments of literacy and official state myths of history."[19] *Volksschule* students were indeed churned into disciplined citizens faithful to the government.

According to Martin van Creveld in *The Rise and Decline of the State*, by 1837, 80 percent of Prussian children were enlisted in school.[20] The population was kept in check and the army's power matured because the soldiers did not think for themselves anymore. "The whole scheme," wrote Thomas Alexander, professor at George Peabody College for Teachers, in his 1919 book *The Prussian Elementary Schools*, "of Prussian elementary education is shaped with the express purpose of making ninety-five out of every hundred citizens subservient to the ruling house and to the state."[21]

HORACE MANN WAS entranced by what he had witnessed in Prussian schools: the routinization and age segregation. After six months of visiting schools in 1843 in countries like England, Scotland, Ireland, Germany, Prussia, Holland, Saxony, Belgium, and France, he sailed back home to Boston at the end of the summer. He organized his observations of European schools into his most famous report, *Mr. Mann's Seventh Annual Report: Education in Europe,* which was published the following year.

Mann showered Prussian schools with nothing but praise: "Arrange the most highly civilized and conspicuous nations of Europe in their due order of precedence, as it regards the education of their people, and the kingdoms of Prussia and Saxony, together with several of the western and south-western states of the Germanic confederation would undoubtedly stand preeminent, both in regard to the quantity and quality of instruction." He did not pose any objections to the Prussian law that says if a parent refuses to send his child to school, the child will be taken away and sent to school, while the parent goes to prison.[22] Overall, Mann implored the board of education to implement the methods of Prussian schooling.

Now the obvious question is, Why institute compulsory schooling when literacy rates and school enrollment in New England were already very high and society was well educated? As Labaree notes in his book *Someone Has to Fail,* "What the system did do was increase the likelihood that young people, in company with a cross section of the local community, would acquire their education in the setting of a formally constituted school, which was publicly controlled, age graded, and run by a trained teacher. The system's primary accomplishment was to provide a shared experience of schooling for the populace. This helped to create a new form of community for a liberal republic; and it also helped to socialize students in new norms of self-control and internalized social values that prepared them to play the role of self-regulating actors in a market economy."[23] In other words, school was an agent of social control.

Compulsory schooling's evangelists, which included many industrialists and financiers, in fact, wanted to "dumb down" the American population to create docile followers, not potentially troublesome freethinkers who questioned authority. In the post–Civil War era, they wanted the working-class children to be trained to labor in the surging industrial economy. They wanted the millions of newly arrived immigrants from Europe to conform and be instilled with common values and traits, fearing that they would otherwise unleash social unrest. Indeed, U.S. commissioner of education William T. Harris warned in 1877, "If we do not 'Americanize' our immigrants by luring them to participate in our best civilization . . . they will contribute to the degeneration of our political body and thus de-Americanize and destroy our national life."[24] Then there was Ellwood Cubberley, an educator and dean of the Stanford School of Education, who in 1909 regarded immigrants from southern and eastern Europe as "illiterate, docile, lacking in self-reliance and initiative" and said, "Our task is . . . to assimilate and amalgamate these people as part of our American race, and to implant in their children, so far as can be done, the Anglo-Saxon conception of righteousness, law and order, and popular government."[25]

Overall, compulsory schooling was not a popular move. For instance, the people of Beverly, Massachusetts, voted to abolish their high school in 1860. Education historian Michael Katz offers the three reasons for this action in his book *The Irony of Early School Reform:* "First, people, those without children especially, protested the raising of taxes; second, the least affluent citizens felt that the high school would not benefit their children; third, they were hostile both to the wealthy leaders of the town and to the onset of industrialism."[26]

Of all the critics of the common school movement, New England philosopher and minister Orestes Brownson was perhaps the most pungent. He was a champion of "democratic localism," the belief that education should be locally controlled. In the *Boston Quarterly Review* in 1839, he tore into Mann's reforms, accusing the board of education of trying to "imitate despotic Prussia" and arguing that the Prussian system was flatly incompatible with American democracy "because, according to our theory, the people are supposed to be wiser than the government. Here, the people do not look to the government for light, for instruction, but the government looks to the people."[27]

One delegate to the Pennsylvania Constitutional Convention of 1837–38 cautioned, "If we ever expect to root deeply this system in the affection of the people, we must make the system voluntary—entirely so. But if we force it upon the people, it will be taken with an ill grace, and will be made use of, if used at all, with reluctance and suspicion."[28] Clearly, this advice was not followed.

Largely self-educated himself, Brownson also asserted that children were already being educated in the community at large: "Our children are educated in the streets, by the influence of their associates, in the fields and on the hill sides, by the influences of surrounding scenery and overshadowing skies, in the bosom of the family, by the love and gentleness, or wrath and fretfulness of parents, by the passions or affections they see manifested, the conversations to which they listen, and above all by the general pursuits, habits, and moral tone of the community."[29]

In 1852, with the stroke of Governor Edward Everett's pen, Massachusetts became the first state in the country to implement a compulsory school attendance law, requiring that all children between the ages of eight and fourteen be forced to attend school for twelve weeks a year with at least six being consecutive. Fines were levied on the parents who failed to comply.[30]

By 1900, thirty-two states and territories in total had some version of compulsory schooling. It would be another eighteen years before the forty-eighth and final state in the country at the time, Mississippi, enacted compulsory school attendance legislation.[31] "The history," Ellwood Cubberley wrote in his 1919 book *Public Education in the United States,* "of compulsory-attendance legislation in the States has been much the same everywhere, and everywhere laws have been enacted only after overcoming strenuous opposition."[32]

Industrialists, financiers, and their private foundations soon became the ones bankrolling the compulsory schooling movement. Between 1896 and 1920, Gatto reveals, they had spent more money on the cause than the actual government.[33] Consider this statement by Frederick Taylor Gates, president of the General Education Board, a philanthropic organization founded by oil magnate John D. Rockefeller, in 1906: "We shall not try to make these people or any of their children into philosophers or men of learning, or men of science. We have not to raise up from among them authors, editors, poets or men of letters. We shall not search for embryo great artists, painters, musicians nor lawyers, doctors, preachers, politicians, statesmen, of whom we have an ample supply . . . For the task that we set before ourselves is very simple as well as a very beautiful one: to train these people as we find them to a perfectly ideal life just where they are."[34] The ruling class used schooling as a tool to control the minds of the masses and perpetuate their own interests.

Many of the same underwriters of forced schooling were also financing the campaign to end child labor. Children, since they could work longer hours for much lower wages, were taking jobs away from adults. The labor unions were among the strongest patrons of compulsory schooling, because if children were mandated to attend school, then they would be out of the factories and adults could have much better chances at receiving employment, and at higher wages.[35]

The 1900 census revealed that 18 percent of all American workers were children under the age of sixteen. The two million children were "working in mills, mines, fields, factories, and stores and on city streets."[36] This prompted a national urgency for child labor legislation. It took another thirty-eight years for Congress to pass the Fair Labor Standards Act, which officially banned the employment of minors in "oppressive child labor."

IN RECENT TIMES, many have used the "school as a factory" metaphor when describing the education system. In both settings, there is a clear hierarchy. In schools, superintendents and principals supervise teachers and students. In factories, owners and managers monitor employees. There is a reward and punishment system. In schools, there are grades, and in factories, there are wages. And in both, efficiency, conformity, and order is demanded.[37]

In the post–Civil War era, while historians argue that it wasn't outright deliberate, schools and factories were structured eerily similarly to each other. It made the transition into industry virtually seamless for working-class children. In his 1978 book, *The Training of the Urban Working Class,* Paul C. Violas, who was professor of history of education in the College of Education at the University of Illinois at Urbana-Champaign, cited studies and the official records of the Chicago school system, which showed that schools were operating under "the assumption that working-class children should be trained by the public schools to stay in their proper class."[38]

So one of the jobs of schools was to prepare children with the habits and skills required for the industrial workforce. When he was superintendent of schools in St. Louis, William T. Harris noted in an 1872 report, "The first requisite of the school is *Order:* each pupil must be taught first and foremost to conform his behavior to a general standard." He pointed out a few duties of students, including punctuality, regularity, and silence, which would all have real-life application in their future work.[39]

Unlike working-class children, the offspring of the affluent followed a classical curriculum and spent many more years in school. As Violas explained, "Their education was designed to prepare them for the positions of community leadership that they were to hold as adults by developing their capacity for independent decision making. The classical curriculum, designed to produce leaders, emphasized cultural education, and rigorous intellectual exercises."[40] Schools, like the society at large, were structured to sustain and reinforce classism and racism. African Americans, in particular, were systemically and historically shut out of schools, educated in segregated, cash-starved schools, or deposited on the vocational track.

Until the mid-twentieth century, most students left school before attending high school. Once high school became universal, going to college became the clearest distinguisher between the social classes.[41]

WHAT ARE THE purposes of modern-day schools? The primary purpose is warehousing—keeping children off the streets, out of the workplace, and out of the home for most of the day to the benefit of parents, some employers, and the general public. Call it the "jail function," as John Holt put it frankly.[42] There is no attempt to cloak this fact. In a blog post bemoaning the number of days her children have off from school, one blogger's headline read: "November Is the Cruelest Month for Moms."[43]

The second purpose is teaching children how to comply with orders, submit to authority, and fit into our consumerist, capitalist economy. This is not usually acknowledged. Schools, educators, and policymakers are not candidly saying that the objective of schools is to produce compliant students, but that's generally what happens.

The third purpose is ranking and sorting students based on their performance in school. It's an efficient way to determine who should be rewarded for her compliance, or in other words, who should go to the top colleges and universities and later hold positions of power and influence in society. As the eminent linguist Noam Chomsky once put it, "The whole educational and professional training system is a very elaborate filter, which just weeds out people who are too independent, and who think for themselves, and who don't know how to be submissive, and so on—because they're dysfunctional to the institutions."

The fourth purpose is a distorted version of education. It really ought to be characterized as indoctrination and conditioning for entry into economic and social systems that have little use for free inquiry and thought, let alone resistance.

AT ITS CORE, compulsory schooling is antithetical to democracy. It tramples on the basic human rights of children. And it is based on the assumption that any kind of schooling, no matter how harmful it could be, is good for you. Please note: I am not romanticizing or advocating for the return of a way of life where women, African Americans, and minorities were shut out of going to school, nor am I advocating for the rollback of child labor laws.

There isn't a more compelling way to explain the folly of compulsory schooling than the way educator John Holt put it in his book *Escape from Childhood:* "The requirement that a child go to school, for about six hours a day, 180 days a year, for about ten years, whether or not he learns anything there, whether or not he already knows it or could learn it faster or better somewhere else, is such a gross violation of civil liberties that few adults would stand for it. But the child who resists is treated as a criminal. With this requirement we created an industry, an army of people whose whole work was to tell young people what they had to learn and to try to make them learn it."[44]

It bears repeating: "such a gross violation of civil liberties that few adults would stand for it." Whenever you force a child to do something, ask yourself whether an adult would comply without objection. Can you imagine if the U.S. government began telling adults that they must stay in their job for the next 180 days each year for the next thirteen years no matter how damaging and dissatisfying it may be? If we were truly in favor of the humane treatment of children, then we could not in good faith support compulsory schooling, which traps them in largely toxic and undemocratic institutions with no means to escape and for no reason other than that the individual is a certain age.

Moreover, it can be cogently argued that these laws violate the U.S. Constitution. The Thirteenth Amendment states: "Neither slavery nor involuntary servitude, except as a punishment for crime whereof the party shall have been duly convicted, shall exist within the United States, or any place subject to their jurisdiction." The definition of servitude is "a condition in which one lacks liberty especially to determine one's course of action or way of life." There aren't many places that fit this description more aptly than school.

In a society without compulsory schooling, what you'd likely see over time is masses of young people exercising their right to refuse to attend school. Many would deliver a clear-cut order to schools: "We're not coming back until you start treating us like human beings."

If schools were actually places of joy, freedom, engagement, and inquiry, you would think that children would want to go to them even if they weren't compulsory. As activist and writer Keith Farnish explained in his book *Underminers,* "No system that is so mentally nourishing, and so beneficial to the individual as the school system's promoters claim, would need to compel, *by law,* anyone to attend on a regular basis. They would just go."[45]

There are obviously many concerns about such a radical proposition. John Holt, in the introduction to *The Lives of Children,* the 1969 book by George Dennison, novelist and teacher at New York's First Street School, quipped, "Proposals to wipe out half the human race with hydrogen bombs do not generate one-tenth as much anger."[46]

The first and most obvious question is, What would working parents do if school were not compulsory? The chief reason why there has been very little pushback against compulsory schooling is that the system works very well for the convenience of parents. Schools effectively serve as baby-sitting factories. Working parents want a physical place to send their children during the day where they are assured they will be supervised, taken care of, and learning something. That is why we need to build accessible alternative physical learning spaces to fill that need.

Now what would happen when a child wanted to attend school but his mother or father refused to send him? There is no hard data on this issue, but I suspect that would be rare. However, a system where children would be able to report complaints or issues to authorities, like the child abuse or neglect reporting system, could be set up to handle such instances.

Another immediate concern is that if school were not compulsory, many poor children would be forced to work to support their families or pressured to leave school early to work. Fortunately, the United States has very strong child labor laws, but we could certainly add a few more legal safeguards to ensure that children would not be exploited by employers in this fashion, or by their parents.

An additional counterargument is that for some children, school is a haven and a place to find safety, food, and shelter for at least a few hours a day. There's definitely some truth to that, but abolishing compulsory school attendance requirements would not impede children from attending school. It would merely give children the right to choose not to go to school. And as we have seen, schools are not absolved of violence, corporal punishment, shame, and abuse; rather, many institutions are active participants in those odious practices. They are far from the idyllic places that some like to portray. As Cevin Soling, director of the film *The War on Kids,* wrote in *Forbes,* "The key to sustaining an abusive, oppressive system is to convince people that it holds merits for the victims."[47]

There's also the worry that if school were voluntary then kids would be out on the streets causing a ruckus and crime would go up. In reality, though, we might see less youth crime. Holt noted in his introduction to *The Lives of Children,* "Paul Goodman once pointed out, in at least one instance statistics showed there was more juvenile crime when school was in than when it was out."[48] And one study found that on the days school was in session, violent juvenile crime increased by nearly 30 percent and property crime decreased by 14 percent.[49]

In the 1880s, Zachariah Montgomery, United States assistant attorney general in the administration of President Grover Cleveland, wrote the book *Poison Drops in the Federal Senate: The School Question from a Parental and Non-Sectarian Stand-Point.* He trawled through government statistics and census data for twelve states—six states with "state controlled education" (Massachusetts, Maine, New Hampshire, Vermont, Connecticut, and Rhode Island) and six states with "parent controlled education" (Maryland, Virginia, Delaware, Georgia, North Carolina, and South Carolina). He found that after a state adopted compulsory schooling, the crime and suicide rate soared. His analysis also showed that there were "over four times as many suicides under State education as under parental education." Montgomery holds the "loss of parental authority and home influence over children" and the "neglect of moral and religious education and training" as responsible, but much of the blame should actually fall on the school environment.[50]

Another concern is that some children are too young to make a decision about attending school or not. I agree. At the younger ages, parents would obviously have more control over this matter.

So where will the children who decide not to attend school be during the day? Who will supervise and care for them if their parents are not available? As mentioned, most children would continue to go to schools where they feel happy, respected, and treated humanely. But for the ones who just choose not to go, that's where my idea for the replacement of the current system comes in. As discussed in detail in Chapter 9, I advocate for reorganizing the city and community to become the school itself and for funding noncoercive forms of public education. Imagine if the money allocated for public education were used to finance community centers, apprenticeships, learning spaces, internships, mentorships, and classes. We could transform our cities and communities into engines for social good, collaboration, and problem solving, where learning shifts from institutions and into the "town square"—museums, libraries, parks, playgrounds, recreational facilities, and community centers. Matt Hern, founder and former codirector of the now defunct Purple Thistle Centre, an alternative-to-school community institution for youth in Vancouver, proposes in his book *Field Day* that we should treat schools as utilities, like public libraries, parks, and community centers. They are supported by public funding and are accessible to the community but are not coercive or compulsory. "The best public institutions," he explains, "those that are universally admired and non-manipulative, are those that do not attempt to mould their users."[51]

Scrapping compulsory schooling is not the first step in a full-fledged learning revolution. It needs to come later down the road. We must first establish alternative, humane spaces of learning and develop legal and economic structures so that working parents are accommodated, every child is able to attend school if he or she wishes, and the most vulnerable children are not browbeaten into labor.

The eradication of compulsory schooling in the United States could not take place without a massive social movement behind it, a radical change in public opinion, and wide-ranging rigorous discourse about means and ends. A noncoercive public education system would not be perfect, but our criterion for judging alternatives is the current system we have in place. The new model would be compared to a system in which children have suffered psychological damage; experienced low levels of love of learning, engagement, happiness, self-worth, and curiosity; and achieved abysmal outcomes. The task is to create a system that performs better than that.

This is finally about creating a more just society. This is about ending the infringement of the rights of children. There are too many problems to solve, too many people to engage with, and too many lives to change to require that young people be holed up in buildings with oppressive conditions for some of the most formative years of their lives.

CHAPTER 3

No Child Left Uncontrolled

As should be abundantly clear by now, I am no fan of the current state of public schools. But these critiques should not in any way suggest that I am against public education. I am staunchly in support of a tax-funded, universally accessible public education system, albeit thoroughly restructured and transformed.

Carol Black, a friend of mine and director of the film *Schooling the World: The White Man's Last Burden,* framed this contrast excellently in a blog post: "The crucial confusion here is between the idea of *publicly supported* education and the idea of *centrally controlled state-administered* education. To really get your hands around this distinction, simply replace the word 'school' with the word 'radio' in the following sentences and see what you get: *I am in favor of publicly supported radio. I am in favor of centrally controlled state-administered radio.* Not the same thing, are they?"[1]

And so in this chapter, I will be laying out a full-throated defense of public education against corporate, neoliberal forces on a quest to privatize and defund it. They want to issue more standardized tests. They want to implement a more structured curriculum. They want to make schools even more punishing and inhumane. They must be stopped. If they're not, it will be much more difficult to adopt the proposals that I and many others want to see executed.

THE MORNING OF January 8, 2002, in Bethpage, a small suburban town on Long Island, was a frigid one. At a little past nine o'clock, after climbing off the yellow school bus with my backpack strapped over my shoulders and lunch bag in my hands, I walked into Charles Campagne Elementary School. It had only been a few days since I had returned from winter break. I made my way through the hallways to my first-grade classroom where my teacher, Ms. Tarkin, was welcoming us. Meanwhile, nearly seven hundred miles west, unbeknownst to me and most of the public at the time, an event that would drastically affect my experience in elementary and middle school was about to unfold.

When the military helicopter carrying President George W. Bush touched down on Hamilton High School's football field, snow dotted the ground. The public school is located in Hamilton, Ohio, a city near Cincinnati that was recognized as the "City of Sculpture" and was then home to roughly sixty thousand people. Inside the school's gymnasium were thousands of students, teachers, and parents, there to witness the signing of a landmark $26.5 billion education reform bill known as the No Child Left Behind Act of 2001. There were speeches from Secretary of Education Rod Paige and Republican congressman John Boehner, who was in his home district and involved in the crafting of the bill. Finally Bush came to the podium to roaring applause and chants of "USA!

USA!" With no fewer than six standing ovations during the speech, he memorably declared, "And today begins a new era, a new time in public education in our country. As of this hour, America's schools will be on a new path of reform, and a new path of results." During the signing ceremony, Bush sat behind a wooden desk, borrowed from an art teacher's room, with the words "No Child Left Behind" emblazoned on a mini-chalkboard attached to its front. He was flanked by all colors of the political spectrum: Democratic congressman George Miller of California, Democratic senator Ted Kennedy of Massachusetts, Republican senator Judd Gregg of New Hampshire, and the Republican Boehner. The bill had drawn unusually strong bipartisan backing in Congress. Only forty-five representatives and eight senators stood in opposition.[2]

While the goal of the law seemed well intentioned— ensuring high academic standards for all children—what transpired was a disaster of epic proportions. Much of the law had actually originated in Bush's home state of Texas. When Bush ran for president in 2000, he discussed the "Texas Miracle." He claimed that as the result of an increased emphasis on standardized testing in the classroom and the threat of punishment for schools that didn't improve, test scores and graduation rates rose. The only problem was that the "Texas Miracle" was a fabrication. Researchers found that tens of thousands of students had been pushed out or dropped out before they needed to take the tests, thereby skewing the numbers, and that there had been no increase in the SAT scores of prospective college students.[3]

However, despite these ominous signs, this became the prototype for No Child Left Behind, and the bill sailed through Congress. The law mandated that all states must test every child in reading and mathematics annually from grades three to eight. There was also an unattainable requirement that 100 percent of schoolchildren reach proficient levels in reading and mathematics by 2014. That year has come and gone and proficiency rates are nowhere near 100 percent.

The full power of the law wasn't actualized until a few years down the road. But when it came fully into effect, it hit American education like a tsunami. As I've said in the past, my elementary school was soon dominated by a culture of "drill, kill, bubble-fill." Everything began to center around the standardized tests in the spring. Beginning in third grade, the amount of instructional time in the arts, music, science, and history was reduced, because basically what was tested got taught, and these subjects were not equally tested.

My school, like others, had to meet "adequate yearly progress" goals determined by New York State. Schools that were unsuccessful at hitting the targets were at risk of being converted to a charter, turned over to private management, or having the entire staff fired. What happened, according to a study by the Center on Education Policy, was that almost half of schools have been labeled as failing under the law. Even Hamilton High School, the school where the law was signed, was branded a failing school.[4] The ruthless accountability structure was driven by carrots and sticks—rewards and punishments—rather than agency and cooperation.

No Child Left Behind (NCLB) was a complete and utter failure. As a former superintendent of a school district in Ohio quipped to *Time* magazine, "No Child Left Behind is like a Russian novel. That's because it's long, it's complicated, and in the end, everybody gets killed."[5] It also marked the federal government's unprecedented intervention in the education system, whose jurisdiction had largely been reserved for local districts and states. Almost two centuries ago, Alexis de Tocqueville in *Democracy in America* had cautioned the United States not to allow locally controlled enterprises, like schooling, to be seized by the national government. In Europe, he observed that individual rights became "more weak, more subordinate, and more precarious" when local authorities were weakened or disappeared. Tocqueville also noted that education became "a national concern," where "the State receives, and often takes, the child from the arms of the mother, to hand it over to official agents: the State undertakes to train the heart and to instruct the mind of each generation. Uniformity prevails in the courses of public instruction as in everything else; diversity, as well as freedom, is disappearing day by day."[6] And this is what has happened under NCLB.

OUR CLASS WAS preparing for the TerraNova exams, standardized tests used across the United States, in reading and mathematics. It was 2003 and I was eight and in the third grade. This was the first brush I had with the testing that resulted directly from the implementation of NCLB. I had never sat for a standardized test before, so practicing for them was altogether a new and unusual experience for me. Bizarrely, we even had to perfect our ability to fill in the bubbles on the Scantron form. One day, my teacher was returning our graded practice reading comprehension tests to us. I had been having difficulty with them, because even though I was a voracious reader, I wasn't able to read as efficiently and closely to the text as was required. Sometimes I would get bored by what I was reading and skim the words. As she came around to my desk and handed me my test, she had a discouraged look on her face. I peeked at my grade. I bombed it. I got a 64. My immediate reaction was shame. I had never felt so dumb in my life. It was the first time I had ever failed a test.

The school day wound down. As I sat on the bus on my way home, I began thinking about how exactly I was going to explain this failing grade to my mother. She expected near-perfect marks from me. I couldn't just not tell her, because my teacher forced us to get our tests signed by our parents, no matter what grade we received. I was a very well-behaved child, and I didn't have the audacity to forge a signature.

When I eventually arrived home, I avoided bringing it up for a while. Then I finally walked up to her, gave her my test, apologized, and told her that I would make sure I did better next time. She was disappointed and a bit shocked. I had always been an outstanding student. I finished my home-work without any prodding from my parents. I performed extremely well on tests—usually in the 90s and above. My report cards teemed with positive comments from my teach-ers that commended me on my work ethic, academic perfor-mance, and ability to follow rules and directions and stay out of trouble. In other words, I was obedient. When it came to school-related work and activities, I did everything my parents and teachers asked of me. Only in retrospect do I now realize that I was living a life that other people had con-structed and laid out for me.

Over the next few months after my failed test, I contin-ued completing more practice reading comprehension tests. I did better each time, but I grew more frustrated. Not only was the exercise of answering multiple-choice questions and neatly filling in the bubbles mind-numbing, it was also demoralizing. My self-esteem waxed and waned depending on how well I did on the test that day.

What often happens in schools is that in a matter of days into a new school year, the students have already been sorted by their fellow classmates and teachers into two categories: the smart kids and the dumb kids. They carry that harmful label as they progress through their schooling career. On one hand, the "failures" learn that they are the only ones to blame for their underachievement. *It is your fault that you are stupid.* This, however, ignores the fact that because there is a predetermined distribution of results inherent in the design of tests, there will always be some percentage of students who fail. "School made these people into failures," explained filmmaker Cevin Soling in a talk, "because they failed at school. School has monopolized the concept of what it means to fail."[7] On the other hand, many of the "successful" kids slowly turn into perfectionists, as I did. Grades feel like life-or-death matters. When these kids score poorly on a test, they are often unable to cope and move on.

Shame in the learning process can be particularly damaging for poor and disadvantaged youth. This topic came up during a conversation I had with Simon Hauger, cofounder and principal of the Workshop School, which serves low-income and minority students in Philadelphia. He put it extremely well: "This is one of the big challenges for dysfunctional communities: You already feel bad about yourself as a learner. As a human being, your whole life is shit. You've been told you're not valuable. Then you go to school and school makes you feel dumb. If that's their experience every day and they go home to something that devalues them and they go to a school that devalues them, then we're failing. They're human beings. They have value."[8]

In the spring of 2003, the TerraNova exams in reading and mathematics were administered to every third grader in my school. It was a significant event, considering the severe repercussions outlined in the law if the students didn't score proficiently. So naturally both teachers and students were stressed and under intense pressure. Shortly after the school year finished, I received my scores in the mail. As expected, I performed well on the mathematics section but didn't fare as well on the reading section. From there onward until the end of the eighth grade, I usually took two standardized tests in reading and mathematics each year. Some years, I also had tests in science and social studies. Fortunately, my elementary and middle school were never labeled as failing. Over the years, I scored better on the reading tests, and later, in high school, I didn't have any issues in my English classes. In total, based on my rough calculation, I sat for more than thirty state standardized tests from kindergarten through twelfth grade. The number of standardized tests administered to students has surged since my days in elementary school. A survey of sixty-seven urban school districts conducted by the Council of the Great City Schools found that students take an average of 113 standardized tests between preschool and twelfth grade.[9]

Standardized testing has become a uniform, detested part of many students' and teachers' lives. "Our children," noted author Alfie Kohn in *Education Week,* "are tested to an extent that is unprecedented in our history and unparalleled anywhere else in the world."[10] It has killed creativity, narrowed the curriculum, dissolved the backbone of genuine teaching and learning, and transformed teaching into a mechanical, routinized operation. Testing has been the centerpiece of both the No Child Left Behind Act and, as we will see, President Obama's Race to the Top program. Each year, states spend roughly $1.7 billion a year on these tests, money that could have been better allocated, perhaps to measures that help trim the child poverty rate.[11] With the introduction of the new Common Core standards, a collection of knowledge and skills that every student needs to gain and master at each grade level, states will need to spend even more money for the creation of new tests. More than forty states have adopted the standards, and they have been the subject of epic resistance from both the left and right.

A grassroots movement led by parents, teachers, and students against standardized testing has caught fire across the United States. (Full disclosure: I am on the board of Fair Test, the National Center for Fair and Open Testing, which has been a leading force in these efforts.) In the spring of 2015, hundreds of thousands of students opted out of the tests, with 200,000 students, or 20 percent of eligible students, opting out in New York State alone.[12]

It is long overdue for our society to begin to think differently about intelligence. "Genius is as common as dirt," writes John Taylor Gatto. "We suppress our genius only because we haven't yet figured out how to manage a population of educated men and women."[13] We need to stop giving so much emphasis to test scores, whether they plummet or escalate. They're artificial, manufactured, and narrow indicators of intelligence. We need to remove all the man-made assumptions about intelligence and view it as a diverse and complex entity, and also treat all talents and abilities as equally as possible. Every time we judge people or schools based on test scores, we yield our authority to testing corporations and we become indentured to them. Why do we trust profiteering companies to decide who is intelligent or not? If you're searching for a prime example of the corporatization of American society, this would be it.

In short, we don't need tests. Instead, we need assessments and portfolios. There's a difference. A test is used to tell whether a student memorized and regurgitated enough material. An assessment, on the other hand, is a process of evaluating, documenting, and reflecting. Many schools are using digital portfolios to showcase students' work—essays, videos, and presentations.[14] In the state of New York, twenty-eight public schools, twenty-six of which are located in New York City, are part of the New York Performance Standards Consortium. The students in those schools, instead of sitting for the five required state Regents Exams for graduation, complete an analytic essay, a social studies research paper, a science experiment, and solve an applied mathematics problem. They are still required to take the English Regents like everyone else, however. A report found that the Consortium schools had lower dropout rates and higher graduation and college acceptance rates than other New York City public schools, even with about the same percentages of minority, low-income, special education, and English language learner students.[15]

THE INFATUATION WITH data, testing, and the introduction of terms such as "chief executive officer" and "efficiency" into the lexicon of education is nothing new. There are indeed stunning parallels in the beginning of the twentieth century, when there was a strong influence of Frederick Winslow Taylor's system of scientific management on the education system.[16]

In the fall of 1910, scientific management began gaining prominence. Hearings were conducted before the Interstate Commerce Commission over an application by various northeastern railroads calling for an increase in freight rates to recoup the higher wages granted to workers the previous spring.

For the opposition, lawyer Louis Brandeis, on behalf of the trade associations, argued that the railroads didn't need to raise rates; they just needed to make their operations more efficient, or in other words, apply Taylor's system of scientific management. To bolster his case, Brandeis brought in a series of witnesses who attested to the fact that the principles of scientific management would increase wages and decrease costs. One of Brandeis's lead witnesses was efficiency expert Harrington Emerson, who testified that the railroads could save up to a million dollars each day with these new methods of efficiency.[17]

Won over by Brandeis's impressive arguments, the railroads' application was rejected by the commission.

After the episode, Taylor, a mechanical engineer by training, became a national icon, and scientific management captured the hearts and minds of the American public. In 1911, he wrote a series of pieces in *The American Magazine* that was later turned into a book called *The Principles of Scientific Management*, which became one of the most influential business books of the twentieth century.

DURING HIS TIME working in factories in various positions like laborer, machinist, and chief engineer, Frederick Taylor was rattled by the lack of efficiency in the production process. Because workers had the ability to make their own decisions and work at their own pace, the process was sometimes sloppy and irregular. Taylor's scientific management required the full unwinding of the old way work had been done. To maximize output and streamline the process, his system denied workers any degree of independent thought and forced them to forfeit their judgment and experience to management. Each laborer, Taylor said, "should receive every day clear-cut, definite instructions as to just what he is to do and how he is to do it, and these instructions should be exactly carried out, whether they are right or wrong."[18]

Managers would perform time-and-motion studies with stopwatches to measure employees' output. The production process would be standardized and surveilled, while individual autonomy, initiative, and creativity would be erased. "In the past," Taylor wrote in his book, "the man has been first; in the future the system must be first."[19]

In his treatise, he outlined the four tenets of scientific management:

First. They develop a science for each element of a man's work, which replaces the old rule-of-thumb method.

Second. They scientifically select and then train, teach, and develop the workman, whereas in the past he chose his own work and trained himself as best he could.

Third. They heartily cooperate with the men so as to insure all of the work being done in accordance with the principles of the science which has been developed.

Fourth. There is an almost equal division of the work and the responsibility between the management and the workmen. The management take over all work for which they are better fitted than the workmen, while in the past almost all of the work and the greater part of the responsibility were thrown upon the men.[20]

In his 1992 book *Technopoly,* Neil Postman nicely condensed Taylorism: "The primary, if not the only, goal of human labor and thought is efficiency; that technical calculation is in all respects superior to human judgment; that in fact human judgment cannot be trusted, because it is plagued by laxity, ambiguity, and unnecessary complexity; that subjectivity is an obstacle to clear thinking; that what cannot be measured either does not exist or is of no value; and that the affairs of citizens are best guided and conducted by experts."[21]

In his own words, Taylor said that scientific management involved "a complete mental revolution."

The first factory graced with the presence of scientific management was Bethlehem Steel, then a military contractor in Pennsylvania. The company had a supply of eighty thousand tons of pig iron in its yard; each worker was loading an average of 12.5 tons a day onto the carts, eventually to be used to supply the Spanish-American War.[22] Taylor, a consultant to the company, immediately noticed inefficiencies in the system. So he assembled a group of ten "large, powerful Hungarians," doubled their wages, and asked them to load 16.5 tons as swiftly as they could. They completed the task in under fourteen minutes. After crunching the numbers, Taylor used the fourteen-minute trial run to determine that the hourly rate of these ten men was seventy-one tons loaded. After accounting for breaks, he somehow came to the conclusion that first-class workers were actually capable of handling 47.5 tons in a ten-hour workday, instead of 12.5 tons.[23]

However, in real life it was virtually impossible for the workers to keep up such a pace day in and day out.

In his book, Taylor offers the tale of a worker he calls Schmidt as a case study:

"Schmidt, are you a high-priced man?"

"Vell, I don't know vat you mean . . ."

"Oh, come now, you answer my questions. What I want to find out is whether you are a high-priced man or one of these cheap fellows here. What I want to find out is whether you want to earn $1.85 a day or whether you are satisfied with $1.15, just the same as all those cheap fellows are getting."

"Did I vant $1.85 a day? Vas dot a high-priced man? Vell, yes I vas a high-priced man . . ."

"Well, if you are a high-priced man, you will do exactly as this man tells you to-morrow, from morning till night. When he tells you to pick up a pig and walk, you pick it up and you walk, and when he tells you to sit down and rest, you sit down. You do that right straight through the day. And what's more, no back talk. Now a high-priced man does just what he's told to do, and no back talk. Do you understand that? When this man tells you to walk, you walk; when he tells you to sit down, you sit down, and you don't talk back at him. Now you come on to work here tomorrow morning and I'll know before night whether you are really a high-priced man or not."[24]

Taylor later writes that Schmidt obeyed orders and successfully completed his work for the higher pay. But many journalists and experts have found that Taylor largely fabricated the character of Schmidt and sensationalized the overall story. First, pay incentives could only go so far. Harvard historian Jill Lepore explains in *The New Yorker*, "Some Bethlehem ironworkers were so wrecked after a Taylor-size day's work that they couldn't get out of bed the next morning."[25] Second, it was undeniable that Taylor had manipulated a man he himself later described as "so stupid that he was unfitted to do most kinds of laboring work."[26]

Taylor was later fired by Bethlehem Steel when new management came in. But that wasn't the end of Taylorism. Between 1901 and 1915, Taylor and his comrades implemented scientific management in more than two hundred American businesses, mainly factories.[27] And as mentioned, it was Louis Brandeis who helped place the system and the man behind it into the national spotlight in 1910.

Before long, there was a massive uproar by the general public and labor unions toward Taylorism. The American Federation of Labor declared, "No tyrant or slave driver in the ecstasy of his most delirious dream ever sought to place upon abject slaves a condition more repugnant to commonly accepted notions of freedom of action and liberty of person."[28] It also says quite a lot that some of the stalwarts of scientific management included the likes of Lenin and Mussolini.[29] Taylorism was simply a new expression of human exploitation uniquely matched to the needs of the nation's growing class of industrial capitalists.

The outrage against scientific management, pent up inside the working class, ruptured in 1911 when a strike broke out at the Watertown Arsenal near Boston. This led to a full-blown congressional investigation into "the Taylor and other systems of shop management."

In January 1912, Taylor testified before the Special Committee of the House of Representatives. The chairman of the committee was William Bauchop Wilson, a former labor organizer. After the grueling hearings, Taylor decided to exit public life. He died a few years later from pneumonia at the age of fifty-nine, but his philosophies barreled onward.

. . .

TAYLORISM WAS NEVER meant to spill over to other parts of American life, but it did. In the decade after 1910, American schools were hijacked by the business community, which was hooked on the credos of scientific management. Raymond Callahan, in his seminal book on the subject *Education and the Cult of Efficiency,* minces no words: "The consequences for American education and American society were tragic."[30]

What was the business community's main objective? Just as Taylor was dedicated to making factories run efficiently, corporate executives wanted to have efficient schools.

Why such an urgency to change the system? Callahan believes there were four trends that interlocked: "that educational questions were subordinated to business considerations; that administrators were produced who were not, in any true sense, educators; that a scientific label was put on some very unscientific and dubious methods and practices; and that an anti-intellectual climate, already prevalent, was strengthened."[31] The business community began its assault by bashing the state of public schooling, employing statistics on the ascending illiteracy rates, low student achievement, and the number of children who didn't finish high school as evidence of failing schools.

Over time, the public rallied in support for corporate-driven education policies. The demands on educators to focus on efficiency in the classroom at the National Education Association conference in the summer of 1911 marked the invasion of scientific management into schools.[32] It took off from there, and by the following year, the movement picked up steam in schools around the country.

School-based metrics aligned with the views and values of business leaders who sought to better control their employees. Newton, Massachusetts, schools superintendent

Frank Spaulding, who applied scientific management in his district, summed up some of them: "I refer to such results as the percentage of children of each year of age in the school district that the school enrolls; the average number of days' attendance secured annually from each child; the average length of time required for each child to do a given definite unit of work; the percentage of children of each age who are allowed to complete their schooling, with the average educational equipment of each; the percentage of children who are inspired to continue their education in high school; and the quality of the education that the school affords."[33] The main figure business leaders were concerned with was per-pupil costs. For instance, administrators would perform cost-benefit analyses on what subjects were most efficient to teach.

What's more, Franklin Bobbitt, professor of educational administration at the University of Chicago, introduced scientific management into the administrative structures by setting up standards and constructing scales for educational services. There were also outside experts who filled out school surveys that would assess the operations of the school and offer corporate-backed solutions. Callahan writes, "Following Bobbitt's plan, schoolmen would become mechanics whose tasks would be to figure out ways and means of doing what they were told."[34] Within a few years, school administrators turned into imitation business executives seeking to get the best bang for their buck.

In 1916, educator Ellwood Cubberley explained what the efficiency movement had resulted in: "Our schools are, in a sense, factories in which the raw products (children) are to be shaped and fashioned into products to meet the various demands of life. The specifications for manufacturing come from the demands of twentieth-century civilization, and it is the business of the school to build its pupils according to the specifications laid down."[35]

Since then, the doctrines of scientific management have never left our education system. They have gained a permanent footing in schools as a result of the education policies over the past decade. In the eyes of policymakers and corporations, children are seen as little more than their scores on standardized tests.

WHEN BARACK OBAMA was elected president of the United States in November 2008, I was grinding my way through the eighth grade, my final year at John F. Kennedy Middle School before I was to move up to high school. While I followed the election closely, the candidates' positions on education policy weren't of much interest to me. And at the time, I didn't give any thought to how my school experience could be different.

Among many progressives and liberals, there were flickers of hope that Obama's election signaled the prospect that his presidency would lead to the reversal of the No Child Left Behind Act and Bush-era policies. It sure seemed that way once he named Stanford professor and NCLB critic Linda Darling-Hammond to head his transition's education policy team.

But then in December 2008, any remaining optimism suddenly vanished. The president-elect appointed the CEO of Chicago Public Schools and his friend (and basketball pal) Arne Duncan to the post of secretary of education. A report by the Broad Foundation, a group that has financed anti–public education reforms, noted that Obama's election and the appointment of Duncan "marked the pinnacle of hope for our work in education reform. In many ways, we feel the stars have finally aligned."[36]

As head of Chicago schools, Duncan shook up the system—in a disturbing manner. He bounced kids around from school to school to make it appear as though schools were "turning around." He did not confront the effect of poverty on learning in a city system where 80 percent of schoolchildren live below the poverty line. He dumbed down standards, misleading the public when he pronounced that test scores had improved. He shuttered "failing" schools, replacing neighborhood schools with charters, often financed and run by fat cats and corporations. This is the man Obama put his faith in to run the Department of Education of the most powerful nation in the world.[37]

The Obama-Duncan duo began their campaign on public education by surreptitiously slipping the Race to the Top program into the stimulus package. Few were aware of the magnitude of this initiative. Race to the Top is a $4.35 billion sweepstakes contest that dangled dollar bills before states that adopted Duncan-backed policies. As with all races, there were many more losers than winners. Obama and Duncan were well aware that states were bleeding red ink, teachers were being laid off left and right, and school budgets were being slashed. States would have little choice but to comply.

In distilled terms, Race to the Top is No Child Left Behind on steroids. Obama's education policies have had a broader and more harmful effect on schools than Bush's policies.

In order to qualify for money, states had to agree to tie teacher evaluations to standardized test scores, implement the Common Core standards, institute charter-school-friendly policies, and expand performance-based pay for teachers. Eleven states and the District of Columbia netted a piece of the Race to the Top money in the first two rounds and another seven states in the third round. Even though many states didn't win a dime, they nevertheless had aligned themselves with Duncan's policies just to compete.

Educators, many of whom had campaigned for the president in 2008, have been utterly alienated by his administration's strategy of bashing and firing teachers. Here's one episode that demonstrates this precisely: In 2010, when the school board of Central Falls, one of Rhode Island's lowest-achieving and poorest school districts, voted to fire the entire high school's teaching and support staff, President Obama and Secretary Duncan rhapsodized about the board's decision.[38] The secretary declared the board was "showing courage and doing the right thing for kids."[39] He, of all people, should know better. As noted, Duncan's policies in Chicago of closing schools instead of fixing them, blaming teachers instead of honoring and supporting them, had all failed to get the desired improvements. A study by researchers at the University of Chicago found that Duncan's school "turnaround" policies only worsened the situation, turning the schools around in the wrong direction.[40]

Perhaps most astonishing is that there have been quite a few incidents where President Obama has publicly denounced his own Department of Education's policies. In 2011, he announced his opposition to "teaching to the test." A year later, in his 2012 State of the Union address, Obama reiterated that point, saying, "To teach with creativity and passion; to stop teaching to the test; and to replace teachers who just aren't helping kids learn." But none of his actual policies reflect these words.

. . .

THE PRESIDENT'S EDUCATION agenda is part of a much broader narrative in this country: the corporate education reform crusade. It is a movement being bankrolled by foundations, Wall Street hedge fund managers, other kinds of billionaires, advocacy groups, and think tanks. They want to send public education off to the guillotine. They champion a free-market, neoliberal orthodoxy, which includes closing schools, privatization, vouchers, charter schools, Common Core standards, high-stakes standardized testing, abolishing locally controlled and elected school boards, performance-based pay, and firing and admonishing teachers. They strive to profit off of schoolchildren and believe that schools should be run more like businesses and corporations. Similar to their predecessors in the "age of efficiency" in the early twentieth century, they treat children like numbers in a spreadsheet, where their worth is derived from how they perform on tests. They want to expand privately managed charter schools, many of which are involved in the resegregation of education; they also expel "problem children" at troubling rates, are mismanaged financially, and often are run by people who have little to no experience working with children.

As one writer observed in *Daily Kos,* "Corporate America sees no reason to educate working class students beyond the most basic level. They are seen as nothing more than future low paid drones in a brutal dog-eat-dog-cat-eat-mouse economy. The war against public education is a class war being waged by the wealthy against a growing working class resistance."[41]

The advocacy groups and networks that dominate the field include StudentsFirst, Democrats for Education Reform, ALEC, Students for Education Reform, Uncommon Schools, Knowledge Is Power Program, Success Academy, Stand for Children, and many others. Whenever you hear any of those names, immediately associate them with the corporate-reform agenda.

Some of the most notable foundations are equally aligned against public education. Let's follow the money. Collectively, private philanthropies currently spend almost $4 billion a year on K–12 education. The triumvirate of the major foundations—or the "billionaire boys club," as education historian Diane Ravitch likes to call them—are the Bill & Melinda Gates Foundation, the Eli and Edythe Broad Foundation, and the Walton Family Foundation. Each has unique goals and strategies, but they all function under the umbrella of market-driven corporate reform. Wall Street financiers have also joined the crusade by investing in charter schools for personal financial gain. Thanks to the New Markets Tax Credit Program established during the Clinton presidency, banks and investors that put money into community projects, like the development of new charter schools, in low-income communities can earn a 39 percent federal tax break over seven years. Journalist Juan Gonzalez revealed in the *New York Daily News,* "The program . . . is so lucrative that a lender who uses it can almost double his money in seven years."[42]

You'll almost never find the people on the front lines of the corporate education movement mucking about the white, wealthy communities where they hail from and live; they're only meddling in working-class and minority ones. I virtually guarantee these people would never send their own children to the schools they advocate for poor black and brown children.

The U.S. Department of Education is permeated with corporate reformers. There is a revolving door among the major foundations, think tanks, charter networks, and the department. For example, Secretary Duncan's chief of staff, Emma Vadehra, previously worked at Uncommon Schools. She replaced Joanne Weiss, who before joining the administration was a partner and chief operating officer at New-Schools Venture Fund. That's why the corporate reformers were so giddy when Obama was elected.

The national media has helped to push the corporate-reform initiatives. Rick Hess, director of education policy studies at the American Enterprise Institute and author of *With the Best of Intentions: How Philanthropy Is Reshaping K–12 Education,* conducted a study on the coverage media outlets gave to the leading education foundations, including the Gates Foundation, Broad Foundation, Walton Family Foundation, Annenberg Challenge, and Milken Family Foundation, from 1995 to 2005. He found that there were "thirteen positive articles for every critical account."[43] The NBC Education Nation Summit held annually in New York City from 2010 to 2013 is another conspicuous example of national glorification of corporate education reform. Critics of standardized testing, the Common Core standards, and privatization schemes were rarely seen on the panel discussions. There were also not many student, teacher, or parent voices. But of course politicians, entrepreneurs, journalists, and college presidents were not in short supply.

WHEN IT COMES to student performance on standardized tests, Dan Goldhaber, education researcher at the University of Washington–Bothell, and his colleagues have found that teacher characteristics account for about 8.5 percent of those results and socioeconomic factors account for about 60 percent. In addition, he wrote, "All the influences of a school, including school-, teacher-, and class-level variables, both measurable and immeasurable, were found to account for approximately 21 percent of the variation in student achievement."[44] The corporate reformers, however, have adopted a "no excuses" doctrine on the role of poverty on schooling. In other words, they deny that being in poverty is an excuse for someone to have poor academic achievement. In doing so, they fail to address the root causes of poverty and the very conditions children are living in. Nearly a quarter of American children live in poverty, putting this country just ahead of last-place Romania in the rankings of developed countries' child poverty rates.[45] It is one of the most disgraceful scandals of our time, yet it hardly matters at all in the calculus of the corporate reformers—or they incorrectly argue that the very measures they propose will lift children out of poverty.

Half a century ago, Michael Harrington published his influential book *The Other America,* a study of poverty in the United States. He noted, "The real explanation of why the poor are where they are is that they made the mistake of being born to the wrong parents, in the wrong section of the country, in the wrong industry, or in the wrong racial or ethnic group. Once that mistake has been made, they could have been paragons of will and morality, but most of them would never have had a chance to get out of the other America."[46] The effects poverty has on children are revolting. Many poor children have difficulty regulating their emotions and experience chronic stress, trauma, and severe health problems. Harvard economist Sendhil Mullainathan, the coauthor of one study on the effects of poverty on the brain, told *The Washington Post,* "Poverty is the equivalent of pulling an all-nighter. Picture yourself after an all-nighter. Being poor is like that every day."[47]

How much can you really expect schools to do when

you have children who are impoverished, hungry, malnourished, more vulnerable to asthma, heart disease, hypertension, stroke, and diabetes, experiencing toxic stress, residing in single-parent households, and/or exposed to violence, crime, lead paint, and secondhand smoke on a daily basis? If the corporate education reformers were really committed to making life better for the poorest and most disadvantaged children in our society, they would stop making asinine comments like "Poverty is not destiny" but rather declare, as activist Kenzo Shibata once said, "Poverty shouldn't be. Period." And they would call for wraparound services, free breakfast programs, early childhood programs for the poor, and adequate numbers of librarians and nurses in schools in order to ameliorate the effects of child poverty, instead of waging a neoliberal jihad on American public education and teachers.

In Cincinnati, Ohio, some public schools have been transformed into community learning centers.[48] Through partnerships with local organizations, social services, health care, mentoring, recreation activities, and parenting and adult education classes are offered year-round at these schools for the benefit of the entire community. The school becomes the anchor of the community, and poverty, malnutrition, and illnesses are mitigated to some degree. Why don't we ask the corporate reformers to pick up the tab on the expansion of this promising approach?

As Harrington wrote, "In a nation with a technology that could provide every citizen with a decent life, it is an outrage and a scandal that there should be such social misery."[49] We can wipe out child poverty in this country. We have the money to do so. We are just lacking the political will.

.   .   .

THE DARLING OF the political left Naomi Klein penned a pathbreaking book titled *The Shock Doctrine* in 2007, offering a sweeping critique of free-market policies and the ascent of what she calls "disaster capitalism." She wrote:

> For more than three decades, [University of Chicago economist Milton] Friedman and his powerful followers had been perfecting this very strategy: waiting for a major crisis, then selling off pieces of the state to private players while citizens were still reeling from the shock, then quickly making the "reforms" permanent. In one of his most influential essays, Friedman articulated contemporary capitalism's core tactical nostrum, what I have come to understand as "the shock doctrine." He observed that "only a crisis—actual or perceived— produces real change."[50]

Klein holds up the dismantling of the New Orleans public school system and the infiltration of privately managed charter schools in the aftermath of Hurricane Katrina as a textbook example of disaster capitalism. But what went down in that city was just the beginning. What has clobbered the cities of Philadelphia and Chicago in recent years is a perfect illustration of shock-doctrine policies—crafting a crisis out of thin air to ram through unfettered capitalistic policies.

In Philadelphia, the state-run School Reform Commission voted in 2013 to close twenty-three schools, almost 10 percent of the city's schools, and shed nearly four thousand jobs, including aides, teachers, secretaries, counselors, assistant principals, and support-services assistants.[51] Seventy-nine percent of the students affected by the school closings are black, even though only 55 percent of the district's enrollment is African American. And 93 percent of students affected are low income, while 81 percent of students in the district overall are low income.[52] The commission claims that in order to cork a $304 million budget shortfall, these unpopular moves were necessary. It doesn't seem to add up when you consider that the district is spending $139 million over five years to increase the number of charter schools.[53]

Philadelphia mayor Michael Nutter, a Democrat in name only, has defended the school closings, giving his "full and unequivocal support."[54] He has also supported the expansion of charters, even though nineteen of the seventy-four operating charters in the city were "under investigation for fraud, financial mismanagement, and conflicts of interest," according to National Public Radio in 2011.[55]

If the state of affairs in Philadelphia seems appalling, consider the much greater devastation being wrought by Chicago mayor Rahm Emanuel. Emanuel manufactured a billion-dollar budget crisis to legitimize slash-and-burn policies of closing schools and laying off teachers. The Chicago Teachers Union claims that the audited budget for the 2011–12 fiscal year showed that the Chicago Public Schools district (CPS) actually had a surplus of $344 million.[56] Meanwhile, the mayor was prepared to pony up tens of millions of tax-increment financing funds—basically a share of property taxes—to DePaul University, a private school, to build a new basketball arena. After an outcry from the public, he opted instead to help fund the development of a Marriott hotel that was being constructed adjacent to the arena.[57]

In May 2013, the Chicago Board of Education voted to shutter fifty public schools—forty-nine elementary schools and one high school—the largest single mass school closing in U.S. history. It is part of the larger scheme to open more nonunionized charter schools.

The school closings devastated communities. They have forced children to cross gang lines on their way to school. University of Illinois at Chicago professor and gang expert John Hagedorn testified before a federal judge saying that as a result of children being displaced by school closings, "it is likely a child will be shot and killed."[58]

In addition, closing schools will not put a single dent in the deficit, contradicting what the district has repeatedly claimed. Chicago radio station WBEZ determined that "all cost savings, plus tens of millions of additional dollars (for a total of $233 million), will be put into receiving schools [schools taking students from the closed schools]." The district also claims that the schools are underutilized—there are some hundred thousand empty desks. The problem is that its calculation is based on an ideal thirty-student class size figure. Any class size below that number is defined as operating inefficiently—having empty seats. Overall, the radio station debunked and labeled as inaccurate nine of the CPS claims about why it needed to close schools.[59]

Emanuel's policies, at heart, are racist and classist. An analysis by the *Chicago Sun-Times* uncovered that about 90 percent of the students affected by school closings are African American, while just 41.7 percent of the overall district's student population is black. Ninety-four percent of the students affected are also low income, while overall, 85 percent of students in the district are from low-income families.[60]

A few months after the school closings vote, the district announced that 2,113 teachers and support staff would be laid off due to budget cuts.[61]

Emanuel has used his power to appoint the seven-member school board, which then rubber-stamps his policies. He fills it largely with investment bankers and businessmen and

-women. Because they are unelected, the members can tune out the public's sentiments without much fear of retribution.

While President Obama's former chief of staff is tormenting his home city, the president has remained mum. Some are wondering: If Obama were still an Illinois state senator today, would he be in the streets protesting against school closings and budget cuts?

Chicago students and teachers are, however, not standing idly by while Emanuel's neoliberal campaign proceeds. They're fighting back. In September 2012, the Chicago Teachers Union strike shook the nation to its core. Since then, students, teachers, and parents have staged mass demonstrations, rallies, and sit-ins around the city. As Rick Perlstein noted in *The Nation,* "The conditions are ripe for such civil disobedience: the bonds of trust within a variegated activist community; a growing culture of militancy extending all the way down to formerly quiescent middle-class parents; strategic smarts, passion, momentum. Brazil, Bulgaria, Taksim Square . . . Chicago. The next battle in the global war against austerity, privatization and corruption just might spark off right here."[62] One manifestation of the public's dissatisfaction with Emanuel was the 2015 Chicago mayoral elections, in which he failed to win a majority of the vote and was forced into a runoff election, the first time in the city's history. His main challenger was Cook County commissioner Jesús "Chuy" García, who was endorsed by the Chicago Teachers Union and ran on a platform that included stopping school closures, putting a moratorium on new charter schools, and supporting an elected school board. While Emanuel did eventually defeat him in the runoff election, what is undeniable is that advocates for public education in Chicago are making waves.

. . .

IN APRIL 2013, the Economic Policy Institute's Broader, Bolder Approach to Education published a fascinating report by Elaine Weiss and Don Long ridiculing the corporate education reforms that have possessed urban school districts like New York City, Washington, D.C., and Chicago. These reforms were put into effect by people such as Secretary of Education Arne Duncan, former chancellor of D.C. Public Schools Michelle Rhee, and former chancellor of New York City public schools Joel Klein.

The report concluded that the market-oriented reforms "deliver few benefits, often harm the students they purport to help, and divert attention from a set of other, less visible policies with more promise to weaken the link between poverty and low educational attainment."

Their major findings:

1. Test scores increased less, and achievement gaps grew more, in "reform" cities than in other urban districts.
2. Reported successes for targeted students evaporated upon closer examination.
3. Test-based accountability prompted churn that thinned the ranks of experienced teachers, but not necessarily bad teachers.
4. School closures did not send students to better schools or save school districts money.
5. Charter schools further disrupted the districts while providing mixed benefits, particularly for the highest-needs students.
6. Emphasis on the widely touted market-oriented reforms drew attention and resources from initiatives with greater promise.

7. The reforms missed a critical factor driving achievement gaps: the influence of poverty on academic performance. Real, sustained change requires strategies that are more realistic, patient, and multipronged.[63]

There you have it: corporate education reform has not and will never work. As Diane Ravitch excellently put it in *Reign of Error,* "No matter how many Hollywood movies the corporate reformers produce, no matter how many television specials sing the glories of privatization, no matter how often the reformers belittle the public schools and their teachers, the public is not yet ready to relinquish its public schools to speculators, entrepreneurs, ideologues, snake-oil salesmen, profit-making businesses, and Wall Street hedge-fund managers."[64]

What this debate over testing and accountability really comes down to is whether we are technocrats or humanists. There was a superb piece in *Education Week* by Jack Whelan, lecturer of business communication at the Foster School of Business at the University of Washington, that pointed out the stark contrast between the two and what it entails for education:

If public-school education is a critical battleground for the soul of the nation, who are the combatants? I see them as broadly falling into two camps: technocrats and humanists. Let's define terms. I mean "humanist" in the broad sense as the affirmation of the value and dignity of particular, individual human beings and of their individual potential to become more densely realized as a Selves in community with other Selves. This contrasts with the technocratic tendency to see humans as abstractions in the aggregate, as data points on a spread sheet . . .

The technocratic mindset feels at home in governmental, corporate, and foundation bureaucracies. It is procedure oriented and lacks practical wisdom or adaptability to the unforeseen or the uncontrollable. It is mentality obsessed with measurement: if it cannot be measured it does not exist . . .

Technocracies as systems are very uncomfortable with what they cannot control or predict. They therefore see the lively, eccentric, and unpredictable as irrelevant or as a problem to be eliminated . . .

Don't be confused by the humanistic rhetoric of technocrats. Look at their policies. Obama talks like a humanist, but Duncan's policies are technocratic through and through.[65]

It will be up to the public to fend off the well-financed corporate war on public education. Students, teachers, administrators, and parents do not have nearly as much money as the other side has lined up. They may not have as many celebratory stories in the national press. They may not be in the White House, Congress, state legislatures, or boardrooms. But they have power in numbers to resist and overthrow the corporate rule of public education.

TOO MANY PEOPLE, lamentably, would be very satisfied if our schools just turned back the clock to the pre-NCLB era. Mission accomplished, they would declare. Yes, schools were a bit better back then. Much less high-stakes testing. Fewer corporatized charter schools. No draconian teacher evaluation systems. Or mass school closures.

But schools were still very much inhumane places in the business of controlling and commanding children (as they've always been and done since their inception in the nineteenth century). They were clearly not utopias. The past decade in education policy has just made schooling more intolerable.

As consequential as the conversations and debates over standardized testing, charter schools, accountability, merit pay, and unions are, we cannot lose sight of the fact that the basics of traditional schooling—grades, tests, lectures, rote learning, lack of learner voice or ownership, and the treatment of the students as "depositories" and the teacher as the "depositor," as Brazilian educator Paulo Freire put it in his incredible book *Pedagogy of the Oppressed*—must also be challenged and ultimately rejected.[66] Until we begin to question our long-held assumptions about learning and schooling, the oppression of our children will continue.

CHAPTER 4

The Right to Learn Freely

Human beings are born incredibly intelligent. However, many believe that children detest learning and can't learn without a teacher or some other authority telling them what to do. To which I reply by asking: Have you ever met an infant? Just look at any one of them. They all play, fail, observe, explore, and once they learn how to talk they ask hundreds of questions a day. They are masters of learning. Curiosity, play, and the awe of living is the compass that young ones use to navigate as they grow and develop. This compass is a wonderful gift that comes with human life.

Until just a few decades ago, the popularly held belief among scientists and researchers was that babies are irrational, selfish, unconscious, and illogical. They would subscribe fondly to the attitudes expressed in a satirical *Onion* piece with the headline "New Study Reveals Most Children Unrepentant Sociopaths." It describes a "study" that found that "an estimated 98 percent of children under the age of 10 are remorseless sociopaths with little regard for anything other than their own egocentric interests and pleasures."[1]

One of the reasons for this ignorance was that "scientists weren't sure how to go about studying the mental life of babies," wrote Yale professor of psychology Paul Bloom in *The New York Times Magazine*. "It's a challenge to study the cognitive abilities of any creature that lacks language, but human babies present an additional difficulty, because, even compared to rats or birds, they are behaviorally limited: they can't run mazes or peck at levers."[2]

In the 1980s and '90s, psychologists began observing the movement of babies' eyes and discovered that they detected objects similarly to adults.[3] This led to pathbreaking research discrediting the centuries-old conventional wisdom and acknowledging that "in some ways, young children are actually smarter, more imaginative, more caring, and even more conscious than adults are," as Alison Gopnik puts it in her fantastic book *The Philosophical Baby*. Gopnik, professor of psychology at the University of California, Berkeley, has conducted extensive research in early childhood development and play. In her book, she notes that due to the plasticity of babies' brains, "Instead of experiencing a single aspect of their world and shutting down everything else they seem to be vividly experiencing everything at once. Their brains are soaked in cholinergic transmitters, with few inhibitory transmitters to allay their effects."[4] Moreover, like adults, they have the ability to daydream. Researchers at Imperial College London scanned the brains of seventy babies, who were between twenty-nine and forty-three weeks of development, and found that their resting state networks—the brain regions active when an individual is awake and at rest but not engaged in a thought-intensive task—were fully formed. One type of resting state network is the default mode network, which is involved with daydreaming.[5]

For most of human history, we weren't aware that babies

could model adult expressions. In a noteworthy 1977 study, Oxford University psychologist Andy Meltzoff and M. Keith Moore of the University of Washington stunned the world with a groundbreaking finding. Experimenters showed a series of gestures to a number of twelve- to twenty-one-day-old infants, and more often than not the subject mimicked them. Disproving previous findings by psychologist Jean Piaget and others, Meltzoff and Moore concluded in their paper, "Infants between 12 and 21 days of age can imitate both facial and manual gestures; this behavior cannot be explained in terms of either conditioning or innate releasing mechanisms. Such imitation implies that human neonates can equate their own unseen behaviors with gestures they see others perform."[6]

Babies can also recognize faces at a remarkably early age. One study suggested that at four months, babies can process faces at adult levels.[7] Another study found that at as young as six months, infants' brains were able to detect the faces of monkeys.[8] Other research shows that at five months old, babies can "follow the gaze of an adult toward an object and engage in joint attention."[9]

Believe it not, babies can even understand probabilities. In a study with six experiments where red and white ping-pong balls were taken out of a box and shown to babies, the psychologists Fei Xu and Vashti Garcia of the University of British Columbia learned that they looked longer at unexpected outcomes than expected outcomes and could make predictions about the content of the box from which the sample of ping-pong balls came from. In a paper published in the *Proceedings of the National Academy of Sciences,* they concluded, "Our results showed that, given a sample, the infants were able to make inferences about the population from which the sample had been drawn. Conversely, given information about the entire population of relatively small size, the infants were able to make predictions about the sample. Our findings provide evidence that infants possess a powerful mechanism for inductive learning, either using heuristics or basic principles of probability."[10]

All human beings are born natural learners. A group of researchers have found that babies begin learning language in the womb.[11] Then in the first year of life, as New York University professor and psychologist Gary Marcus notes in a piece for *The New Yorker,* before saying actual words, they babble, repeating the same individual syllable, like "ga-ga," and then linking a few syllables together over time, like "ga-doo-gee."[12] Regularly, they are eavesdropping on conversations and sounds in their environment. Soon thereafter, babies can put together real words. When it comes to learning how to walk, babies are constantly falling over, picking themselves back up, and experimenting. It's fascinating to watch. Children learn how to both walk and talk when they are ready, and they do so largely by instinct and on their own.

"Hardly an adult in a thousand, or ten thousand, could in any three years of his life learn as much, grow as much in his understanding of the world around him, as every infant learns and grows in his first three years," explained John Holt in *How Children Fail*.[13] And as writer George Dennison wrote in *The Lives of Children,* "Consider, too, how shocking it would be if for two minutes we adults could re-experience the powers of mind—the concentration, the memory, the energy for detail, to say nothing of the physical élan—we possessed at the age of ten. Our vanity in relation to the young most certainly would not survive."[14]

Developmental psychologist John Flavell once told Gopnik that he would sacrifice all his degrees and honors for the opportunity to "spend just five minutes inside the head of a young child—to genuinely experience the world as a two-year-old once more."[15] There isn't anything quite like the powers that children possess. As we will see, the way most of our schools teach children is unsound. They brush off all the research and evidence that show that children learn through play, curiosity, and imagination.

THE FIRST TIME Gever Tulley rebelled from a classroom experience was in the third grade when he was forced to memorize the multiplication tables. "I remember I was so intensely offended that I should do this memorization just because that's what you have to do," he said. "It was like I was taking a political stance."[16]

Tulley grew up in Northern California. When he was about six years old, his family moved to Canada. That was because his father detested President Richard Nixon, who had just been reelected to a second presidential term. They moved back to California when Nixon was impeached a couple of years later.

Now in middle school, Tulley entered the Community School, an alternative program in the Mendocino Unified School District. This was the 1970s, an era of experimentation in public schools across the country. The original conception of his school was to create a place that would attract the children who were bored and the truant children, sometimes referred to as "the feral children of Mendocino," who resisted going to school. There was a staff of about eight teachers, one of whom was each student's mentor. That person was responsible for tracking the student's work and helping him understand its purpose and find resources and experts. For the fifty or sixty students enrolled, it was entirely project based. "So you would come to school," Tulley explains, "and when a good idea came to you, you would just start working on it." With an abundance of lightly supervised time, he was able to work on activities like writing, playing with the Apple computer, or coding in the electronics lab. As long as they were doing something, there weren't any restrictions on what the students could do. Once or twice a week, the teachers would have a meeting with the students to codify what they had learned into curricular categories. "Say you started this game of Dungeons and Dragons," he said. "Well, that's math and probability. Put down the number of hours spent in those categories." This reflective aspect was something the students looked forward to all week.

Tulley noted, "We had a sense of parenthood for this school. That was true for every student that went there. We helped make it. This was our school." He went to the Community School for his middle and high school years.

The fall after his graduation in 1980, he matriculated at the University of California, San Diego. He hadn't met some of the typical college entrance requirements. Since the UC system made accommodations for poor students, he got waivers on requirements, like taking a foreign language. By that point, Tulley had been programming professionally (for money) for four years. The university, however, would not let him test or interview out of the Computer Science 101 class. He figured that when he went to that class, he would just talk to the professor, who would realize the waste of time that this was.

"When I arrived at the first class," he said, "I noticed that there were over three hundred students taking the same class that I was. That alone was peculiar." The other part that astounded him was that it was going to take an entire year to learn this "elementary level computer science textbook." To him, it felt eerily similar to the time he was told to memorize the multiplication tables in elementary school. "I couldn't understand why anybody would roll over and accept that you have to put your time in doing this boring activity in order to get the right to do something interesting," he said. By the way, skipping the computer science course didn't fly with the professor either.

Tulley lasted only one quarter at the college. He dropped out, moved to Santa Cruz, and worked in a computer repair job and did freelance programming gigs. For the next few decades, he worked in a dizzying array of jobs in the technology industry as a game engineer, developer, software architect, consultant, and computer scientist. He would never return to the halls of ivy.

In 2004, Tulley and his wife, Julie Spiegler, who worked at Adobe Systems, attended the Adobe Christmas party. He started a conversation with a group of acquaintances and friends about the adventures they had had as children—unsupervised play for hours every day. He told me, "I remember saying something to the effect of how remarkable is it that in a generation and a half, our behavior when we were children is now seen as crazy and irresponsible on the part of parents?" He proposed to the group that somebody should start a summer camp where kids would be separated from their parents and be able to play, go on adventures, and do dangerous things. And that's of course what he did. "By the end of dinner," he said, "I already had five children signed up." He personally knew all of them, but he wanted to have a few kids he hadn't previously been familiar with. He put an announcement on a blog and found three more. Two of them jetted in all the way from Connecticut.

The following summer, Tinkering School was brought

to life. Tulley converted his guest bedroom into bunk beds for eight children. He said, "Without any clear pedagogical framework, we just decided to build things as a context for learning." On the first morning, at the workshop near his home, the children came together and he told them, "Everybody take a seat," but there were no chairs, so their first task was to construct chairs. The first couple were terrible and broke immediately, but by the end of the day, they had sturdy chairs. Throughout the week, they also built bridges, twenty-foot freestanding towers, and even 120 feet of roller-coaster track and a tiny car to ride in.

"A little bit after that, I was getting e-mailed asking when the next camp was," Tulley said. The following summer, he grew the group to twelve children. During camp, he was regularly blogging about the day's events and began garnering considerable interest from educators, parents, and children around the world. With 100 percent reenrollment, he received more than one hundred applications for four spots and held a needs-blind lottery. In general, he wasn't organizing the camps in order to make extra money. He was just genuinely curious about how these learning experiences work.

A few years after delivering a very popular talk, "Five Dangerous Things You Should Let Your Kids Do," at the TED conference in 2007, Tulley and Spiegler expanded it into a book, *50 Dangerous Things (You Should Let Your Children Do)*, which was published by Penguin. It could be best summarized by a few sentences from a talk he gave at TEDxBloomington in 2011: "Children today are increasingly treated like exotic animals: kept in special cages and fed a diet of pre-digested ideas, lest they skin a knee or have an original thought but there is great value in the minor scrape or bruise and the lessons that they teach."[17]

It was at Tinkering School where he heard students

expressing dissatisfaction with their experiences in regular school. "I was starting to wonder," he said. "Here are these obviously very smart, self-actualized kids who are bored in school and are starting to resent the fact that they have to go to school." After doing some research on alternative education, he came across a man named Bryan Welch, director of a summer camp in San Francisco called A Curious Summer. In 2010, they met up and had a conversation that spiraled into entertaining the possibility of creating a year-round school. They decided to do it. They rented a tiny office in Maritime Hall in San Francisco and bootstrapped a new school driven by the same principles as their respective programs: play, experimentation, and self-directed learning. Tulley spent most of his time raising money from donors. Welch met with prospective families and explained the vision for what would be called the Brightworks School, named after the polished metal or wood surfaces of a boat.

In the spring of 2011, Tulley signed a lease on a nine-thousand-square-foot building with eighteen-foot ceilings, formerly a factory for Best Foods mayonnaise. Each day, thousands of gallons of mayonnaise had been processed there. Later, a month before the opening of Brightworks in September, Welch and Tulley's partnership ended. They had overlooked some of their incompatibilities. "I put no blame on Bryan," he said. "I would not have started Brightworks without that spark. I look back to those days as some of the most productive." The school opened that fall.

Tinkering School is still in operation. It holds five-week sessions in Northern California each year and has partner programs in cities like Chicago, Buffalo, Baltimore, Madrid, and Austin.

.   .   .

WHEN I ENTERED the Brightworks school one morning in the fall of 2012, the sounds of children shouting and dancing echoed throughout the former factory building. Sprawled across the cork floor, they were learning *capoeira,* a Brazilian martial art, from an instructor. The students begin the day with Morning Circle, when general announcements are made and some physical exercise occurs. At the end of each Morning Circle, they have a simple daily mindfulness exercise where a collaborator strikes a metal bar and everyone sits still and listens until the sound fades away. That is meant to help the students learn how to focus and pay attention to detail.

Tucked in the Mission District of San Francisco, the Brightworks school is unlike any school you have ever experienced. Some jokingly refer to it as "the school where children refuse to leave." Replicating the feel of a one-room schoolhouse, the space features a fabrication lab, art studio, kitchen, science lab, library, wood shop, individual workspaces, and tree houses. There's also a lofty ceiling, a myriad of windows and skylights, tree trunks, and plenty of woodwork scattered throughout.

I first learned about the school a few years ago. Then in November 2012, Gever Tulley and I appeared on a panel at the Fast Company's Innovation Uncensored conference in San Francisco with then–StudentsFirst CEO Michelle Rhee and former president of the Washington Teachers' Union George Parker. Since then, I have paid several visits to the school.

During the 2014–15 school year, the forty-nine enrolled students ranged in age from five to fifteen. The high sticker price—$25,095—and lack of racial diversity are two concerns that the school continues to confront. Regarding the former, Tulley said that nearly 40 percent of the families receive some tuition assistance. The reason the cost is so high is that the school has no other source of income, beyond some private donations. And regarding the latter, Tulley says that in the past they did direct outreach to low-income and minority families, but many of those families were not comfortable sending their kids to this "weird school."

After Morning Circle, they branch out into their bands to begin work. Grouped by age, each band has up to eight kids. There is ample time for age mixing and collaboration. Teachers are called "collaborators." The student-collaborator ratio is about eight to one.

Before lunch, the students walk over to a nearby park to play. The students end their day with Closing Circle for reflection. On Fridays, there is traditionally a community lunch with everyone in the school. A parent or community member prepares the food.

One of the unique staff positions is the "libero," after the player in volleyball who can replace any other player. The libero is a collaborator who isn't assigned specific students but moves around the bands and assists the students who are in the crux of their projects.

For the 2013–14 school year, the libero was Sean Murray. Murray, who is in his thirties, is affable and lanky with blond hair and blue eyes. After graduating from Duke University in 2004, he taught at the Churchill School in Manhattan for four years, which is exclusively for kids with attention deficit hyperactivity disorder (ADHD). During his final year at the school, he opened the Bamboo Bike Studio in Red Hook, Brooklyn, with two friends. They held workshops to teach people how to build their own bicycles out of bamboo. Then he spent two years exploring carpentry and woodworking. He worked for Varian Designs, a Bay Area–based boutique furniture design and manufacturing company and also did carpentry work for a few contractors.

One day, a couple with a young child who were friends of Murray's suggested that he check out this new school called Brightworks. He just went and knocked on the door. He couldn't believe it actually existed. In February 2013, he started as a volunteer at the school with the explicit intention of eventually working there. "My dream was to start something like Tinkering School by the time I was sixty," he told me. "Not only does [Tulley's school] exist and is way better than mine could ever be, but I get to work with him and Josh [director of Tinkering School]."

ZADA HATHAWAY IS considered a "Brightworks native." She's been enrolled at the school since its genesis. Her mother is Ellen Hathaway, director of the school. Their family became familiar with Tulley after reading his book.

Zada is a teenager and has short-cropped brown hair, braces, and purple fingernails. She was dressed in a gray Brightworks shirt, jeans, and red shoes when we were sitting and talking on a couch one morning.

Until fifth grade, she attended a traditional public school in San Francisco. She was a perfectionist and got all A's. The transition to Brightworks was a bit difficult and confusing for her. "I was like, why aren't people telling me what to do all the time?" she said. "I had gone to a school where you have to do everything people are telling you to do." This is a subject that Tulley and I discussed at length. "Most kids are not used to managing their own time," he told me. "They've come from an environment where every moment is scheduled: before, during, and after school." So you need to give them a period of time, usually about six months, with no obligations. "I've got an hour of my time and I'm going to sit here and stare into space."

The first day of the first year at Brightworks was memorable. Zada said they made mayonnaise to "pay tribute to our history," constructed "a fake mountain out of paper and spritzed water on it to see how the water would come down," and sang songs. The overall curriculum is based on what they call an arc. An arc is a central theme to be examined in multiple angles over many weeks. In each arc, there are three phases: exploration, expression, and exposition.

When I visited Brightworks in November 2012, the arc at the time was the topic of salt, and the students were in the midst of the expression phase. Before that, Zada's band had completed the exploration phase. During that phase, Tulley explains, "The idea is to create an experiential and intellectual landscape where that topic is very prominent and the students get a chance to find something that they are fascinated by in that topic." Eventually, they create project declarations, which fully state and outline what they want to accomplish with their projects. One activity Zada's band did was watch a video about synesthesia, which is a condition in which a stimulation of one sense causes a sensation in another sense. Zada, who was eleven at the time, actually has the condition herself. Christie Seyfert, her collaborator, told her how synesthesia related to salt, and she decided to do her project on the effect of salt on the nervous system. She did research online and sought out experts, including neurologists, psychologists, and professors. She met with them and recorded her interviews and ultimately typed up her findings into a research paper. Then during the exposition phase, parents and community members come to the school and check out the projects and listen to the students' presentations.

After the salt arc came the fairness arc. Zada and her band volunteered at the food bank and the needle exchange, an optional activity. They learned about homelessness, sweatshops, and workers' rights. For her main project, Zada was inspired by Haight-Ashbury, the neighborhood she lives in. "There are a bunch of homeless people," she said. "A lot of people are scared of them and I didn't understand why, because they are just normal people. They just happen to not have houses. I wanted to make a project showing people why it's not fair that people mistreat them." She went on a quest for places where she could volunteer. She discovered the Homeless Prenatal Program, which was located just a few blocks from the school. Later, she met the founder and was permitted to volunteer for a few hours a week.

"I'm the girl who sat on the street telling people about the prenatal program and asking them whether they wanted to donate to it," Zada said. Over a span of six weeks, she raised six hundred dollars. Then she penned a research paper about her experience.

No grades or tests are given at Brightworks. By the time a student graduates from Brightworks, she will have a rich portfolio that documents all of her projects.

I asked Tulley why Brightworks has more learning requirements than a free or democratic school, where there isn't a curriculum and kids can learn whatever they want. He said, "Two reasons. One is that you have to make a school where parents will put their children in. San Francisco parents are not interested in a free school. Two is that it's a bit selfish. I wanted a place where adults and kids could play with these ideas together. Co-curated learning." However, there is some flexibility. One day, during the fairness arc, a parent called up the school and said, "My friend is in town. He's a famous cheese maker and I thought I would bring him by the school. He's offered to do a cheese-making session with the kids." Ellen Hathaway had taken the call and was about to ask Tulley whether they should do it but stopped herself and told him, "Screw the arc, let's make the cheese!" And they did. The cheese maker showed up with a baby goat in a pet carrier and the kids had a wonderful time making cheese for an afternoon. "We don't treat the pedagogy as dogma," he said. "We put it aside when an opportunity comes."

WE LOVE LEARNING until someone interferes inappropriately with this process. For most children, this interference is known as formal schooling, which kicks in around age five and increasingly even earlier. If you wanted to create a place that would be least conducive to the conditions of robust learning and teaching, you would look no further than a traditional school. Students are endlessly measured like meat products—given grades and test scores, herded room to room every forty minutes, and told to be quiet, sit still in their seats, and pay attention to their teacher. Who wouldn't hate learning after going through that insanity for thirteen years?

Here's how Swedish teacher and writer Ellen Key eloquently summed it up in *The Century of the Child:*

> The modern school has succeeded in doing something which, according to the law of physics, is impossible: the annihilation of once existent matter. The desire for knowledge, the capacity for acting by oneself, the gift of observation, all qualities children bring with them to school, have, as a rule, at the close of the school period disappeared. They have not been transformed

into actual knowledge or interests. This is the result of children spending almost the whole of their life from the sixth to the eighteenth year at the school desk, hour by hour, month by month, term by term; taking doses of knowledge, first in teaspoonfuls, then in dessert-spoonfuls, and finally in tablespoonfuls, absorbing mixtures which the teacher often has compounded from fourth- or fifth-hand recipes.

After the school, there often comes a further period of study in which the only distinction in method is, that the mixture is administered by the ladleful.

When young people have escaped from this régime, their mental appetite and mental digestion are so destroyed that they forever lack capacity for taking real nourishment.[18]

As a society, we make a number of wrongheaded assumptions regarding learning in school. The first assumption is that children need to be forced to learn things they don't like in order to be prepared to do the boring things in adult life. However, I've never met an alumnus of a free or democratic school who wasn't able to do the boring, annoying parts of adult life—like filing taxes, taking out the garbage, or doing laundry—because he wasn't forced to learn things he didn't like in school. It doesn't equate. Alternative education advocate and author Wendy Priesnitz in her book *Beyond School* points out that this line of thought is "suggesting that a bad experience is a good preparation for another bad experience."[19]

The second assumption is that if we just let kids do whatever they want, they will play video games or watch television all day. They might do so at first, but most get sick and tired of it after a while and find something else to do. (In chapter 6, we will see a similar scenario with the students at the Brooklyn Free School.) It's very important for them to discover that dissatisfaction for themselves.

The third assumption is that there is a common body of facts and information that every person should know and some subjects that should be compulsory in school. Consider the Common Core standards, a set of academic standards for English language arts and mathematics. In essence, the standards stem from a position of arrogance—a handful of people have the right to decide what knowledge is essential or not. As Daniel Greenberg noted in *The Crisis in American Education,* "For every subject we painstakingly arrange to have our children exposed to in school, a thousand other subjects lie at hand, ignored by our schools, but no less significant in real life than the few that were somehow selected." In addition, he asks, "Can anyone really say what a child of six needs to learn today to be an effective adult twenty years from now?"[20] Absolutely not.

As we will see, children in free and democratic schools do learn the "basics"—reading, writing, and arithmetic—through peer-to-peer learning, play, real-world experience, and sometimes structured lessons, but without being coerced.

Much of the curriculum and course sequencing found in high-ranking high schools strongly resembles what something called the Committee of Ten advocated more than a century ago. In 1892, the National Education Association assembled the Committee of Ten to establish a uniform curriculum for schools. Chaired by Charles Eliot, president of Harvard, the commission was made up of U.S. commissioner of education William T. Harris, college presidents and professors, and high school principals. In a report, the committee made several recommendations, including that there should be twelve years of schooling—eight for elementary school and four for secondary school—and the subjects English, mathematics, history, science, and foreign language should be made requirements for college entrance. Defending standardized teaching methods, they insisted that "every subject which is taught at all in a secondary school should be taught in the same way and to the same extent to every pupil so long as he pursues it, no matter what the probable destination of the pupil may be, or at what point his education is to cease."[21] But most of the subjects taught in school beyond writing, reading, basic algebra, history, and biology will not be relevant in adult life unless you are working in a field that requires extensive knowledge of that subject. What is fundamental for life is learning who you are, what you are most passionate about, how to self-direct your education, think critically, collaborate, and make decisions. And if you have these things, you can learn anything. As the author and activist William Upski Wimsatt nicely put it in his book *No More Prisons*, "There are no sex classes. No friendship classes. No classes on how to navigate a bureaucracy, build an organization, raise money, create a database, buy a house, love a child, spot a scam, talk someone out of suicide, or figure out what was important to me. Not knowing how to do these things is what mess people up in life, not whether they know Algebra or can analyze literature."[22]

The fourth assumption is that learning occurs only within the walls of a school building. You see this playing out every time somebody says, "You go to school to learn," or argues that we should increase the amount of time children are required to be in school. Quoting Ivan Illich, John Holt remarked in *Reason*, "The one thing schools really teach, all over the world, and they teach it to everybody—is the superiority of the schooled over the unschooled. So all these people who in their own eyes are dropouts, all the people who have failed to take advantage as they see it of a legal opportunity, a legal obligation, can then blame themselves. So you can see, we have here an instrument which can separate society into chiefs and braves, sheep and goats, high and low—an instrument which can effectively condemn the vast majority of society to a kind of permanent inferiority and convince them it is their own fault."[23] But learning is happening always, not just in the confines of a school, even if you are not conscious of it.

The fifth assumption is that children won't learn unless there are carrots and sticks, like grades, rewards, honor rolls, and valedictorian and salutatorian honors. With these extrinsic motivators, the student becomes intensely afraid of failing, making mistakes, and getting poor grades. But fear is a poor goad to actual learning. As American filmmaker Stanley Kubrick once said, "Interest can produce learning on a scale compared to fear as a nuclear explosion to a firecracker." Children can learn a subject or topic months or even years quicker if they have a personal urge to learn it rather than if they are forced to do so when they aren't really ready.

The sixth assumption is that only a few children are motivated to learn on their own. That may be true for children who have experienced many years of schooling, but we must remember that human beings are born intrinsically motivated. For example, how do babies start learning to walk? There isn't an adult howling at them: "Dammit, walk already." Babies begin by observing activities happening in their environment and naturally try to model them for themselves. The retention of that self-motivation in childhood into the rest of life is what's crucial. That's why extrinsic motivators found in schooling—like grades, rubrics, punishments, and bribes—are so pernicious. They finish off much of the intrinsic desire for and love of learning.

The seventh assumption is that all children should learn by rote memorization, filling out worksheets and being lectured at. Some indeed prefer structured learning, which is absolutely acceptable, but many kids don't learn that way. As flawed as the measures to determine proficiency are, large swaths of public school students are not proficient in reading and mathematics after going through thirteen whole years of schooling. And according to U.S. Department of Education statistics, 2.7 million undergraduates took at least one remedial level course in the 2011–12 academic year.[24] Some of this has to do with the effects of poverty, of course, but this still indicates the ineffectiveness of passive, teacher-directed instruction. When such methods are employed, retention is usually very low. The night before the test, you cram the material, and just days later, most of it has escaped your memory. Ask yourself: How much of what you learned in school can you recall today? Likely not much, beyond what is required for use in your profession.

In the 1950s, renowned educational psychologist Benjamin Bloom came up with a framework to categorize learning objectives. Called Bloom's Taxonomy, from bottom to top in increasing complexity, it lists knowledge, comprehension, application, analysis, synthesis, and evaluation. Bloom defined knowledge as the recall of information. Comprehension is defined as the understanding of concepts and ideas. Application is defined as putting knowledge into practice. Analysis is defined as deconstructing ideas and identifying patterns. Synthesis is defined as putting together different ideas and theories. Evaluation is assessing the ideas and methods. Decades later, in the 1990s, a group of cognitive psychologists embarked on a mission to update the taxonomy for the twenty-first century. Published in a book in 2001 with the title *A Taxonomy for Learning, Teaching, and Assessing,* Bloom's Revised Taxonomy is arranged in increasing importance from lower- to higher-order thinking skills: remembering, understanding, applying, analyzing, evaluating, and creating.[25] Our schools' priority should be focusing on the application and production of knowledge, not memorization.

At amazing schools, learning is done with and by the learners. And it is done with their consent. In other words, they can choose to quit at any time. And through project-based, experiential learning, they are applying and creating knowledge. As the taxonomy shows, in this way, higher-order thinking skills are most fully cultivated.

As John Holt put it so well, "Young people should have the right to control and direct their own learning; that is, to decide what they want to learn, and when, where, how, how much, how fast, and with what help they want to learn it. To be still more specific, I want them to have the right to decide if, when, how much, and by whom they want to be *taught* and the right to decide whether they want to learn in a school and if so which one and for how much of the time." He then enunciates, "No human right, except the right to life itself, is more fundamental than this."[26]

One common response to this point of view is: Why should children be able to choose what they want to learn when teachers and adults have more experience and knowledge? Because much research and anecdotal evidence shows that when learners have autonomy and control, they learn more effectively, are more intrinsically motivated, and show higher levels of self-determination.[27] In an experiment in

1930, some of the most troubled boys in a city were rounded up and put into a classroom. The average IQ was eighty-two. There were tables, blackboards, books, and textbooks in the room. As long as the boys stayed busy and refrained from disturbing others, they could do almost anything they wanted. An achievement test was administered at the beginning and end of the four-month experiment. The results were stunning. In even this short time frame, because of the self-directed learning they embarked on, the students' achievement increased an average of fifteen months in reading, arithmetic, and other subjects, four times what was expected of a cohort with this level of intelligence. As the study concluded, "A group of delinquent boys of varying ages and capacities, if given the opportunity and supervision, will improve more in educational age when left alone than they will under ordinary schoolroom conditions with formal instruction."[28]

There's a popular misconception that self-directed learning is a solo activity. That couldn't be more incorrect. Peers, teachers, and mentors are critical components to the process, as we will see from the schools I report on later. The role of the teacher is to advise, mentor, and, sometimes, directly teach. Learners absolutely need guidance, but there are times when it's better that they are left alone to figure things out by themselves. Structured learning environments should not be the default choice for our schools, as they are today.

There are also some who say, "How can a five-year-old possibly know what she enjoys learning?" It is through exploration and play that children discover what they are most interested in. And how are young people ever going to learn how to make decisions, take responsibility, and live on their own terms after school if they are almost never given an opportunity to do so? As Alfie Kohn has written, "The way a child learns how to make decisions is by making decisions, not by following directions."[29]

We need to trust children and give them agency.

We need to immerse young people in environments with adults, professionals, and people of a wide range of ages and backgrounds. Age segregation in schools was originally conceived as a tool to keep children docile. And docile children are not children who are truly engaged in learning.

We need to let them learn in the real world itself rather than be stuck in a school building. If you grow up in a privileged community, you will be caged in a well-funded school for thirteen years in the company of largely affluent kids, with minimal contact with those who are marginalized and poor. Your worldview will be extremely limited and perhaps even perverted. (In impoverished communities, children are also confined in school buildings, but some of that has to do with the fact that public spaces are not very safe. There is at least that logic to it.)

If young people were allowed to spend most of their time in the world around them, participating in apprenticeships, internships, and volunteer activities in libraries, day-care and senior centers, community centers, food banks, orphanages, hospitals, churches, prisons, museums, and art galleries, they would see the massive injustices in our society and, as naturally curious people, ask questions and investigate these issues and perhaps become outraged to the point that they have no other choice but to do something about them. And I believe we would have a more socially conscious citizenry.

Finally, we need to let children, in the words of educator A. S. Neill, "live their own lives."[30]

CHAPTER 5

The Right to Play

What are the best conditions for learning to flourish naturally? Advocates and practitioners of progressive education have long known and proclaimed the answer: spaces where the learner's curiosity, creativity, and intrinsic motivation are nurtured. This wisdom is finally being confirmed by scientific evidence.

Curiosity

Thousands of years ago, in the opening to the *Metaphysics,* Aristotle stated, "All men by nature desire to know." He was correct. According to a study conducted by psychologist Michelle Chouinard, when four children ranging in age from thirteen months to five years were recorded engaging with adults for more than two hundred hours, it was estimated that the children asked a total of nearly 25,000 questions.[1]

When we're very young, we're exploring our surroundings, discovering unknown lands, tinkering with objects and toys, and ultimately trying to make sense of the world.

Then gradually, we become less skeptical, less inquisitive, less excited, less spontaneous, and less willing to turn things inside out. We don't ask as many questions as we once did. We start taking life at face value. We don't go the extra mile and investigate a little deeper. We become passive human beings. Why? Obviously school itself is a major reason. In school, correct answers are prized over asking good questions, because the latter won't directly help your performance on tests, nor will it put you on good terms with your teacher, who fears stopping the class and answering your question because he or she is rigorously trying to cover all of the mandated curriculum within a very short time period. There isn't much time for lengthy inquiry and debate.

Creativity

This superb line is attributed to the artist Pablo Picasso: "All children are artists. The problem is how to stay an artist when the child grows up." We are all born creative. The world is not split between the creatives and noncreatives. Creativity is more valued in today's world than ever before. A groundbreaking 2010 IBM survey of more than 1,500 global CEOs found that it is the most important leadership quality for success.[2]

Like curiosity, creativity is all too often beaten out of children in school. In 1968, educators George Land and Beth Jarman had 1,600 five-year-olds sit for a creativity assessment used by NASA to locate the most creative engineers and scientists. Ninety-eight percent of the five-year-olds scored at the genius level of divergent thinking—the ability to generate many solutions to a problem. They were then retested at ages ten and fifteen. The percentage of students who attained genius level slumped to 32 percent at age ten and 10 percent at age fifteen. When 200,000 adults were given the same test, a mere 2 percent hit genius level. As Land and Jarman concluded in their book *Breakpoint and Beyond,* "Non-creative behavior is learned."[3] In other words, we once had a creative population with enormous potential to be tapped, but schooling largely extinguished it.

While this problem is systemic, some of its responsibility lies with the classroom and teachers. First, according to research carried out by Wellesley psychology professor Beth Hennessey and Harvard Business School professor Teresa Amabile, the biggest killers of creativity are constant surveillance, expected evaluation, rewards, competition, and restriction of choice.[4] Not coincidentally, these are the characteristics of the average traditional school. Second, many teachers aren't actually very fond of creative students. A study conducted by psychologists at Union College and Skidmore College asked elementary school teachers to rate their favorite and least favorite students based on characteristics associated with creative children. What they found was that while the teachers said they liked having creative students in their class, "judgments for the favorite student were negatively correlated with creativity; judgments for the least favorite student were positively correlated with creativity. Students displaying creative characteristics appear to be unappealing to teachers." The psychologists then asked the teachers to note the characteristics associated with creative children to understand why the teachers originally stated they enjoyed working with creative children. Paradoxically, some of the characteristics teachers said applied to the least creative children were "makes up the rules as he or she goes along," "is impulsive," and "is nonconformist," demonstrating that they really didn't know or value what truly creative students were like or how they behaved.[5]

As classroom management guides show, students are expected to follow school rules and their teachers' directions without question. Disruptive behavior is not tolerated and has consequences. This is why kids with extravagant imaginations rarely fit in well in school. True creativity partakes of some level of disorder and messiness, and that does not sit well in traditional classrooms.

Schools have a simple choice in front of them. They can choose to continue to crush one of the greatest inclinations of human nature or begin to nurture children's creativity and try to repair the enormous damage they've done to it.

Self-Control and Grit

Consider how *The Washington Post* describes one middle school, DC Prep public charter school, in the nation's capital: "Fourth- through eighth-graders at this Northeast Washington school are expected in their seats by 8 a.m. No excuses. The children do not speak in the hallways or classroom unless spoken to by a teacher. They navigate the hallways single file. Throughout their eight-hour school day, they bring to each class charts on which they record, as the teachers decree, behaviors, both good and bad, listed on a key. This key lists 26 behaviors, A through Z. Failure to meet any of them results in detention . . . At the end of class, students file out in silence. Two boys wearing green mesh pinnies over their navy-blue polo shirt leave last. They are serving in-school suspension."[6]

Is this a prison, a military academy, or a school?

In recent years, terms like "self-control" and "grit," defined by University of Pennsylvania psychologist Angela Duckworth as "perseverance and passion for long-term goals," have entered the lexicon of education reform conversations, fueled by our growing fetish with character education and the publication of books like Paul Tough's *How Children Succeed*. In response, some schools have implemented boot-camp-like routines, setting rigid schedules, forcing students to concentrate punctiliously on the task at hand and abide by strict and precise rules pertaining to speaking and sitting in class, sometimes not permitting students to use the bathroom, and punishing or suspending those who fail to follow orders, all in an attempt to teach character traits and raise test scores. Nearly all of these schools work with mostly poor children of color. One network is called Success Academy Charter Schools, which has dozens of schools across New York City. A 2015 *New York Times* investigation by reporter Kate Taylor exposed some of the schools' inhumane, troubling practices. Here are a few observations made by Taylor: "Rules are explicit and expectations precise. Students must sit with hands clasped and eyes following the speaker; reading passages must be neatly annotated with a main idea." "Incentives are offered, such as candy for good behavior, and Nerf guns and basketballs for high scores on practice tests." "Success has stringent rules about behavior, down to how students are supposed to sit in the classroom: their backs straight, and their feet on the floor if they are in a chair or legs crossed if they are sitting on the floor." There have also been incidents where students have wet themselves during practice tests, because teachers wouldn't allow them to use the bathroom or "the students themselves felt so much pressure that they did not want to lose time on the test."[7] Then there are Knowledge is Power Program (KIPP) schools, which have created character report cards with a rubric consisting of twenty-four statements that students are graded on. What this has done is annihilate intrinsic motivation and turn school into a game with an end goal of amassing character points.

John Holt has argued that good behavior is mistaken for good character by teachers and schools.[8] To put it plainly, in its current format in most schools, character education is producing subservient children who knuckle under to authority, follow directions blindly, and do as they are told. Why would we ever want to mold such people? The problem is that, as author Alfie Kohn notes in *Phi Delta Kappan*, "Character education's 'fix-the-kids' orientation follows logically from the belief that kids need fixing. Indeed, the movement seems to be driven by a stunningly dark view of children—and, for that matter, of people in general."[9] This has led some to argue that self-control equates to social control.

The point is that lifelong self-control and grit is not learned best through obedience training, but through exploration and play.

AT EIGHT A.M. on a Monday morning in October 2013, Brightworks students, staff members, and a few parents of the younger kids congregated outside the school. Luggage in tow, they began boarding a school bus one by one. They were on their way to Mendocino Woodlands Camp. A few staff members also drove in private cars.

Since 2012, the entire school has been going on an annual five-day trip filled with camping, hiking, and canoeing at the beginning of the school year. Its purpose is for students to learn how to bond as a community, foster strong group relationships, get out of their element and into an uncomfortable, foreign environment without the Internet and technology, and explore nature. "Hanging out with your new cohort hour after hour, day after day," said Tulley, "you get to work through very quickly a lot of those social hiccups and figure out who you are." For these city kids, it was one of their first experiences in the woods, and for some of the younger children, it was their first time away from home for an extended period of time. Some of the children told me that it was also a bit difficult to adjust to because they were not used to having their days be so structured and directed. The trip has become a school tradition, and returning kids look forward to it each year.

After a four-hour journey, the bus rolled up to their campsite in a large redwood forest. They unpacked and settled into their cabins. The cabins, "works of art" as one collaborator put it, were built by the Works Progress Administration and Civilian Conservation Corps during the Great Depression in the 1930s. Each had a stone chimney and bunk beds.

Dinner was held in the dining hall. At the end of the meal, a naturalist dressed up as the "Waste Wizard" unexpectedly shows up, collects all of the uneaten food into a bucket, and indicates how much food is being wasted to encourage everyone to waste less food during the next meal. "We have a love-and-hate relationship with the Waste Wizard," says Tulley. "We appreciate what they do, but as a school, we're intolerant of canned curriculum." Later that evening, the school split into groups and went on a night hike.

The next day, students, staff members, and the naturalists all went on guided hikes together. On Wednesday, the students repeated this, but the staff members stayed behind and participated in a professional development day in the dining hall. They talked about the next arc, which was clocks, and some ideas to explore with the students.

That evening, there was an improv night of skits and drama around the bonfire. More hikes and team-building exercises took place on Thursday. That evening, there was a big closing ceremony run by Richard, a naturalist, around the fire. He presented a candle in the shape of the Earth, lit it, and explained how it symbolized the world and how it was in our hands. It got passed around and each person shared his or her reflections of the experience. "It was set up in a way in that it feels you have tremendous power to influence the world and people around you," Keaghan Townsend told me. "It was definitely the most visceral thing I remember from the trip." In his early twenties, Townsend was an after-school collaborator and Cañada College graduate with disheveled brown hair, half-rimmed glasses, and a beard. He had just been hired a month before after having worked with young people in after-school programs and two summer camps for a few years. Because he had past experience in the outdoors, the trip was a perfect way for him to get assimilated into the community.

As people began packing their bags and getting ready for bed, Christie Seyfert, another collaborator, brought out an old beach towel with a picture of a troll on it. Someone would ask the troll a question and she or one of the older kids would "translate" the troll's answer. It soon turned into kids sitting around asking deeply personal questions and adults or older kids dispensing advice to them.

The following morning, they departed for San Francisco, and when they returned to school, it was clear the trip had made its mark on the students. "They had healthier group dynamics and were more patient with each other," said Ellen Hathaway, director of Brightworks. "When conflicts arose, it was like conflicts between siblings, rather than like 'I don't want to be around that person.'" Townsend also told me that during after-school hours, the students' abilities to self-organize games and activities had improved noticeably.

WHAT DISTINGUISHES SCHOOLS like Brightworks from traditional ones is how much time the students spend engaged in free play. This brings us to the questions: What is play? And why is it so pivotal to children's social, emotional, intellectual, and physical development? The dictionary definition of play is to "engage in activity for enjoyment and recreation rather than a serious or practical purpose." I disagree. Play very much so has "a serious and practical purpose."

There's nothing wrong with children playing all day. The problem we run into is that it doesn't fit many parents' limited criteria of what real learning looks like: children in school sitting at a desk, head facing the chalkboard, and a teacher telling them what to do. They say there's a stark difference between work and play. In those parents' eyes, children are wasting time and not doing anything productive when they play. Child psychologist Bruno Bettelheim dispelled such folly in *The Atlantic Monthly:* "A common mistake adults make in reacting to a child's play is taking it as 'not real.' But in more than one sense play is the child's true reality, and we have to respect it as such."[10] The eminent Italian educator Maria Montessori once said, "Play is the work of the child." By playing freely, children are learning self-control, empathy, collaboration, how to make decisions, follow rules, and resolve conflicts. Children who play more behave better. Play is full of laughter, excitement, happiness, curiosity, and wonder. And learning.

Play is not a waste of time. Play is what makes us human. As Stuart Brown, the founder of the National Institute for Play, wrote in his book *Play,* "Play is a *state of mind,* rather than an activity."[11] It also brings us into a state of flow where nothing else seems to be more important.

As J. Madeleine Nash explained in *Time* magazine, "Researchers at Baylor College of Medicine, for example, have found that children who don't play much or are rarely touched develop brains 20% to 30% smaller than normal for their age."[12] The dearth of play in a child's life can seriously disrupt brain development and lead to catastrophic consequences in adulthood. In his research, Brown noticed that one common thread that linked mass murderers was an absence of play in their childhoods.[13]

Does play make children smarter? Of course it does. During free play, studies have found that children use more advanced vocabulary than during other activities. Psychologist Jerome Bruner wrote that "the most complicated grammatical and pragmatic forms of language appear first in play activity."[14]

Much research lends credence to the notion that we need more free play in schools. The landmark 1997 HighScope Preschool Curriculum Comparison Study followed the lives of sixty-eight low-income children. Each child was randomly assigned to one of three different schools. One group attended a Nursery School model with lots of "self-initiated play in a loosely structured, socially supportive setting." Another group attended a Direct Instruction model in which children were directly taught by teachers and expected to obediently follow the teacher's instructions and lessons. And the last group attended a HighScope model in which children learned in a traditional classroom but had some autonomy.

By age twenty-three, the researchers found that only 6 percent of the children in the HighScope and Nursery School groups needed "treatment for emotional impairment or disturbance during their schooling," as compared to 47 percent of the children in the Direct Instruction group. They also found that only 9 percent of the Nursery School group had been arrested for a felony at the ages of twenty-two to twenty-three, as compared to 34 percent of the Direct Instruction group. And not a single member of the Nursery School group had been suspended from work, as compared to 27 percent of the Direct Instruction group.[15] The results unequivocally show that self-directed, play-oriented classrooms serve children the best and end up creating responsible adults.

Moreover, Brown, after recording six thousand "play histories" of his patients, noticed a direct correlation between play behavior in childhood and happiness in adulthood.[16]

The same is similarly true with animals. As educator James Herndon notes in his 1971 book *How to Survive in Your Native Land,* one psychologist of rat behavior discovered that to make rats more intelligent, he needed "to allow them to roam at random in a spacious and variegated environment."[17]

So it's safe to conclude, as play scholar Brian Sutton-Smith once famously said, "The opposite of play is not work. It's depression." We could all use a little more play in our lives. And responsibility, it turns out.

FOR WEEKS, NINE-YEAR-OLD Izzy kept nagging his mother, Lenore Skenazy, to drop him off somewhere and let him find his way home. One day, she felt he was ready and gave in to his pestering. During a trip to the original Bloomingdale's on the Upper East Side of Manhattan, Lenore left Izzy in the handbags section with a subway map, a MetroCard, a twenty-dollar bill, and some change if he needed to make a call.

"No, I did not give him a cell phone," Skenazy wrote

in a column for the *New York Sun* a few weeks after the episode. "Didn't want to lose it. And no, I didn't trail him, like a mommy private eye. I trusted him to figure out that he should take the Lexington Avenue subway down, and the 34th Street crosstown bus home. If he couldn't do that, I trusted him to ask a stranger. And then I even trusted that stranger not to think, 'Gee, I was about to catch my train home, but now I think I'll abduct this adorable child instead.'"[18]

Forty-five minutes later, the nine-year-old made it home to his family's New York City apartment without a scratch and "ecstatic with independence." Shortly after her column describing his adventure was published, Skenazy was slammed with a torrent of criticism, dubbed "World's Worst Mom," and then appeared on national television to defend her parenting style.

The firestorm of uproar targeted at Skenazy can be summed up in one sentence: How dare you let your child out of your sight for even a second, let alone ride the spine-chilling New York City subway full of lurking murderers and kidnappers?

In 2014, a Florida mother was arrested and charged with child neglect for letting her seven-year-old son walk to and play alone at a park half a mile from home. Charges were later dropped. Then in 2015, a Maryland couple, who are part of the "free-range" parenting movement, made national headlines when they were put under investigation by Child Protective Services for child neglect for the "crime" of letting their two children walk home alone from a neighborhood park. Shockingly, they were found responsible for "unsubstantiated" child neglect. But fortunately, they were eventually cleared of all charges.

Incidents such as these point to two major issues in

education and society. The first is the waning of unstructured, make-believe, and spontaneous play and the growth of manufactured, structured play. The second is that today's children are more supervised and sheltered than past generations. We are losing the battle for free play in many communities.

Brown University professor of history Howard Chudacoff, in his book *Children at Play,* designates the period from 1900 to 1950 as "the golden age of unstructured play." Child labor laws were in full effect, so children had more time for leisure. And parents were content with letting their children roam free within clearly understood limits. But by the second half of the twentieth century, what he calls "the commercialization and co-optation of children's play" began occurring. There was also the problem of adult intervention in play. He writes, "Adults increasingly tried to restrict and control children's pleasure by obliging them to follow adult rules, presumably for reasons of rationality and safety. The result was a constriction of autonomous, unstructured, or self-structured play."[19]

Childhood is in danger of going extinct. "The Wilderness of Childhood is gone; the days of adventure are past," wrote author Michael Chabon in *The New York Review of Books.* "The land ruled by children, to which a kid might exile himself for at least some portion of every day from the neighboring kingdom of adulthood, has in large part been taken over, co-opted, colonized, and finally absorbed by the neighbors."[20] Journalist Jennifer Senior commented in a *New York* magazine piece on childhood in New York City, "Today, we think of . . . children as fragile, vulnerable creatures, sensitive to sunlight and best stored in Styrofoam peanuts and bubble wrap."[21]

After surveying mothers of 2,400 children in sixteen

countries, Yale psychologists Dorothy and Jerome Singer found that 72 percent of mothers believe their children are "growing up too quickly." That included 95 percent of American mothers, the highest figure of any country studied. In the study, they concluded, "As the primary protectors of their sons and daughters, mothers are deeply concerned that their youngsters are somehow missing out on the joys of childhood and experiential learning opportunities of free play and natural exploration. Children seem to be rushed too rapidly into the rigors of adult life. For lack of safe outdoor play spaces and unstructured free time, children are deprived of the excitement and social interactions of a healthy youth."[22] Ironically, parents are one of the largest contributors to this problem. Many have turned days of freewheeling, unsupervised play into wall-to-wall tutoring sessions and structured play dates.

According to the *Archives of Pediatrics & Adolescent Medicine,* the amount of time children participate in free play declined by 25 percent between 1981 and 1997.[23] And David Elkind writes in *The Power of Play,* "Over the past two decades, children have lost twelve hours of free time a week, including eight hours of unstructured play and outdoor activities."[24] Unstructured free play is not some aimless activity. It is defined, as psychologist Peter Gray puts it in *Free to Learn,* as "play in which the players themselves decide what and how to play and are free to modify the goals and rules as they go along."[25]

Play, over the past few decades, has also become more fixated on manufactured toys and prepackaged experiences. Research psychologist Mary Ann Pulaski found that minimally structured toys, like wooden blocks, paint, and pipe cleaners, evoked richer fantasy and a greater diversity of themes than structured toys, like a metal dollhouse and Barbie dolls.[26]

AS FOR THE other major problem—the Orwellian surveillance of children—a series of statistics chronicle the circumstances: Only 13 percent of children walk or bike to school, down from nearly 50 percent in 1969.[27] About half of three- to five-year-olds are not taken outside to play every day.[28] Only 6 percent of children aged nine to thirteen play outside on their own in an average week.[29] Less than 10 percent of British children play in "natural places, such as woodlands, countryside and heaths," whereas 40 percent of adults did in their youth.[30] Half of British children polled are not allowed to climb trees.[31]

According to a piece in *Boston Magazine*, child psychologist Michael Thompson once asked a cafeteria thick with middle school parents to remember their happiest childhood moments. Then he told them, "Okay, now raise your hand if there was an adult with you in that moment." Only 10 percent of them raised their hand. Thompson said, "Modern parents feel that more time with Mom and Dad is always a positive—this is the single biggest change in American childhood—but the truth is that more time with you isn't always a positive. In fact, it's annoying."[32] This overparenting and oversupervision is deleterious to a child's development. A study found that unsupervised children are more often found playing outside and have better social skills.[33] Kids need time for solitude as well as time with their peers.

What caused these disturbing trends in the decline of free, unsupervised, and unstructured play? One primary culprit is the media. Television and radio airwaves are regularly filled with stories of children being abducted or drowning in pools. That has caused parents to be terrified of letting their children be unsupervised at any moment.

Media scholar George Gerbner calls this the "mean world syndrome," which says that the mass media induces fear, anxiety, and depression into the public, making the world seem more perilous than it actually is.[34] He once said, "You know, who tells the stories of a culture really governs human behavior. It used to be the parent, the school, the church, the community. Now it's a handful of global conglomerates that have nothing to tell, but a great deal to sell."[35] We never hear the stories of children who come home alive after climbing trees or playing unsupervised outside in the neighborhood with friends. That certainly won't boost ratings.

Crime rates, including murder rates, are at their lowest levels in decades.[36] America is actually likely the safest it has ever been.

What about child abductions? According to the National Center for Missing and Exploited Children, roughly 800,000 children are reported missing each year, but that number can be easily misconstrued. A quarter of them were abducted by family members, and more than 58,200 were abducted by nonfamily members. As Christopher Beam notes in *Slate,* "Even these categories can be misleading: Overstaying a visit with a noncustodial parent, for example, could qualify as a family abduction." But just 115 children were victims of "stereotypical kidnapping," defined in the study as "a non-family abduction perpetrated by a slight acquaintance or stranger in which a child is detained overnight, transported at least 50 miles, held for ransom or abducted with the intent to keep the child permanently, or killed."[37]

The British writer and author of *How to Live Danger-*

ously, Warwick Cairns, estimated that "it would take your child, left outside, 500,000 years to be abducted by a stranger, and 1.4 million years for a stranger to murder them."[38]

Nobody is saying that we shouldn't be cautious when it comes to our children's safety, but we risk crippling their well-being by locking them up and inappropriately surveilling them.

If we don't let children engage in unbridled, self-governing free play, ask yourself: What will a world look like without children acting like explorers and pioneers, knights and dragons, pirates and sailors? "What will become of the world of adventure, of stories, of literature itself?" ponders Michael Chabon.[39]

UPSTAIRS IN THE Brightworks space referred to as the Mezzanine one April afternoon in 2014, Tytus was sitting at his desk sketching the last page of the four-page storyboard of a comic. Brown haired and slim, he was sixteen years old and wore a gray sweatshirt over a red and white shirt and beige pants. He is reserved and speaks quietly. Tytus's parents helped bring Tulley to speak at TEDxKraków in Poland in the fall of 2013. They decided to move to San Francisco for the first half of 2014 and enroll Tytus at Brightworks.

In Poland, he went to a traditional public school with lectures, grades, and tests. There were about forty kids in each class. When he returns in the fall, he will be a junior and specialize in social studies, physics, and mathematics.

When I asked him how the transition and experience at Brightworks has been, Tytus paused for a minute and said, "It's hard to put it into words. I like that I can do what I wouldn't be able to do in Poland. I'm drawing comics right now. I'm spending half a day just working on this. It certainly wouldn't be possible in my other school." He adds, "This is a really cool place to be."

The comic he was working on was an adaption of "The Gift of the Magi," a short story by O. Henry. Soon, he planned to visit the art store, pick up some inks, and finish drawing the comic by the following week. He was treating this project as a "war map"—an opportunity to learn the necessary skills to create a comic book based on a plot from scratch.

Tytus was one of five students who were part of "Brightworks University," the newly minted high school program at the school, which started in September 2013. They occupied the Mezzanine, a cozy loftlike space that overlooks the dining area. Their schedule seemed more structured than the rest of the bands. In the mornings, they had two-hour workshops with a collaborator on a range of subjects that relate to the arc. Those began midway through the school year. In the afternoons, they had independent study time and sometimes a writing class.

On Monday mornings, the high school students had math and science class with Tulley. During the mirrors arc, they explored geometry and how mirrors work. Engineering class was held on Tuesday mornings with Sean Murray. They worked in the wood shop. One of the questions that guided the workshop was: "How would you experience the world if your eyes were three feet apart?" The answer is that it would be much more three-dimensional. So each student created his or her own telestereoscope, a device that presents a three-dimensional view of distant objects. Wednesday mornings was when philosophy class was held. A few students told me that it was the most popular class. Each session began with an interesting question or quote, which they would then deliberate over. On Thursday mornings, they had visual communications class with Tulley, and on Friday mornings, they had Community Friday, where there is no division between the bands and students can join any collaborator for an activity.

One Thursday morning, I participated in the visual communications class. Five students and Tulley were seated around a dark wood whiteboard table in the Mezzanine, above the fray downstairs. The class got under way with a warm-up exercise. Tulley asked us to draw an upsetting shape on a sheet of paper in under a minute. Then we had to pass it to the person sitting to our left. The task was to alter the other person's drawing and make the upsetting shape angry. This repeated for a few minutes until Tulley said, "Finish the drawing!" I now had my original drawing back. It was basically a blob.

Next, Tulley presented a paper that came out of the box of Coloud headphones. He went downstairs and brought back the actual headphones. "Why did Julie [his wife] choose these headphones?" he asked. "Because they don't tangle," said one girl. "Well advertised," said another.

Then he asked, "Why did they design this sheet?" On one side, there's a unique design, and on the other, there are instructions and a Sudoku puzzle. The group had a discussion about why the company spent so much effort on the packaging and instruction sheet. "The truth is that they are trying to make a moment out of unpacking the thing, like Apple does with its bento style packaging," he said. Madison added, "They're trying to make it magical." They also talked about how companies are striving to get your attention, and the number of advertisements you see daily, and compared the Coloud packaging to the box of the Canon

EOS 60D camera. Their assignment for the next week was to find four positive and two negative brand associations and write a paragraph about each.

After the class ended, I met with Max, a fourteen-year-old who wore a white T-shirt, black jacket, and jeans. He was in his second year at Brightworks. He previously attended Stuart Hall for Boys, which he calls "the most strict Catholic school on the planet." Very unhappy at school, Max struggled in his classes and didn't fit in. In the sixth grade, his family began to search for a new school for him. They visited many traditional schools as well as Brightworks, after a recommendation from Max's friends at San Francisco Rock Project. He loved it. He said, "I knew that after I walked in, this was the only place I could ever like going to school in." He told his parents, "I learned more stuff in one day here than I have in two weeks at school." After some prodding, they agreed to let him enroll.

Outside of school, Max's two main interests have been music and film. When he was seven, he produced two films, *Roadkill* and *Jaws 4: Stay Away from My Doggy Door*. He actually made those on a day he faked illness to stay home from school. In fourth grade, he joined the San Francisco Rock Project, a music school. He was there until 2013. That's where he met Kai. In 2011, they started a rock band called Spotted Botanists with Kai's brother Zak and three people who took turns playing bass. Max played guitar and was sometimes the lead singer. They did shows in bars, schools, and fund-raisers all over the city. They cut a demo in a recording studio and even tried to go on America's Got Talent but didn't get accepted. Over time, Max's music tastes evolved from British rock to math rock, defined as "a style of rock music characterized by complex and technically demanding instrumentation," and thus he lost interest in the music the band was playing. They split up in early 2014.

For Max, the leap from Stuart Hall to Brightworks was tough. "Coming in here, I was definitely a Stuart Hall kid," he said. "I thought I wasn't when I was at Stuart Hall. So it took time—four to five months—for me to adjust. It was more of opening my mind and accepting that I had a lot more freedom." His time at the school has been dominated by film. One film that strongly influenced him to pursue this field was *The King's Speech*. He said that the camera work in the scenes deeply resonated with him.

His first film at Brightworks was called *Boarded*. It was about a poor kid and a rich kid who end up rooming together in a boarding school. Both of them had problems with their fathers. Another film was called *The Horologist,* which he made during the clocks arc. The main character is a man named Bennett who has trouble finding his way. He pours his emotions into clocks and tries to make his dream clock. The film Max was working on when I met him was going to be the last one of the year and "the most complex thing" he's ever worked on. He was still in declaration phase and hadn't finished writing the script yet. The story was going to be about a man who works at a twenty-four-hour fitness center. In it, two mirrors face each other. Every day, as he walks out of the place, he's "one reflection into the mirror." His life improves. His car, house, and family get better. "But at the end of the infinity mirror, there's a curve, and it starts running out of light, and once he goes back around the curve, his life starts to get really bad," Max explained. "Now he has to fight his way back through the curve to get back to where he was before all of this happened."

Project-based learning gets results.

. . .

ONE DAY IN April 2014, I asked Tulley if he had heard about that morning's mass stabbing at Franklin Regional Senior High School in Pennsylvania, where a sixteen-year-old sophomore stabbed twenty students and a security guard. He had. I told him that I would presume that such an incident would be nearly impossible at his school. "Yes," he said. "By the time you got your backpack hung up, four or five people would have noticed you weren't feeling well. It's very hard to accumulate rage here."

I've visited public, private, and charter schools all over the country and I don't think there's a place that I have felt more comfortable reporting in than Brightworks. The students and collaborators were not only friendly but eager to spend time and share their knowledge and experiences with a stranger like me. As Tulley put it, "We are, in the truest sense of the words, an intimate learning community." There is something magical happening at a school where students wield power tools and harness the power of their imaginations.

In sum, our schools should strip away every element that they are known for: grades, tests, compulsory classes, periods, bells, age segregation, and homework. And then we should craft institutions that are grounded in the attributes we want to see in citizens in our society and designed to foster critical thinking and lifelong learning.

CHAPTER 6

Schools Where Children Can
Be Themselves

Imagine a school where the students are not required to take any tests or classes. Imagine a school where the students are not given grades. Imagine a school where the students and staff members together run it democratically. Imagine a school where the students are given full freedom over how they learn. Around the world, there are hundreds of schools that embody those very principles. They're called democratic and free schools. And they've been in existence for almost a century.

One of the oldest free and democratic schools in the world is the Summerhill School. It was founded by Alexander Sutherland Neill in 1921 and is currently located in Leiston, England. It "is possibly the happiest school in the world," as he once put it.[1] The school is made to fit the needs of the child rather than the child made to fit the school. Lessons are optional. The school is self-governing through democratic meetings a few times a week. Every student and staff member has one vote.

This is the general policy statement of the school:

1. To provide choices and opportunities that allow children to develop at their own pace and to follow their own interests. Summerhill does not aim to produce specific types of young people, with specific, assessed skills or knowledge, but aims to provide an environment in which children can define who they are and what they want to be.

2. To allow children to be free from compulsory or imposed assessment, allowing them to develop their own goals and sense of achievement. Children should be free from the pressure to conform to artificial standards of success based on predominant theories of child learning and academic achievement.

3. To allow children to be completely free to play as much as they like. Creative and imaginative play is an essential part of childhood and development. Spontaneous, natural play should not be undermined or redirected by adults into a "learning experience" for children. Play belongs to the child.

4. To allow children to experience the full range of feelings free from the judgement and intervention of an adult. Freedom to make decisions always involves risk and requires the possibility of negative outcomes. Apparently negative consequences such as boredom, stress, anger, disappointment and failure are a necessary part of individual development.

5. To allow children to live in a community that supports them and that they are responsible for; in which they have the freedom to be themselves, and have the power to change community life, through the democratic process. All individuals create their own set of values based on the community within which they live.

> Summerhill is a community, which takes responsibility for itself. Problems are discussed and resolved through openness, democracy and social action. All members of the community, adults and children, irrespective of age, are equal in terms of this process.[2]

Imagine if every single school adopted and abided by this mission statement.

IN 1960, A. S. Neill published his manifesto *Summerhill,* which pieced together for a wider audience the philosophies behind the school and his thoughts on education. The book became an instant international bestseller, with millions of copies sold. It is known as one of the catalysts that galvanized the 1960s and '70s free school movement in the United States. The epoch was marked by the countercultural tides of antiwar, civil rights, feminist, and free-speech protestors, all fanning the flames of rebellion against the status quo and our technocratic society.

Free-school stalwarts aimed to create small alternative schools outside of the government's clutches and without grades, tests, or undemocratic structures. They reckoned that the education system couldn't be salvaged by making tweaks in instruction or curriculum. "So long as schooling was set up to serve the interests of a competitive, consumerist, mass-mentality society, it could never fully educate young people for lives of meaning and personal integrity, no matter how well-intentioned were its reformers," as Ron Miller explained in his outstanding book *Free Schools, Free People.*[3] By their reasoning, education should be "entirely devoted to the happiness of the individuals who lived, loved, and played within each intimate community." By 1973, according to sociologist Frank Lindenfeld, there were over eight hundred free schools in the United States.[4]

Progressive education had previously seen its heyday during the first few decades of the twentieth century. Led by school reformers John Dewey and Francis Parker, the philosophy of child-centered and experiential learning took root in the country. The movement had gone from being "a tiny and, in many eyes, a crackpot movement quarantined in a handful of private schools," as *Time* magazine put it in 1938, to one that impacted every school in some fashion.[5] Montessori education, developed by Italian educator Maria Montessori; Waldorf education, established by Austrian philosopher Rudolf Steiner; and the Reggio Emilia approach, developed by Italian educator Loris Malaguzzi, are three other models of progressive education established in the twentieth century. Today, though, more often than not, progressive schools fail to live up to their name. Overall, they are certainly much better than traditional schools (it's hard not to be), but many give students letter or number grades or assess them with a strict rubric, have a rigid curriculum and course requirements for graduation, administer tests, and control students' learning rather than allowing them to have full autonomy and choice. In his book *Someone Has to Fail,* Stanford professor David Labaree explains, "Students may experience this softer approach to classroom management as more benign and friendly than the heavy-handed use of authority in the traditional approach. It may even be more effective in general as a way to motivate students to learn what the teacher is teaching. But it is no less a mechanism for controlling student behavior."[6] Those are some of the key differences between many so-called progressive schools and free schools, as we will see. On the alternative education spectrum, free schools are the most "radical."

During the 1960s and '70s, several educators and writers gained a national audience with their searing indictments of conventional schooling. Some called them the "romantic critics of education," others called them the "deschoolers." It is on their shoulders that advocates of alternative education stand today. Of the critics, the most famous one was John Holt. After teaching in private schools in Colorado and Cambridge, Massachusetts, he wrote two bestselling books, *How Children Fail* (1964) and *How Children Learn* (1967), drawing from his experience and observations in the classroom. Book critic Eliot Fremont-Smith wrote in his *New York Times* review of *How Children Fail* that it was "possibly the most penetrating, and probably the most eloquent, book on education to be published in recent years."[7] Holt soon became a notable figure in American education and went on to pen many more books. He is also widely considered the father of the homeschooling movement.

In 1967, Jonathan Kozol, after teaching mainly poor black children in a Boston public school, wrote *Death at an Early Age*. It chronicled his first year of teaching and the systemic racism and inequality ingrained in the school system and won the National Book Award in 1968. A few years later, his book *Free Schools* was published, offering a damning assessment of free schools and excoriating many for their lack of accessibility for poor and minority children. He wrote, "In my belief, an isolated upper-class Free School for the children of the white and rich within a land like the United States and in a time of torment such as 1972 is a great deal too much like a sandbox for the children of the SS guards at Auschwitz."[8] Since then, he has continued writing and speaking about education, inequality, and race in America.

In 1969, novelist George Dennison wrote *The Lives of Children,* which recounted his time as a teacher at the First Street School in Manhattan, a free school with twenty-three poor children that was founded by his wife. Half of the students previously had behavioral and learning difficulties in public schools. The school rejected the fundamentals of traditional education—grades, report cards, tests, and homework—and crafted an environment that would best kindle students' intrinsic motivation to learn. Dennison explained, "We made much of freedom of choice and freedom of movement; and of reality of encounter between teachers and students; and of the continuum of persons, by which we understood that parents, teachers, friends, neighbors, the life of the streets, form all one substance in the experience of the child."[9]

Then there was Ivan Illich, a Roman Catholic priest who eventually left the priesthood. As we'll discuss in detail later, he wrote the 1971 polemic *Deschooling Society,* in which he lambasted formal schooling and imagined a society without it.

Other significant books about the issue of education included the social critic Paul Goodman's *Compulsory Mis-Education* (1964), educator Herbert Kohl's *36 Children* (1967), and educator James Herndon's *The Way It Spozed to Be* (1968) and *How to Survive in Your Native Land* (1971).

All of these individuals have appreciably shaped my perspectives on schooling and society, and it astounds me how relevant their writings are today.

As the countercultural movement waned and the Vietnam War ended, the number of free schools dwindled. They were also hamstrung by a lack of funding and disorganized leadership within the overall community. The free school movement didn't achieve mass acceptance or cause public schools to change, but it was nowhere near a failure. Its philosophy has permeated the larger world of education and provides a powerful alternative way of thinking about education.

Today, there are more than two hundred democratic and free schools in many countries across the world. One type is called Sudbury schools.

A THEORETICAL PHYSICS professor at Columbia University in the early sixties, Daniel Greenberg found himself disgruntled with the field he was in. Years later, he would write, "I would be able to crank out a lifetime of publications, but the joy of creation would be missing."[10] He also felt like a failure as a teacher after his students did not successfully grasp his course material. After five years of contemplation, the professor arrived at this conclusion: "A person can only focus their attention, learn, and hope to be good at what they are doing, if they are engaged in a pursuit for which they are passionate. And they will only be passionate about things that give meaning to their lives." He realized that his greatest pleasure was making sure that others would be in the best position to discover their own passions. And thus, Greenberg hoped to one day create an environment where "children could search for meaning in their lives."[11]

In the mid-1960s, Greenberg left his professorial position at Columbia and moved with his family to live in Framingham, Massachusetts, less than an hour's drive from Boston. His wife, Hanna, had been accepted into a graduate biochemistry program at MIT.[12] Soon, they began searching for a school for their son, Michael, but couldn't find "anything like the kind of school for a democratically based society that we were interested in," he wrote.[13] That's when they began considering the possibility of starting their own school. In the summer of 1966, Greenberg put together a document called "Education in Transition," which described his views on education and offered an outline for a potential school. Slowly, some interest in a new school began to burgeon in the Framingham community, and a core group of founders was established. Then, after two years of planning, preparation, and hiring, Sudbury Valley School was officially born in the summer of 1968. One of its flyers explained that its mission was "not to produce people who will fit in, but to fit out people who will be able to produce something—with skill, enthusiasm, and pleasure, as a natural outgrowth of their initial curiosity."[14]

Located in an old stone Victorian mansion in Framingham, the school sits on a beautiful ten-acre campus. During the 2014–15 school year, they had more than 150 students, aged four through nineteen, and nine staff members. Tuition was $8,400 a year for the first child in the family, $7,000 for the second, and $5,600 for the third and any others. This is much less than nearby private schools, but financial aid is not available. Age-mixing flourishes. As we will see in more detail shortly, at democratic and free schools, during the weekly school meeting, students and staff members vote on the policies that run the school, and the judicial committee enforces the rules. There are no grades, tests, homework, or traditional classes. Throughout the world, there are now dozens of Sudbury schools modeled after Sudbury Valley, but they operate independently.

At the 2005 International Democratic Education Conference in Berlin, Germany, participants agreed on this statement to define democratic education: "We believe that, in any educational setting, young people have the right: 1. to decide individually how, when, what, where, and with whom they learn 2. to have an equal share in the decision-making as to how their organizations—in particular their schools—are run, and which rules and sanctions, if any, are necessary." In other words, children should be trusted, should have autonomy, and are capable of learning without compulsion. Yaacov Hecht, founder of the Democratic School in Hadera, Israel, explained in his book *Democratic Education* that the three components of democratic schools are "a choice of areas of learning," "democratic self management," and "evaluation focusing on the individual."[15]

As A. S. Neill put it succinctly, "I have never yet seen a lazy child. What is called laziness is either lack of interest or lack of health. A healthy child cannot be idle; he has to be doing something all day long."[16] Free and democratic schools install the appropriate stimuli into the environment in the form of books, art, tools, games, computers, toys, and instruments to catalyze learning and teaching naturally. Kids are playing, dancing, laughing, reading, writing, governing, exploring, questioning, and discovering. Staff members are advising and helping students in their learning endeavors.

Here's how one Sudbury Valley alumnus described his school experience: "The school gave me the gift of time to let my own interests rise to the surface. When you sit down to paint, you don't just sit and paint. You have to think about what you're doing and why. Any creative effort, perhaps any effort at all, requires a great deal of thought, even reading a book. You don't just read a book. You think about what you read. Otherwise you're doing it for nothing. The school gave us the gift of time to relax, to have those things come to the surface that were there; it gave us the time for reflection, for the introspection that you need to really develop your own creativity."[17] Some famous alumni of the school include Laura Poitras, the Academy Award–winning documentary filmmaker of *Citizenfour*; Nikole Beckwith, actress and playwright; and Mark Christianson, professional musician with the United States Marine Band ("the President's Own").

IF YOU WALK into a free school without dropping your preconceived assumptions or having much knowledge of how they work, you will likely be startled at what you observe. My first visit to the Brooklyn Free School (BFS) was on a chilly February morning. I trekked over to the school, which occupies a five-story brownstone in Clinton Hill. (Full disclosure: I spoke at a TEDx event organized by the school in 2012. I did not receive compensation.)

When I first walked in, I felt uncomfortable. Where were the metal detectors? The security guards? The bells? The cells—I mean classrooms? The suffering children? None were to be found. After some time, I felt very much at home. This couldn't possibly be a school, I thought. But indeed it was.

When the school was founded in 2004 by Alan Berger, a former public school assistant principal, it became the first free school to open in New York City in three decades. In 2006, *The New York Times* dubbed it "arguably New York's most radical center of learning."[18] Since its humble beginnings, the Brooklyn Free School has become the largest free school on the East Coast. During the 2014–15 school year, eighty-two students were enrolled, with twelve in the new prekindergarten program and twenty-five in the high school program. Overall, there were six full-time teachers and two assistant teachers. Tuition was $18,000 a year for the preschool, $20,000 for the general school, and $22,000 for the high school. Payment works on a sliding scale based on a family's income, ranging from $100 to the full sticker price. About a quarter of the students pay full tuition, which helps subsidize the cost for others. Nearly all of the school's funding derives from tuition, supplemented by fund-raising and grants. As for the racial demographics of the school, 55 percent of the students were white and 45 percent were of color.

There are no grades, tests, or required classes. In the mornings and afternoons, there are three to five formal classes and workshops offered. Most students attend at least one class every day. Students are divided into advisory groups of no more than fifteen students; they are age based and meet briefly twice a day in the morning and afternoon. On Fridays, most students go on field trips, usually with their advisory groups, to various attractions in the city. There are also school-wide activities and events, like the annual musical, talent shows, wrestling tournaments, field trips, and, of course, the weekly democratic meeting, where, as we'll see, school policies and rules are deliberated over. Many high school students also have internships.

Within a short time spent at the school, it will become obvious to any visitor that Brooklyn Free School students love their school. One student told me, "I cringe at the thought of going to any other school." Students' complaints about the school are few in number, because problems are so transparent and students have the power to fix them.

AT THE SCHOOL, I chatted with dozens of students and was particularly interested in understanding how they adapted to such a free environment. Educator Yaacov Hecht argues that there are three types of situations that usually arise in this type of school: students who experience a "freedom shock" upon entry, students who are trying to "achieve more than they could have in a regular school," and students who "seem to have been born in a democratic school."[19]

The time it requires for a student to adjust and heal depends on how damaging his or her former school was. The students at the Brooklyn Free School have coined the adjustment period as nothing less than a "detox." There is often much difficulty in breaking a traditional school mindset that conditions students to resist having freedom and choice in their learning and their own lives.

For eighteen-year-old Louise, detox took about six or seven months. She had been a student at Poly Prep Country Day School, a prestigious private school in Brooklyn, for almost a decade. In middle school, she got straight A's but suffered from major anxiety issues. She was a perfectionist, craving high grades and her teachers' approval. "I need to get approved by outside sources because I was getting none of that from within myself," she explained. In seventh grade, Louise visited the free school for a trial week. She spent most of her time reading the Harry Potter books in a corner, having found the social scene "terrifying." She did not have much experience meeting new people her own age. So at the conclusion of the week, she told her parents she didn't want to go to the school and continued at Poly Prep; she remained a student there until her freshmen year of high school. During this period, she was still miserable and had frequent panic attacks, but she was able to cope sufficiently by detaching herself emotionally from school.

Then, during the summer before what was going to be her sophomore year, Louise met a few BFS students and learned more about the school's values and culture. She began rethinking her original stance on the school, and eventually she realized that it might be just what she really needed. She told me her decision to switch schools was more "impulsive" rather than one that fully embraced the free school. It was her only alternative at the time.

At the beginning of detox, many students spend time "consuming massive amounts of what was previously controlled or limited," according to unschooling advocate Dayna Martin.[20] Louise's first few weeks at the school in the fall of 2012 were pretty tough. She intentionally shunned most people. She told me, "Detox is a confusing period for you. I spent it watching television on my laptop. After a while, it doesn't feel good to watch television for twelve hours a day. It's not satisfying." She participated in literature and Model United Nations classes and by the spring had read dozens of books. In her transcript for college admissions, Louise wrote, "In the beginning of my first year, I used books primarily as an escape from the more intimidating social aspects of the school. I quickly fell in love with the books themselves and ended up spending the majority of my days in the library, simply because I couldn't get away. After a while, I got the courage to use what I was reading as a tool to engage with others, instead of treating it as something isolating."

During detox, the students ask themselves questions like, Who am I? What do I like to do? They're slowly rediscovering their true self and identity and learning how to be and think for themselves. The process can take all the way from days to months to years for the "freedom shocked." By the spring of 2013, Louise had emerged out of her shell and become an active member of the school community, taking on roles in several committees. During her senior year— the 2014–15 school year—she applied to several liberal arts colleges, like Oberlin, Reed, and Kenyon. In her essay, she wrote about being a feminist and how she has become more aware of the relationships among race, class, and gender. She decided to attend Reed College.

ONE CENTRAL FEATURE that separates free and democratic schools from other self-appointed alternative schools is the absence of coercion in learning. Nobody will compel a child to learn something she is not interested in. For instance, classes at Sudbury Valley aren't like typical classes where kids are lectured at by a teacher and sit in desks in rows. As Daniel Greenberg explains in his book *Free at Last,* "At Sudbury Valley, a class is an arrangement between two parties. It starts with someone, or several persons, who decide they want to learn something specific—say, algebra, or French, or physics, or spelling, or pottery . . . Those who initiate the deal are called 'students.' If they don't start it up, there is no class . . . The class deals have all sorts of terms: subject matter, times, obligations of each party . . . Classes end when either side has had enough of the deal."[21] There's a clear difference between being forced to be in a structured environment and choosing to be in one.

Some schools, like the Brooklyn Free School, have a list of classes available for students to take and provide the opportunity for students to propose their own classes. Classes run in cycles of six to ten weeks.

In free and democratic schools, there isn't a set, prescribed curriculum, nor are there any grades given or tests administered to the students. One question that often comes up is, But how are we going to tell whether a child learned something or not? Well, the problem is with the question itself. We get far too caught up with trying to prove or measure learning: What grade did Johnny get on the chemistry midterm? How many students passed the state tests? Which school got the highest average test scores? How many Advanced Placement courses did Suzy take? How far behind are American students from Chinese students on the Programme for International Student Assessment rankings? We forget there is no real value in using arbitrary, quantitative indicators to pit students against one another. Learning should be free of fear and be engaged in for its own sake. Not to please parents. Not to impress other people. Not to get good grades. Not to accumulate degrees or awards. Imagine if all the time people spend grade grubbing and résumé padding was instead allocated to actual learning by pursuing one's passions and interests. A great deal of learning would be taking place, and a lot less psychic damage done.

This, however, is not an argument against portfolios and evaluations. Of course, students should know how to document their work and receive constant feedback and support from peers, experts, mentors, and teachers. But evaluations should not be reducible to a number or a letter, and they should serve the purpose of growth and improvement rather than demoralization.

In order to graduate from one of these schools, there are some requirements that must be met. The Brooklyn Free School has had a total of thirty-one graduates. During the 2014–15 school year, seven students graduated, the largest graduating class the school has ever had. Director Lily Mercogliano explained to me that when a student feels that he or she is prepared to leave and move on to future endeavors, the student can declare his or her intention to graduate. The student must "be in accordance with the school's community responsibility policy"—that is, participation in democratic process, cleanup, and mediation—"and attendance policy," she said. Then the student needs to write a graduation essay that answers the question, Why are you ready to graduate and move on to the next stage of your life?, and consult with a committee of staff members and mentors. Next, the essay and a narrative transcript, which includes self-evaluations of activities engaged in at the school, is defended before the general school community in a voluntary meeting. The community votes to allow the student to graduate or not. A three-quarters majority is required. At the Hudson Valley Sudbury School in New York, students must defend a thesis with the topic "How I have prepared myself to be an effective adult in the larger community."

After I visit any school, I always ask myself the question, If I ever had a chance to redo my youth, would I want to attend this school? And the answer is, I would only be satisfied if I went to a democratic or free school.

ONE AFTERNOON AT the Brooklyn Free School, I met Mia, a sixteen-year-old African American girl. She has bounced in and out of public and private schools and homeschooling. During middle school, she was regularly stressed out and turned off by the rote learning in her classes. When eighth grade came around, she and her mother began searching for a high school, because her middle school ended at eighth grade and she didn't want to attend any of her district's high schools. One day, her mother googled "free school"—free in terms of price—and the Brooklyn Free School popped up. After a trial week at the school, Mia told me that it reminded her of homeschooling and she wanted to be a student there.

It took a whole year for her to truly adjust to the school. At first, she says, "The fact that I had the freedom to make my own curriculum scared me a little bit. I didn't trust myself to do that. There was always a sense of not wanting to fall behind, and at that time, I decided to push myself to do all this schoolwork that was even harder and more advanced than what they would be doing at public school anyway." Soon, it became way too much work for her to manage. It finally occurred to her that this was nobody's fault but her own. "I decided that I didn't always have to be doing something academic at every second of the day," she said. "I got a little more relaxed. I started to sink into the freedom."

Once Mia began taking classes, she said, "I started to think about what I actually wanted to learn and what I felt like I needed to learn so that when I go out of BFS, I know that I'm comfortable with what I've learned at school." In 2014, she and another student founded a record company that promotes antiracist, antisexist, and antihomophobic music. They have engineers, a studio, and potential artists standing by, but they realized that they don't have a full grasp of the fundamentals of business. That's what they hope to study in college. Mia ended up attending Kingsborough Community College in Brooklyn and concurrently takes a few classes at BFS.

What she considers to be the most powerful experience during her time at the school has been the race and gender affinity groups. They were launched when Alan Berger was director but have expanded since Mercogliano became director in the 2013–14 school year. She had already been a teacher at the school for eight years and had graduated many years earlier from another revered New York free school—Albany Free School. The affinity groups grew out of a larger schoolwide conversation around racism and microaggressions at the school. Students who chose to opt in met once a week or every two weeks in mixed or segregated groups by race or gender to discuss the issue. They have learned about oppression, privilege, power, cultural appropriation, and other social justice topics. Students of color told me that having a safe and open space to talk about race has helped them become educated on how to spot discrimination and what to do when it happens. However, a few students told me that the affinity groups sometimes feel a bit "forced upon" the students. Louise, a white student, said, "Generally, people who are saying that it's forced upon them are the people who have privilege and aren't aware of it. The pushback you get from race affinity groups is never from people of color. It's always white people. In gender affinity groups, the pushback is always from men." Such conversations can be uncomfortable, she adds, but they have been some of the "most rewarding" parts of her school experience. "I've realized that I'm never done learning about oppression, and that the work to undo it is never finished," Louise wrote in her college application.

Social justice is an integral component of the school, and it's mentioned in the very first line of the school's mission statement:

> Brooklyn Free School's mission is education for
> social justice. Always advocating for young people's
> voices to be heard, BFS engages students and staff in
> democratic decision making and problem solving. We
> honor student choice and facilitate student-centered
> learning through play and exploration, constructivist
> teaching, collaborative course work and self-directed
> student initiatives. We support social and emotional
> development through conflict mediation, personal
> reflection, diversity awareness and community
> responsibility. BFS works in the service of students and
> their families, partners with progressive educators,
> and embraces our larger community.

Mercogliano noted that in recent years the school has doubled down on improving equity by strengthening student voices, diversity, and its relationships with public schools. She said they wanted "this to be an accessible school for all students and to really represent Brooklyn, and also be a school that is working with public schools and teachers and trying to own an identity about students having power in education . . . There is a lot of desire to work with public schools and a strong wish for public schools to be different." But above all, the goal is to be a place where every student is "able to be their full selves" and "get to be who they are and who they want to be."

SOFTWARE DEVELOPER Jeff Collins went on a quest to find a school for his daughter where she would be engaged, treated with respect, and be able to choose what she wanted to learn instead of being told. He couldn't find one, so he decided to start a school himself.[22]

Collins spoke with his wife and a few friends and formed a small founders group. He picked up some books on how to start a Sudbury school from the Sudbury Valley School Press. The founders group organized a meeting in their local town of Woodstock, New York, and put out a notice in the newspaper that they were starting a private school but refrained from revealing the details of what the school was going to be like. About one hundred people came to the meeting, and Collins spoke of a school with no grades, tests, homework, or mandatory classes—a place where the students were free to learn with few constraints.

"We found a few people who agreed entirely with our philosophy," he recalled. "But there was skepticism to fear to downright hostility from some. 'How can you do this? This is so dangerous to a child's education' or 'This will damage a kid's education. You aren't teaching them all the things they need to learn to be a real person.'"

The first batch of parents who signed up for the school were those who really craved this type of schooling, wanted something different for their kids, or were trying to have their child leave the school he or she was currently in. Collins and his team swiftly received permission from New York State to start a school but had some trouble finding a building.

Finally in 2002, Hudson Valley Sudbury School began with sixty-five students in a building that had housed a local school administration office. Later, they discovered that the building wasn't constructed properly and getting it up to code wasn't worth the cost.

So the school closed down for a bit while a brand-new building was constructed, financed by Collins personally. In June 2004, they restarted operations unofficially in a trial run with twenty-five students. Then in September, they officially reopened with thirty-five students. More than a decade later, in the 2014–15 school year, enrollment hit eighty pupils. The maximum capacity for the building is one hundred students, and there are eight staff members. The school is housed in a cozy five-thousand-square-foot ranch-style building enveloped by natural vegetation on a sixty-plus-acre property. There is ample space outside for the kids to play—whether on the basketball court or the lawns.

While tuition is $6,300 a year for the first child and $4,725 for the second child, the school has a generous financial aid policy. "If you can't pay the full tuition," Collins explained, "then you have to submit documentation [tax returns] indicating your financial situation. We then make a judgment call based on your income." The school is technically private and operates as a nonprofit.

Just as Woodstock was one of the cultural centers of the bohemian, counterculture phenomenon of the 1960s, the Hudson Valley Sudbury School today is devoted to shaking traditional education to its core.

AT ONE MOMENT of the school day, kids were reading in the library, a boy was working on his laptop in the dining area, two were playing basketball outside, two girls were rolling around in the grass, and others were sitting at a picnic table playing Scrabble. In the computer room, six students, ranging in age from eight to twenty-two, were playing the online video game League of Legends on their laptops. Down the hall in the library, a band of kids and staff members were sitting on the floor in a circle playing cards. Nearby, two young girls, Ava and Kaya, were working on the computer. They had found the Percy Jackson and the Olympians series on the bookshelves. After reading them, they decided to compose a Greek mythology story of their own. The two made up their own characters and gave them names after using Google Translate.

Those were some of the myriad mixed-age interactions that were happening at the school. In traditional schools, on the other hand, children are separated by age, or as prominent education thinker Sir Ken Robinson put it, according to "their date of manufacture," from the time they begin school. Bringing age segregation into schools was, as we've seen, actually a calculated scheme by the father of the public school system, Horace Mann, to breed efficiency and standardization, a feature that has remained in schools ever since.

When he visited schools in Prussia in 1843, Mann made this observation: "The first element of superiority in a Prussian school . . . consists in the proper classification of the scholars. In all places where the numbers are sufficiently large to allow it, the children are divided according to ages and attainments; and a single teacher has the charge only of a single class . . . There is no obstacle whatever . . . to the introduction, at once, of this mode of dividing and classifying scholars, in all our large towns."[23] A few years later, replacing the multiage one-room schoolhouse, he introduced the concept of "age-grading" into schools in Massachusetts, beginning with the Quincy Grammar School. This meant that students were sorted and classified into their "graded" classes based on their age, with one year's age difference between each class.[24]

In 1913, Frederic Burk, president of San Francisco State Normal School, vibrantly critiqued the "class system" in these words:

> The class system has been modeled upon the military system. It is constructed upon the assumption that a group of minds can be marshaled and controlled in growth in exactly the same manner that a military officer marshals and directs the bodily movements of a company of soldiers. In solid, unbreakable phalanx the class is supposed to move through all the grades, keeping in locked step. This locked step is set by the "average" pupil—an algebraic myth born of inanimate figures and an addled pedagogy . . . The class system does permanent violence to all types of pupils. (1) It does injury to the rapid and quick-thinking pupils, because these must shackle their stride to keep pace with the mythical average . . . (2) The class system does a greater injury to the large number who make slower progress

than the rate of the mythical average pupil . . . They are foredoomed to failure before they begin.[25]

Prior to age-graded schools, many children did not attend school at all, and the ones who did often learned in one-room schoolhouses with a wide age range of students. Doing an apprenticeship was a popular route for many young people, so they spent most of their time alongside adults. With the dawn of compulsory schooling and age segregation in schools, historian Joseph Kett writes in his book *Rites of Passage,* "Their contacts with adults are likely to occur in highly controlled environments such as the classroom, and the adults encountered are usually conveyors of specialized services such as education and guidance." He defines adolescence as "the period after puberty during which a young person is institutionally segregated from casual contacts with a broad range of adults."[26] Five Calvin College professors pose this question in their book *Dancing in the Dark:* "How are youth going to mature except by contact with adults?" They go on to argue, "In the long run, isolation and market segmentation stall or retard maturity because they separate youth from the broader society, especially from the real world of adults."[27]

In the 1930s, psychologist Lev Vygotsky devised the term "zone of proximal development," referring to the distance between what a learner can master independently and what the same learner can do with the help of an adult or other peers. Boston College research professor of psychology Peter Gray likes to apply this concept to age-mixed interactions among children. After spending a great deal of time at Sudbury Valley, Gray notes in an article for the *American Journal of Play,* he and his colleague Jay Feldman "found that more than half of the social interactions among students spanned age gaps greater than twenty-four months, and a quarter of them spanned gaps greater than forty-eight months . . . In a subsequent long-term qualitative study, we documented and coded nearly two hundred separate interactions that occurred specifically between adolescents (age twelve and older) and younger children (defined as less than twelve years old and more than four years younger than the oldest adolescent in the interaction)."[28] Numerous studies have found that mixed-age classrooms foster more play and reading and writing activity than same-age classrooms.[29]

Daniel Greenberg likes to say that age mixing is Sudbury Valley's "secret weapon." He is indeed correct.

WITH ALL THIS freedom, you might ask, how do students in these free and democratic schools learn to read?

Our schools do everything fundamentally backward when it comes to teaching kids how to read. "The only way you can stop a child from learning to read and liking it—in the densely verbal culture which surrounds us all with printed language anywhere we turn—is to teach it the way we teach it," proclaimed John Taylor Gatto in *Weapons of Mass Instruction*.[30]

First, we force kids to read when they may have no interest in it. My blood boils every time someone says that we need to get all kids reading on grade level. "For non-schooled children there is no critical period or best age for learning how to read," writes Peter Gray in *Psychology Today*.[31] Some kids are early readers, some take more time. When we push reading too early, it may turn off kids for the rest of their time in school. It isn't until many years later that many recover from their "bibliophobia" and discover the joy in reading. Second, we teach reading through worksheets, grammar exercises, and oftentimes humdrum books.

At democratic and free schools, like the Brooklyn Free School and Philly Free School, many students learn to read naturally without formal instruction. They are immersed in an environment free of coercion and teeming with books and literate people, young and old. Because younger children are constantly interacting with older children, they often learn to read by example and observation. There is also some peer pressure to learn to read, because students want to be able to communicate with everyone and be part of activities that require basic literacy. However, if a student wants to receive reading instruction from a teacher, he or she of course has the option, and some do.

As Paul Goodman once put it, "According to some neurophysiologists, given the exposure to written code in modern urban and suburban conditions, any emotionally normal child in middle-class surroundings will spontaneously learn to read by age nine, just as he learned to speak by age three. It is impossible for him not to pick up the code unless he is systematically interrupted and discouraged, for instance by trying to teach him in school."[32] Children who do not have books at home or have not been raised by parents who read to them regularly may need formal instruction and additional attention. But that does not refute my overall argument, which is that most children do not need traditional reading instruction in order to learn how to read.

Brazilian educator Paulo Freire taught three hundred illiterate sugarcane workers how to read and write in just forty-five days by making connections and using vocabulary relevant to their lives. This led to the creation of thousands of "cultural circles" across Brazil to expand literacy.[33]

There are some simple things schools can do to develop lifelong readers. Research shows that when children are read to and allowed to choose what they read, they are more likely to read more often for pleasure. A study by Scholastic found that just half of children aged six through seventeen are currently reading a book for fun. When it comes to the predictors of reading frequency, 41 percent of frequent readers aged six through eleven (frequency is defined as reading for fun at least five days a week) reported being read aloud to, while 13 percent of infrequent readers said the same. Additionally, 78 percent of frequent readers aged twelve through seventeen reported reading "a book of choice independently in school," while the same was true for just 24 percent of infrequent readers.[34] Freedom and enjoyment, in short, produce frequent readers.

CONTRARY TO POPULAR belief, it doesn't take years to teach children basic arithmetic if you ignore some of the ways it is traditionally taught in schools. For instance, one day at the Sudbury Valley School, a dozen students, aged nine to twelve, asked Daniel Greenberg to teach them the four basic operations of arithmetic: addition, subtraction, multiplication, and division. He held an hourly class once a week and used an old math book with thousands of exercises as a resource. It took two classes for the kids to learn addition, two more classes to learn subtraction, and after just twenty contact weeks, they learned a few years' worth of material. Every single one of them.[35]

In the fall of 1929, L. P. Benezet, superintendent of schools in Manchester, New Hampshire, tried an experiment where he dropped all formal instruction of arithmetic below the seventh grade and began "concentrating on teaching the children to read, to reason, and to recite." By recitation, he "meant speaking the English language," where students would engage in oral composition by speaking about books they read, places they visited, and movies they saw. Benezet wrote in the *Journal of the National Education Association* that he "picked out five rooms—three third grades, one combining the third and fourth grades, and one fifth grade."

"For some years," he explained, "I had noted that the effect of the early introduction of arithmetic had been to dull and almost chloroform the child's reasoning faculties."

In the experimental rooms, the superintendent gave the students various problems in "estimating heights, lengths, areas, distances." Most of them answered the exercises correctly. He expanded the experiment to six or seven rooms. Again, there was no formal arithmetic instruction and the "emphasis was placed on English expression, on reasoning, and estimating of distances." Then in the fall of 1932, researchers from Boston University began conducting a study of Benezet's methods with 200 sixth graders in Manchester schools, 98 from experimental rooms and 102 from the traditional rooms. The first arithmetic test administered at the beginning of the year showed the traditionally trained pool performing better than the experimental pool. By mid-April, the groups were neck and neck. In June, the experimental pack overtook the traditional group. "In other words," Benezet wrote, "these children, by avoiding the early drill on combinations, tables, and that sort of thing, had been able, in one year, to attain the level of accomplishment which the traditionally taught children had reached after three and one-half years of arithmetical drill."[36]

· · ·

ONE SPRING EVENING, I went out to dinner with some of the Hudson Valley students and staff members at an Italian restaurant in town. The conversation ranged from topics like compulsory schooling and how Sudbury schooling can become a part of the mainstream to, yes, dyed hair. Dyed hair was the latest trend sweeping the school. If you arranged the kids in a row according to their hair color, a rainbow would appear.

I was later shelled with questions from the kids, who were eager to learn about what I was working on, my future plans, and some of the schools I had visited. They were very interested in hearing what other students' school experiences were like.

During my visit to the school, whenever I interviewed a student, I posed the question, What is the worst part about school? Each time, the student either stumbled, froze in place, or didn't have an answer for me. They all loved going to this school.

One of the most interesting students I encountered was a ten-year-old boy named Emmet. Dressed in a purple-and-teal plaid shirt, faded jeans, and, of course, purple hair, he was sucking on an orange lollipop when I first met him. He had been coming to Hudson Valley since he was three. His favorite pastime is playing the Adventure Time Card Wars game with his friends. Emmet does this twice a week for about half an hour. Like many boys his age, he also loves playing the indie open-ended video game Minecraft, which lets players create their own virtual worlds out of blocks. Emmet was building a giant sandstone pyramid—learning architecture, planning, and social skills through engaging with fellow users on the servers. "It's really hard and sometimes a little boring," he admits. "But it's great to use my imagination.

It's fun and makes me happy." And isn't that one of the most important qualities we should want all our children to have?

"IS THIS CASE serious or moderate?" asked the judicial clerk.

"Serious," replied one student.

"Yeah, serious," said another.

The judicial meeting was in session at the Philly Free School. Located in Graduate Hospital, a middle-class neighborhood in southwest Philadelphia, the private school became a member of the alternative education scene in 2011. By the 2014–15 school year, it had grown to educate nearly fifty students aged four to nineteen with four staff members, an intern, and a few volunteers. Tuition, which is on a sliding scale, ranged from $0 to $12,000 depending on the student's financial situation. Twenty-one percent paid nothing. Half of students were white, half were of color, a figure almost unheard of in other private schools. Having lots of racial and socioeconomic diversity in the school was central to the founders' mission. That's why they chose to be in a city—and because "the mix of people that you get in the city is the hugest learning opportunity," said Michelle Loucas, cofounder of the school. In public schools, because they suffer from class and racial segregation, she says, there's very little interaction or understanding of people across races or classes. "That's a critical failing of our education system."

Four judicial committee members serve on a rotating basis: one kid under eight, one kid eight or older, one staff member, and one judicial clerk, who is usually a student and is replaced every six weeks. They meet daily to settle disputes and disciplinary problems. The clerk doesn't vote.

The case involved a student who accidentally busted the ceiling fan in the basement. She didn't shut the fan off or tell a staff member about the problem. This was a very serious case, because it was a fire hazard. A few witnesses testified before the committee. Shortly after, the committee voted and came to a consensus: "There will be nobody allowed in the basement until the school meeting, where the case will be decided." The school meeting is the governing body of the school, consisting of all students and staff members. Each member of the school has one vote. During the meetings, school policies, issues, and rules are discussed and voted upon. There are, however, some admissions and administration-related policies that are not decided democratically.

The next case involved a petty offense. A twelve-year-old student kept touching the computer screen, violating one of the school rules. And yes, a five-year-old student noticed the offense, wrote up a complaint, and gave it to the judicial committee for review.

During the meeting, the student pled guilty to the offense and the committee delivered a minor sentence: the student would need to get recertified to be permitted to use the computer. Loucas says everything at the school is transparent, but they try to let students "make mistakes without the watchful gaze of their parents." The judicial meetings go on until the committee finishes ruling on all the complaints. That day, however, the meeting was cut short to make time for the upcoming school meeting.

A majority of the judicial meeting cases are mess related—something is untidy or disorganized. The point is to hold people accountable and reinforce community norms. If a rule is broken, then the student is charged and an investigation is launched.

What sets schools like these apart from the rest is that they are truly democratic institutions. The learners govern the school through the school meetings. A student usually chairs the meeting and puts together the agenda. As noted earlier, when 94 percent of a population has no control over its government and no voice, we call that a totalitarian regime or dictatorship. Yet in a supposedly democratic nation, where about 94 percent of the population of schools—students—has virtually no voice in how its institutions should be run and governed, we fail to recognize the irony. As Yaacov Hecht puts it in *Democratic Education,* how can we expect to have active, engaged citizens in democracy when we put kids through a dictatorship for thirteen years of their lives?[37]

Evoking some of the spirit of the eighteenth-century New England colonial town meetings where community members organized to construct policy and set budgets, the school meeting is one of the cornerstones of democratic education. Attendance and voting in meetings are optional at most democratic and free schools. Students can just come to the meetings when they have an interest in the issues on the agenda. Likewise, in most democracies, you are given the right to vote, but you are not obligated by law to vote. You simply have the power to vote if you wish.

Interestingly, in order for me to get permission to visit these democratic and free schools and conduct interviews, the students and staff members had to vote whether to let me in or not.

At the Sudbury Valley School, the set of rules and behaviors drawn up for adults and children in the community are:

1. A person cannot infringe on another's rights.
2. A person cannot disturb another's activities.

3. A person cannot use another's private property without permission.

4. A person cannot endanger the safety of another.[38]

Students are also surrounded by nurturing, supportive adults at all times. At Sudbury schools, students have the power to hire and fire staff members, who do not have tenure. Every spring, there are staff elections held where students vote by secret ballot. As Peter Gray explains in *Psychology Today,* "The staff who survive this process and are re-elected year after year are those who are admired by the students. They are people who are kind, ethical, and competent, and who contribute significantly and positively to the school's environment. They are adults that the students may wish in some ways to emulate."[39]

After lunch, the school meeting at the Philly Free School was brought to order. About ten kids and staff members sat around a table in the sunny art room with the cacophony of construction work in the background. Passing a motion requires a simple majority, while suspensions require a two-thirds majority. The meeting barreled on for a while, ticking off complaints and various issues. Students regularly walked in and out of the room. One motion that overwhelmingly passed stated that students are allowed to walk around in bare feet beginning in the springtime. The case of the student breaking the ceiling fan that was previously heard by the judicial committee was resolved with a ruling that the family of the student would be forced to replace the fan.

Democracy is not always neat and efficient. The time devoted to meetings, which are often laborious, could be trimmed, but democratic meetings are at the heart of free schools and should begin to be emulated more widely. Students from the Philly Free School and others are so much more prepared for and interested in participating in civic life compared with students from schools where they are stripped of their basic civil liberties and rights for thirteen years, because they learn and engage in schools where their rights are respected and upheld.

In the country of Colombia, there are thousands of Escuelas Nuevas (New Schools), which have a democratic decision-making process that includes the voices of students, teachers, and parents. As David L. Kirp, professor at the University of California, Berkeley, wrote in *The New York Times,* "In the schools, students elected by their peers shoulder a host of responsibilities. In a school I visited in a poor neighborhood in the city of Armenia, Colombia, the student council meticulously planned a day set aside to promote peace; operated a radio station; and turned an empty classroom into a quiet space for reading and recharging."[40] This model of schooling provides further grist for the argument that democratic schools can successfully educate poor children, not just upper-middle-class and wealthy ones.

Can public schools with hundreds and sometimes thousands of students implement some kind of democratic governance process where students have real power, unlike the charade known as student government? One high school in New Hampshire with nearly eight hundred students has operated largely democratically since the 1970s. At Hanover High School near Dartmouth College, after the student council voted to abolish itself in June 1970, there was a group of teachers and administrators who were interested in setting up a new governance system. Some saw a gross contradiction between raising young people in a democratic society and students learning in undemocratic institutions. As Marilyn Blight, the school's media specialist, recounted in a 1996 article for the *Democracy & Education* journal, in September 1971 the principal "announced the formation of a new democratic governance system in which students and faculty would share decision-making power with the administration."[41] In 1977, the Dresden Board of School Directors approved the Hanover High School Council unanimously. As the school's student handbook explained, "The Council shall have the authority to act on all matters at Hanover High School not controlled by school board policy, state law, administrative regulations established by the Superintendent of Schools, and rules and regulations published in the Student Handbook of Hanover High School." When it was adopted, certain provisions stated that in order for Council to be dissolved, there would need to be an internal motion in support of disbandment from the body itself and approval from the principal and the school board. That was to ensure that in the future, if a new principal didn't support it, that individual couldn't singlehandedly get rid of Council.

One afternoon I spoke with Kelsey, a Hanover senior and the moderator of Council for the 2014–15 school year.[42] Council comprises more than forty members, and the exact number varies by year. There is an at-large delegation made up of the twelve students with the highest overall number of votes. Then sophomores, juniors, and seniors each have five voting members and one alternate, while freshmen have four voting members and one alternate. There are also a few staff and community members, including at least one parent of a current student in Council. Every spring, elections are held. Anyone can run. The officers include a moderator, an assistant moderator, a secretary, a treasurer, a public relations person, and a Dresden School Board student representative. They are all students and are elected internally by

Council at the end of each school year, beginning their term the following fall.

In Council, there are also several committees that deal with specific issues, including the class, student life, student activities, judiciary, organizational engineering, curriculum, administrative, and executive committees.

During the school year, meetings occur once a week for about an hour. They are open to the whole school. Kelsey told me her job is to bring the meeting to order and start going through the issues on the agenda. She only votes in order to break a tie. A simple majority is required for a motion to pass. Motions that come from committee need a two-thirds majority vote from the members present. Once a motion passes, it goes to the principal, who has veto power. With a two-thirds majority vote, the council can override a veto. Only particularly noteworthy motions, such as ones that affect the school curriculum, teachers, and the overall community, need to receive the approval of the school board.

Kelsey said that for motions where it's unclear whether Council has jurisdiction or not, a review board agreed to by the principal and the moderator has the power to make a decision. This board consists of two staff members, two students, a representative of the superintendent's office, a representative of the Dresden School Board, and a community member. Later, a vote on the conclusions is taken, with a majority required to pass.

In the past, motions have ranged from requiring that teachers return tests and quizzes within a certain time frame to banning plastic bottles to changing the academic integrity policy.

While it has faced some backlash from teachers and administrators in the past, Council has endured for nearly four decades. Kelsey says that it's defined her high school experience. "In terms of preparing people for the real world," she explained, "it's something we should all know how to do: have proper discussions, be willing to talk about things that might be uncomfortable . . . and go through this process democratically and fairly [to come] up with decisions, even if we aren't happy about the outcomes." For such a privileged community, she added that it's given students an opportunity "to challenge things we've accepted at school."

In public schools, students should demand power in the school decision-making process. They should collectively organize and try to form a student union. Recently, students at the London School of Economics, King's College London, the University of Amsterdam, and others have held protests and occupied spaces demanding the democratization of the university. A school's authority figures will not relinquish power willingly. They will only give it up when they have no other choice.

AFTER VISITING MANY democratic and free schools around the country, I have concluded that I had never met more articulate, unorthodox, curious, and happy children before. The students at these schools have a purpose. They are lifelong learners. They love reading books and playing and learning. They can go on for hours about their interests and passions. They can communicate better than most adults can. And they haven't lost much of their curiosity and creativity.

The two questions parents are always anxiously waiting to ask are: That's great and all, but do these kids get into college? And what types of careers do they end up in? In fact, a large majority of the graduates of democratic and free schools enroll in college and/or live happy and satisfied lives without having misery inflicted upon them or being coerced to do the things that students of traditional schools must do—testing, ceaseless homework, and mandatory classes, to name a few.

Graduates of a public alternative school called the Jefferson County Open School in Lakewood, Colorado, were surveyed by Rick Posner and the results were documented in his 2009 book *Lives of Passion, School of Hope*. The survey included responses from 431 former students from 1976 through 2002 (out of a total of 865 former Open School students). Ninety-one percent of the respondents went to college, and they ended up being very successful there. Eighty-five percent of them completed their degrees. Moreover, Posner found that 89 percent of the alumni said "they are happy with their jobs" and 84 percent said their Open School experience "has had a positive influence on their work lives."[43]

Take one graduate of the Sudbury Valley School. Raised in New Hampshire, Brooke Newman was a straight-A student and played on her public school's junior varsity soccer team. She was the "golden girl," as she likes to say.[44] But Newman hated the drudgery of school, despised the hours of homework, felt alienated by the culture of makeup and fashion, and noticed that there was a lack of depth in her relationships. School didn't appeal to her.

Her older brother, on the other hand, neatly fit into the Bart Simpson ethos of the time: "underachiever and proud of it." He was miserable in school and got bullied by other students.

Newman's parents took him to see a psychologist, who recommended that they send him to Sudbury Valley, which they eventually did, albeit begrudgingly. And her brother ended up loving his new school. There wasn't any bullying and he was able to play music all day.

Meanwhile, Newman was growing quite jealous of her brother and wanted to go to the school as well. "My brother had a permanent recess while I was busting my ass to get straight A's," she said. Her father, a Vietnam War veteran, wasn't very open to democratic schooling, and there was an expectation in her family that Newman was going to grow up to become a doctor, lawyer, or stockbroker, and this type of education wasn't going to get her there.

But then one evening, there was a panel discussion of Sudbury Valley alumni, including a doctor. The fact that many of the school's graduates lead successful, happy lives sold her parents on allowing her to join her brother at the school.

In February 1993, at age fourteen, Newman enrolled at Sudbury Valley. She told me, "I became a human being again. I realized that I could learn and do anything I wanted." She would never go back to public school.

When she first arrived, she was more involved in the structured learning activities, but that decreased over time as she became more comfortable with the free environment. She helped organize the school dances and once she earned her driver's license, she did administrative work for an online bookstore and later started her own cleaning company—cleaning people's houses and apartments a few times a week.

After graduating in June 1996, Newman took a gap year to continue her cleaning business, which had expanded greatly. The next fall, she matriculated at Northeastern University, where she studied political science. A year and a half in, she transferred to Eugene Lang College at the New School and graduated with a bachelor's degree. From there, she sampled a potpourri of professions—working for a German-based international media monitor in New York, the Red Cross in Florida as a service coordinator, and the *St. Petersburg Times* (now known as the *Tampa Bay Times*) and the *Citrus County Chronicle* as a freelance journalist. She moved back to New York and landed a job as a research assistant for the Children's Environmental Health Center at the Icahn School of Medicine at Mount Sinai. Then in 2006, she was recruited to work at the World Trade Center Medical Monitoring and Treatment Program, which was based out of Queens College, and was there until 2011. In the meantime, she also completed her master's degree in public administration at the Baruch College School of Public Affairs, taking classes at night. Brooke Newman surely turned out fine.

Researchers Peter Gray and David Chanoff conducted a landmark study of the graduates of the Sudbury Valley School in Massachusetts. They sought to survey the students who graduated from the school at least a year earlier. With a response rate of 84 percent of the total number of graduates, sixty-nine subjects filled out a questionnaire or were interviewed. Publishing their findings in the *American Journal of Education* in 1986, Gray and Chanoff found that 75 percent of the total graduates had pursued some form of formal higher education. They wrote, "None of the graduates who had gone to college claimed to have a problem adjusting to the formal structure of college—the required courses, assignments, tests, and so on . . . The same people who had rebelled against required schoolwork before coming to SVS, when they had no choice in the matter, were not rebelling against required work in college because it had been their own desire to go to college."

Some of the benefits of the Sudbury Valley education, as noted by respondents, were "motivation to continue learning was greater as a result of attending SVS," "more responsible for or more in charge of his or her own education as a result of attending SVS," "lack of fear of authority figures," "development of skills and knowledge in specific fields of interest to a greater extent than would have been possible at another school," and "developing personal strengths or overcoming personal problems."[45] Remarkably, not a single graduate said his or her life would be better off had he or she attended a traditional school instead of Sudbury Valley.

For a more comprehensive and updated study, Sudbury Valley itself orchestrated an analysis of 119 graduates and organized their findings in a 2005 book called *The Pursuit of Happiness: The Lives of Sudbury Valley Alumni*. The interviews took place in 2002 and 2003, and the cutoff date for eligibility was 1998 to "allow for several years of life experience after leaving Sudbury Valley." The median age of the respondents was thirty.

Graduates attended colleges and universities like Boston College, Boston University, Brandeis, Carnegie Mellon, Columbia, Emory, Harvard, Lehigh, MIT, New York University, Tufts, Northeastern, University of Massachusetts–Amherst, and Wesleyan. Eighty-two percent of the alumni pursued some form of formal higher education. Compare this with the statistic that less than 70 percent of graduates from the public school system matriculate into college. The main reason that Sudbury Valley students chose not to go to college was that "they felt ready to go directly into the fields they wished to pursue as adults," not that they were unprepared.

Close to half reported working in jobs where they have autonomy and fluid schedules. By and large the alumni of Sudbury Valley were in professions that gave them pleasure. As one former student put it, "Have a hard time going home at night. Too much fun working." And only 14 percent of the alumni weren't satisfied with their financial situation.

There were several salient conclusions from the study: The "vast majority felt very secure in the level of control they had over their destiny," "the alumni reveal in all their diversity a tremendous depth of satisfaction with their lives, together with a life-long striving for beauty and excellence," "they are, one and all, seeking happiness in their lives," and, finally, they are "a wonderful collection of human beings— contemplative, purposeful, clear, happy, and able to cope with change, challenge, and setbacks."[46] Set this image against the bleak landscape of the rest of America. According to a study by Emory University sociologist Corey Lee M. Keyes, more than half of U.S. adults were "moderately mentally healthy," but less than 20 percent were "flourishing," which means having "high levels of emotional, psychological, and social well-being."[47] A Gallup poll found that only 20 percent of people in the United States can give a strong "yes" to the question, "Do you like what you do each day?"[48]

There is a selection bias to be considered when it comes to making sweeping statements about the alumni of democratic and free schools. Based on my interviews with people who work at these schools, families who send their children there are generally college educated and are middle or upper class. And as adults, many of the alumni have the access to resources and programs and family support that allow them to "do what they love," unlike others who are forced to take on taxing, low-wage jobs because they have no alternative.

But at the very least, when I scan through the list of alumni from democratic and free schools, I observe something quite fascinating. It is rare to come across someone whose profession is politician, chief executive officer, or financier, three professions associated with money, prestige, and power. I believe their educational experiences helped them realize that there are other purposes in life: fulfillment, meaning, happiness, and belonging. It was A. S. Neill who wrote, "To sum up, my contention is that unfree education results in life that cannot be lived fully. Such an education almost entirely ignores the emotions of life; and because these emotions are dynamic, their lack of opportunity for expression must and does result in cheapness and ugliness and hatefulness."[49]

NEARLY ALL OF the democratic and free schools in the United States are privately run. Some schools would prefer to be part of the public system, but they would have to compromise too many of their principles in order to function legally. They would need to give standardized tests and grades, follow state standards, and have compulsory classes. There isn't as much flexibility today as there was before the No Child Left Behind Act went into effect.

Because they charge tuition and often have limited financial aid, these schools generally attract students from upper-middle-class and affluent families. You can't expect a poor family to be able to spend thousands of dollars on tuition on top of the money they pay in school taxes. That's the reason why there are few low-income children in some of these schools.

In her 2000 book *Left Back,* education historian Diane Ravitch railed against free schools and argued that they were not appropriate for poor children:

> An educational philosophy of "do your own thing"
> was the worst possible prescription for poor children,
> because it left to their own devices the very children

who were most in need of purposeful instruction. Poor children in classrooms where teachers "facilitated" instead of teaching were at a terrific disadvantage as compared to privileged children who came from homes where educated parents read to them, took them to museums, surrounded them with books, and supplied whatever the school was not teaching.[50]

However, what I have observed is that once these poor children's basic needs are met and they undergo detox, which can often take some time, many do succeed in a more free and open school environment. As psychologist Abraham Maslow noted in his hierarchy of needs theory, human beings' needs for food, water, shelter, and safety must be satisfied first, and then they can move to love, friendships, achievement, and self-fulfillment.

Do disadvantaged students crave structure, bearing in mind that they have so little of it at home and in their lives overall? Some, of course, feel more comfortable learning in a traditional, structured environment, but that varies by subject and student. Most crucially, poor youth and youth of color need democratic schooling the most because they are almost always confined in the most authoritarian learning settings and do not have the experiential learning experiences at home that most middle- and upper-class kids have. In the Global South, there are outstanding locally run institutions, such as Universidad de la Tierra in Oaxaca, Mexico; Swaraj University in Udaipur, India; Barefoot College in Tilonia, India; and the aforementioned Escuelas Nuevas in Colombia, which serve as additional evidence that the principles of freedom, trust, and autonomy in learning are applicable universally.

Finally, why aren't many people aware of democratic

schooling and why hasn't it caught on with the general public? There is such a small number of these schools and they are isolated in pockets of cities and communities without much of a relationship with local entities. I've also noticed that the people who run these schools sometimes don't persuasively depict their model of education and its many successes, which is the most vital element in persuading parents who can afford to enroll their child in the school. They have to realize that democratic schooling is a foreign concept and trusting children is something most parents just don't have the courage to do easily.

MOST FREE AND democratic schools have a pretty small student population—usually fewer than two hundred. Compare this to most elementary schools, which vary in size from two hundred to six hundred students. Some people wonder how we could scale the free-school model to larger institutions. One way would be to break up mammoth schools that have thousands of students and create much smaller schools within them with no more than two hundred or so students. According to "Dunbar's number," a concept coined by Oxford evolutionary psychologist Robin Dunbar, the "mean group size" for human beings, or "the number of individuals with whom a stable inter-personal relationship can be maintained," is about 150 people.[51]

Such a process would require converting and transforming already existing spaces, not closing or privatizing them. As I'll elaborate in Chapter 9, the school building can be a place where students and teachers can meet, organize, work, and learn. But for much of the time they would be out in the community or city, places where a tremendous amount of learning takes place naturally.

. . .

WHEN I GIVE speeches, I often field questions from students who are feeling trapped in school and dying for a way to escape. If they don't have access to a democratic or free school, there are some alternatives: homeschooling, unschooling, and self-directed learning centers.

Since 1993, homeschooling has been legal in all fifty states, with each state having a different level of oversight. According to 2012 data from the National Center for Education Statistics, homeschooling is on the ascent, with more than 1.77 million homeschoolers in the country, or roughly 3.4 percent of school-age children. Sixty-eight percent are white, while 15 percent are Hispanic, 8 percent are black, and 4 percent are Asian. Of the reasons parents gave in a survey for why they homeschool, the three with the highest percentages were "a concern about environment of other schools," "a desire to provide moral instruction," and "a dissatisfaction with academic instruction at other schools."[52] There's no doubt that many families, mainly from among the Christian right, homeschool with a religious or moral intent, but that percentage is on the decline. Lisa Miller reported in *New York* magazine that "the greatest proportion of homeschool parents in the United States earn between $50,000 and $75,000 a year and have a bachelor's degree or more."[53]

Many homeschoolers unfortunately learn pretty much the same way kids in public schools are learning: reading textbooks and filling out workbooks and dittos. But Jude Steffers-Wilson isn't like most homeschoolers.[54] He's closer to someone we would call an unschooler, a term coined by John Holt in the 1970s. There's a small bloc of homeschooling families, about 10 percent, who subscribe to the unschooling philosophy. President of Holt Associates Pat

Farenga, who worked closely with Holt, defines unschooling "as allowing children as much freedom to learn in the world as their parents can comfortably bear."[55] No grades, no tests, no structured curriculum.

For seven years, Jude, a lanky seventeen-year-old biracial boy, was a student in the New York City public school system. In school, he didn't behave and learn like the other kids in his classes. His teachers in elementary school made him read fiction books, which he loathed. Instead, he loved history and other sorts of nonfiction. In the second grade, he was assigned a project on historical figures in America. Instead of choosing to research Martin Luther King Jr. or Rosa Parks, like most of the other students, he studied Malcolm X, indicating an innate sense of rebellion. In school overall, he was appalled by how much pressure the state standardized tests placed on students. As his mother put it bluntly, "I have never known a kid who hated school more than my son."

In his first middle school, Robert F. Wagner Middle School on the Upper East Side of Manhattan, Jude, who was in the sixth grade, only made it through three months of the year before he transferred to another school. "The teachers really demeaned and belittled me," he said. His new school, Global Technology Preparatory, was located in his home neighborhood of East Harlem. The Title I school had just opened in 2009 and serves predominantly poor Latino and black students. When Jude was enrolled, the school's principal was a young, ambitious white woman. "For her," he claims, "it was a feel-good position. *I'm going to save these poor black and brown kids by giving them a good education.*" For the more than one hundred students in the school, the day ran from eight in the morning to six in the evening as the result of a partnership with the nonprofit organization

Citizen Schools and participation in its Expanded Learning Time program. In the seventh grade, Jude said things got out of hand. "Kids were out of control. They were screaming and yelling. They were making fun of each other. And my mom was like, 'You're getting out of here.'" He said that his friends who are still at the school told him that the principal quit and moved to Rwanda to work on a new hybrid education program. Virtually all of the original teachers also threw in the towel.

Jude's mother had always wanted to homeschool him, but since he is now old enough to stay home alone, it is finally possible. Judging from my conversation with him, he is more of an unschooler than a traditional homeschooler. His mother curates resources and offers a wealth of support, but most of what he is learning is in a very self-directed fashion.

Unschoolers, in large part, contend that learning and living are inextricable. On a typical day, Jude is involved in a variety of activities—not in a school building, but in the real world. On the more academic side, he is learning math through an online education program called Time4Learning, Japanese mythology by watching documentaries and reading books, and painting and drawing. There is also an art teacher in the neighborhood who helps him out. In the afternoons, he often goes to the boxing gym to work out for an hour and then heads to his daily hour-and-a-half martial arts class. For the past few years, he had been learning *jeet kune do,* a form of martial arts that combines the elements of boxing, *wing chun,* and fencing. He loves it. He earned his black belt in the fall of 2014.

Many unschoolers go to college, do well there, and lead happy and fulfilled lives. But Jude is undecided on whether he wants to go to college. If there's one thing he knows for sure, it's that he wants to pursue a profession that allows him to work with his hands.

I don't have any doubt that he will, all the more so when weighing the overall data on homeschoolers: On average, they beat their public school counterparts on standardized tests. And they have superior social skills. (As we saw earlier, most of the "socialization" that happens in schools is very unhealthy.) Homeschoolers generally earn higher grade point averages and have higher college graduation rates than their peers.[56] In fact, colleges and universities like Stanford, Harvard, Duke, MIT, and Yale actively recruit homeschoolers, because they know that they are more self-motivated, educated, mature, and involved in their communities.[57]

Homeschooling and unschooling are obviously not solutions for the masses. It isn't very accessible for children who have both parents working long hours, something that is particularly common in low-income and minority communities. And it puts heavy demands on those parents.

There are also resource centers in some communities for children who are registered as homeschoolers. For example, in Hadley, Massachusetts, there is North Star: Self-Directed Learning for Teens, a learning center. Each teenager is assigned an adviser who helps craft a personal learning path. Optional classes, workshops, and tutorials are offered a few days per week. There is a membership fee depending on how many days the child spends at the center.

For children who cannot be homeschooled, unschooled, or attend a democratic or free school or a resource center, what can they do? Hack school. Find ways to spend as little time as possible in school. I graduated from high school six months early. I took some extra classes in my junior year and then I only had to take four classes during my senior year in order to graduate. Many traditional public and private schools offer independent study options as well as credit for completing community college classes. It's not easy, but there are loopholes to get around the one-size-fits-all system and build a more meaningful learning path.

DEMOCRATIC AND PROGRESSIVE education is among the most humane and successful models of education in existence. In these schools and programs, unlike in conventional ones, the rights, interests, and opinions of the children are respected and of prime concern. They view children as people, too.

The challenge is how to bring these schools to more communities, cities, and countries to rescue young people from the clutch of traditional education. Godspeed.

CHAPTER 7

Not Your Father's Shop Class

Around the nation, in the past several years, the maker movement—a shift from consumption to actual making and doing—has been prospering. Its effects have been felt particularly in the education field, as many consider it to be giving credence to the importance of what is commonly referred to as vocational education.

The origin of the maker movement may be found in the 1970s in the San Francisco Bay Area. On March 5, 1975, the Homebrew Computer Club held its first meeting in Gordon French's garage in Menlo Park. It was largely inspired by the introduction of the Altair 8800, the first personal computer on the market. Computer hobbyists assembled in numbers to exchange information, circuits, and parts. The club attracted Steve Wozniak and Steve Jobs, later cofounders of Apple Computer; legendary hacker John Draper, better known as Captain Crunch; and Lee Felsenstein and Adam Osborne, subsequent inventors of the first commercially produced portable computer, the Osborne 1.[1]

The goal of the club was to "give to help others." Each

meeting, according to Wozniak, got under way with a "mapping period." Each member would introduce a certain topic and there would be a lively discussion. He once remarked that "without computer clubs there would probably be no Apple computers." Early prototypes of the computers were exhibited at each meeting, and feedback was offered.[2]

The Homebrew Computer Club gathered regularly until its last meeting in December 1986. Today, the soul of the long-gone computer clubs can be found in the maker movement. Chris Anderson, former editor-in-chief of *Wired,* has predicted that it heralds the arrival of the third industrial revolution. That's highly unlikely and hyperbolic, but there's no doubt that more people than before (even though they are still mostly college-educated white males) are gaining access to affordable tools and machines.[3] In his book *Makers,* Anderson outlines three fundamental forces that led to the emergence of the maker movement:

1. People using digital desktop tools to create designs for new products and prototype them ("digital DIY").
2. A cultural norm to share those designs and collaborate with others in online communities.
3. The use of common design file standards that allow anyone, if they desire, to send their designs to commercial manufacturing services to be produced in any number, just as easily as they can fabricate them on their desktop. This radically foreshortens the path from idea to entrepreneurship, just as the Web did in software, information, and content.[4]

We are all makers at heart. Some of us just don't realize it yet. Making is not limited to the science, technology, engineering, and mathematics (STEM) fields. It also encompasses art, design, cooking, sewing, farming, and others.

Makers are rebelling against a culture that has become prepackaged, standardized, and deprived of the ingenuity that comes from working with the hand. They are creating or building physical things, be it with 3D printers, Raspberry Pis, laser cutters, or other tools, in kitchens, garages, makerspaces, or hackerspaces. A "makerspace," a relatively new term, is a physical place where people with common interests work on projects and have access to many tools and materials. It is a mashup of shop class and the computer lab. A hackerspace, however, is a physical place that is specifically for programming, hardware, and electronics. They've been around for decades now. Embedded in cities and communities around the world, the number of hackerspaces and makerspaces is on the rise, estimated to have topped more than a thousand.[5] Some libraries are also beginning to create makerspaces.

THE INDIVIDUAL WHOM many would consider to be the pioneer of the modern maker movement is Dale Dougherty.[6] He is the founder and CEO of Maker Media and creator of Maker Faire. When we spoke at the South by Southwest Education conference in Austin, Texas, in March 2014, he was wearing half-rimmed glasses and a black windbreaker. He is tall and has graying hair.

Born in southern California in the 1950s, Dougherty lived there until he was twelve, when he moved to Louisville, Kentucky. He spent much of his youth reading books, playing with electronics, and building models. In high school, his favorite subject was English. His demanding teacher would make him rewrite everything until it was perfect. "When you realize that this isn't stuff that comes naturally, you have to work for it," Dougherty said. "You develop an analytical mind for your own work." He applies the same principle to making, where you are iterating ideas over and over again.

At age fourteen, he began working in restaurants, where he felt he was his "own agent." As a busboy, waiter, cook, or bartender's assistant, he learned how to take on responsibilities, make decisions, and act professionally. Over time, he developed a love for food. Cooking, he said, is "one of the most satisfying things for me."

After graduating from high school, Dougherty went off to Bellarmine University, a small liberal arts school in Louisville, for two years. Then he transferred to the University of Louisville and graduated with a bachelor's degree in English in 1979. As in high school, he found himself bored and discontented in college. "Obviously I got some foundation in school, but I didn't have a lot of formative experiences," he explained.

Dougherty moved to Boston after college and continued working in restaurants and writing on the side. After getting married, he became a copywriter at an ad agency, a "pretty dull job," he noted. He took a technical writing course at Northeastern University and got connected with Tim O'Reilly. O'Reilly was searching for writers for his technical firm, and Dougherty took a position as an independent contractor.

In 1978, the pair launched O'Reilly & Associates and began publishing computer manuals. "Our goal was to make it accessible," Dougherty said. "We often learned from our own experiences and tried to write it clearly for other people. There were technical topics that had a relatively small audience at the time."

The Internet had been growing rapidly, and Dougherty

took note of its enormous potential. In 1993, he developed the first commercial website, Global Network Navigator (GNN). Two years later, it was sold to AOL. His next endeavor was Songline Studios, an online publishing company that produced technical manuals and was an affiliate of O'Reilly & Associates.

Next, he wrote the Hacks series of books for O'Reilly to "reclaim the term 'hacking' for the good guys." As he was working on the books, he realized that hacking was not limited to software. We can also hack the physical world in similar ways. Dougherty realized there was a huge audience of people who loved working on projects in technology and electronics, often in their spare time, who weren't being recognized or served. He called these people "makers" and pitched to Tim O'Reilly the idea of a publication that would be a "Martha Stewart for geeks." In 2005, Dougherty started *Make* magazine at O'Reilly to give makers resources, tools, and knowledge to help them work on their projects.

The next year, Maker Faire was born. The first Maker Faire was held in San Mateo, California, and drew 18,000 people. There have now been hundreds of Maker Faires convened around the world, attracting a total of more than three million attendees. As its motto goes, it is "the Greatest Show (and Tell) on Earth" and celebrates "arts, crafts, engineering, science projects and the Do-It-Yourself (DIY) mindset." Chris Anderson calls Maker Faire "the Woodstock of the new industrial revolution." Unlike your traditional local county fair with deep-fried butter on a stick, corn dogs, games, and thrill rides, the Faires show off makers and their DIY drones, 3D printers, and robots. On a warm Saturday afternoon in September 2013, I made my way to the New York Hall of Science, on the grounds of the old World's Fair in Queens, with about 650 makers and 75,000 antsy children and parents and other attendees for the annual New York Maker Faire. In my time at the event, I noticed intense go-kart races, a life-size Mouse Trap board game, the Deep Imager 5 (a 3D printer), Popcade ("a mini arcade cabinet that packs all the fun of a full-sized classic arcade game into a cabinet that's just half the size"), and plenty of aerial drones. One of the most popular exhibits was Air Rockets, where hundreds of four- to thirty-year-olds scrambled to construct foam Air Rocket Gliders and compete against one another. Seated around wooden tables under a tent, groups of four made rockets out of tape and paper. The assistants helping them were dressed in Air Force uniforms. Later, the rockets were launched and a leaderboard was put up to display the flight altitudes.

Dougherty wanted to create a space for all ages to feel accepted in and help people discover the joy and love of learning that transpires from making. He says, "There's almost no other place where we can bring science, technology, art, and craft together and celebrate it as a sort of human achievement." He also sees Maker Faire as a response to the mass consumerism that dominates our society. "I want everyone to see themselves as a producer, a creative person, a builder, a shaper," he said.

In 2013, Maker Media, whose troika of brands includes *MAKE* magazine, Maker Faire, and Maker Shed (an online store for project kits, tools, and books), spun off from O'Reilly Media into an independent company. Dougherty is the founder and CEO. His vision of a revolution in hands-on "making" is becoming a reality.

WHEN THE WHITE HOUSE hosted its first Maker Faire in 2014, it was a sign that the maker movement had officially gone mainstream. The White House Office of Science and Technology Policy, which in the past has run science fairs, became aware of the mounting national interest in making and decided to put a call out to makers around the nation.

On a sweltering day in June, more than a hundred makers, young and old and from more than twenty-five states, descended upon the White House. The thirty-plus exhibitors were dispersed around the premises: on the South Lawn, along the West Colonnade, in the Rose Garden, hallways, and various rooms.

In the morning, President Obama toured a handful of the exhibits. In the Rose Garden, he sat with creator Sandra Richter on a solar-powered bench called a Soofa, named one of the "six wonders of Obama's 'Maker Faire' tour" by *The Wall Street Journal*.[7] It charges phones and collects environmental data, like noise levels and air quality. Richter, visiting scientist at the MIT Media Lab and cofounder and CEO of Changing Environments, the company that developed Soofa, spoke with the president about creating more smart, sustainable, and social cities.[8]

In the West Colonnade, Obama met and chatted with Partha Unnava, a student at the Georgia Institute of Technology and the CEO and cofounder of Better Walk.[9] Founded in 2013 by three Georgia Tech biomedical engineering students, the company offers innovative crutches that reduce the amount of pain in the underarm and wrist areas caused by traditional crutches. They used 3D printers to produce prototypes and accelerate the turnaround time. As the only undergraduate student at the event, Unnava personally delivered a letter, which had been 3D printed on a piece of metal, to Obama on behalf of 150 colleges and universities saying they would commit to advancing the maker movement on their campuses.

Some of the other inventions Obama checked out included a seventeen-foot-tall, 2,200-pound electric giraffe, a biodiesel-powered sports car built by students at Philadelphia's Workshop School, and a 3D pancake printer.

Soon after, Obama headed to the East Room of the White House to give a short speech to the participants, entrepreneurs, business leaders, and national and state officials. In the beginning, he joked, "What on earth have you done to my house?" and then mentioned some of the more peculiar inventions. Throughout the fifteen-minute speech, he also dropped the names of principal Simon Hauger and students from the Workshop School, Dale Dougherty, and Partha Unnava.

Obama declared the day "A National Day of Making" and called for expanding American manufacturing and making tools like laser cutters and 3D printers more accessible to the general public. Clearly passionate about the maker movement, he said, "I hope every company, every college, every community, every citizen joins us as we lift up makers and builders and doers across the country."

THE MAKER FAIRE and other making-related events and programs are all contributing to the creation of a new generation of makers. Dale Dougherty once wrote, "The biggest challenge and the biggest opportunity for the Maker Movement is to transform education. My hope is that the agents of change will be the students themselves." This is the comeback of shop class, retooled for the twenty-first century.

A piece on KQED's MindShift blog ran with the headline "Can the Maker Movement Infiltrate Mainstream Classrooms?"[10] Bringing making culture into schools would be wonderful, but one legitimate worry is that teachers will establish a standardized making curriculum, institute restrictive standards, and insist on giving tests. Instead, schools should create makerspaces or similar physical spaces for making that are accessible to everyone, not age segregated, and that are free of compulsion and the foolish rules and routines found in traditional classrooms.

Making is the epitome of educator John Dewey's philosophy of learning by doing. Instead of completing textbook problems or having a teacher spoon-feed you information, you're given the freedom to experiment, tinker, build, and create.

I spoke with Steve Davee, director of education and communications at the Maker Education Initiative.[11] It works with museums, libraries, schools, hackerspaces, and communities to fulfill its mission of providing opportunities in making to young people. "We have to recognize what children have been showing for the entire history of humanity," he said. "They learn through playing, autonomy, freedom, and taking risks."

Maker Education's flagship program is Maker Corps, which trains and places members in organizations and gives them a "possibility box," which is filled with tools and materials, to help introduce making. The pilot program launched in the summer of 2013. One hundred and eight Corps members worked as mentors in thirty-four host sites: children's museums, schools, libraries, and makerspaces. Over 90,000 young people and families in nineteen states were reached.[12] The following summer, the number of corps members inched up to more than one hundred and twenty. A majority of the members are college students, but there are also many teachers and people from other fields.

Davee argues cogently that the most powerful element of the maker movement is that it's bringing "an increased sense of child empowerment, agency, empathy, and perspective that comes from actually feeling like you have a form of expression." Like him, I find that making can be a unifying force in education and a mechanism for allowing the doctrines of natural learning to permeate institutions and society at large. The most telling example of this is that we have a president who has executed education policies that are fundamentally at odds with the curious and imaginative nature of children, yet that same man hosted an event at his home that celebrates those very qualities and values.

One public school in Philadelphia that serves predominantly low-income and minority students is riding the maker movement wave and achieving much success.

TWO STUDENTS WERE romping around outside in the cool rain. Indoors, one was monitoring the worms in her compost bucket. A band of three girls was working on their MacBook laptops. Some students were ticking through solutions to problems in food transportation and distribution. Upstairs, a few students and a teacher were having a rigorous discussion about their upcoming project. Principal Simon Hauger was tending to a student who needed a bandage for a small cut. And a teenage boy was hard at work, sewing some eco-friendly T-shirts. Those were just a handful of scenes one morning at the Sustainability Workshop School in Philadelphia. Sitting on the edge of the Navy Yard, the school's building, Quarters A, is a gorgeous white Victorian-era mansion that towers above the various ships docked in the Delaware River nearby.

On my first visit, I arrived at the school on a muggy and drizzly morning in March 2013. I was taken aback by an aura of comfort. At the time, the school was in the second year of its pilot program. It was an alternative senior-year program with twenty-nine students aged mostly seventeen or eighteen. The students were still technically enrolled at their former high schools, received graduation credits, and were permitted to participate in sports, clubs, prom, and graduation. Since it was technically a public school, there was no extra tuition. Mirroring the frequently evolving demographics of the city of Philadelphia, there was exceptional ethnic, socioeconomic, and cultural diversity at the school. More than half of the students lived at or below the poverty line.

Founded by a crew of four teachers, the mission of the Sustainability Workshop School is to "unleash the creative and intellectual potential of young people to solve the world's toughest problems." Three simple principles guided the axioms of learning: "Putting the work first, trusting students to make decisions, and making the most out of failure." Project-based learning was used with a focus on students' interests. In the first year of the pilot, which was the 2011–12 school year, the curriculum had a sustainability bent. Students collaborated with people at Philadelphia's Drexel University on various projects. In the second year, there was more flexibility, and the students' projects weren't constrained to the sustainability sphere.

The first room I stumbled into at the school is called the Big Room. Every morning, a school-wide meeting was held there for thirty minutes. Usually, there was a discussion in response to an article or current event. Before I arrived, they read an article that profiled my writing and activism and had a conversation on reforming the education system.

On one of the walls, I noticed a large sign with the words "We are the Workshop School. We will be known as: Inspirational, Passionate, Risk-takers, Innovative, Community, Determined, Open-Minded, Trustworthy." At the beginning of the school year, the students brainstormed some terms that described the group. Interestingly, the words were very similar to the ones the previous year's class of students came up with. "This idea of thinking about how you want to be known," said Simon Hauger, the school's cofounder, "it's one of the fundamental shifts early on; they feel that their ideas are really important and they have this first step into shaping their own community. That process really empowers them, not the actual words themselves."

A SHORT-SLEEVED PLAID or solid-colored shirt tucked into blue jeans held up by a belt is Simon Hauger's classic garb. In his forties, he is a lanky and plain-faced man with graying hair. Raised in Philadelphia during the 1970s, he endured a rough family life. After graduating from high school, Hauger studied electrical engineering at Drexel University. At the age of twenty-one, while in college, he participated in a co-op program, doing some circuit design work for General Electric. He had an epiphany after observing that many of the older men were doing the same work that he was doing and realized that he didn't want to be stuck in by-the-numbers engineering for the rest of his life. For Hauger, college was "mental gymnastics," where there wasn't much depth in learning. In his senior year, he had a meeting with his counselor. He jokes that it was like waterboarding: "You run in. He lays you on the table and starts pouring water on you."

"What do you want to be?"
"I don't know. Tell me what I should be."
"You're good at math and science, be an engineer."
"I'll go to school for engineering."

"And then you run out," he said. "Five years later, you're like: what the hell am I doing?" A religious conversion soon after inspired him to enter teaching. "I felt freed up to think about what I was passionate about—not what was prestigious," he told me. "One of my arguments is that school should connect students with their passions and interests. It shouldn't take a religious experience to do that." He picked up an engineering degree and then a teaching certificate to teach in an inner-city school. He himself had firsthand experience coping with social injustice and inequality, living in a single-parent household and being friends with low-income and minority kids. The hiring process was hell for him, and in frustration, he sent in résumés to engineering companies. Eventually, the district got back to him and placed him in a position at South Philadelphia High School for half a year. The following year he was transferred to a school in the neighborhood he grew up in—West Philadelphia High School.

"My first year at the school was tough. I struggled to do meaningful work in the classroom," he admits. "I got into a place where the students respected me and I ran just a traditional math and science class." For his own sanity, he spearheaded an after-school science fair club in the automotive shop, where students discovered and learned with their hands, a far cry from what the rest of the school day was like. In 1998, the kids built an electric powered go-kart and won second place in the city science fair, the first time the school had won something in the competition, he said. The year after, they changed it up, entering a 1995 Jeep Wrangler that they converted to 100 percent electric into the fair, and they won top honors. In the third year, the students decided to take part in the American Tour de Sol, "the nation's oldest and most prestigious competition for alternative fuel vehicles." While they didn't win, Hauger said it was a great learning experience. But then in 2002, the team outshined more than forty teams, including MIT, by designing and building an electric Saturn SL2 that averaged 180 miles per gallon.

After winning multiple national titles, forging the world's first hybrid supercar, and starting an annual tradition of defeating MIT, the team undertook the herculean task of entering a $10 million competition called the Progressive Insurance Automotive XPRIZE, which "challenged competitors to build safe, affordable, production-capable, super-fuel-efficient cars." Two vehicles were registered: one was a converted Ford Focus gasoline plug-in hybrid and the other was a Factory Five GTM biodiesel hybrid kit car. And they beat MIT once more and made it all the way to the semifinal round.

The fifteen-person team's extraordinary efforts in the 2010 XPRIZE competition landed three students, Simon Hauger, and Ann Cohen, Sustainability Workshop School board member and retired longtime president of the American Federation of State, County and Municipal Employees (AFSCME) Local 1637, a trip to the White House. At the launch of a 2010 STEM initiative, President Obama spoke about the team's successes: "Now, they didn't win the competition. They're kids, come on. But they did build a car that got more than 65 miles per gallon. They went toe to toe with car companies and big-name universities. They went against big-name universities, well-funded rivals. They held their own. They didn't have a lot of money. They didn't have the best equipment. They certainly didn't have every advantage in life. What they had was a program that challenged them to solve problems and to work together, to learn and build and create. And that's the kind of spirit and ingenuity that we have to foster. That's the potential that we can harness all across America. That's what will help our young people to fulfill their promise to realize their dreams and to help this nation succeed in the years to come." (We can only hope that Arne Duncan took heed.)

The idea of starting an actual school began a few years earlier. "Winning the Tour de Sol in 2002," Hauger said, "gave us the confidence that any student can do anything [he puts his] mind to. We were having a lot of fun and saw a lot of the educational value in the program. Soon enough we stumbled upon the project-based learning approach and started reading [about] what other folks were doing."

Around the same time, Hauger, Michael Clapper, Aiden Downey, and Matthew Riggan, all of whom became friends working together at West Philadelphia High School, had dinner at a restaurant in Chinatown. The conversation slowly evolved into one question: If we all could start a school, what would it look like? That discussion would culminate into an actual school less than a decade later, grounded in the same principles—project-based learning, autonomy, and engagement—that defined the West Philadelphia High School after-school program. The two-year pilot program from 2011 to 2013 received private funding from the Barra Foundation, the Greater Philadelphia Innovation Cluster, and others, and support from the School District of Philadelphia and Drexel University. But the journey hasn't been without hurdles. As Hauger told CNN, "Believe it or not, it is easier to build cars that get over 100 miles per gallon than to start a school in Philadelphia."[13]

JOEY, NATE, AND JESÚS were building an electric go-kart. NJ^2, the group's official name, has its territory in a small enclave of the Big Room. Nate and Jesús told me that the point of the project was to show the world we need more electric cars and thereby decrease the amount of pollution in the atmosphere. Not engineers by trade, the three found the learning curve steep. Fortunately, the year before, a group of students had also built a go-kart, so they had some leftover parts to work with. Wearing a blue hoodie, jeans, and black shoes and sporting a goatee, Jesús told me that the first step was to do a lot of research, particularly on the types and sizes of metals and parts to use and where to purchase them.

Once the parts arrived, they measured the frame out of aluminum, made sure it fit precisely, and cut it correctly. While I was chatting with Jesús, Nate was toying with the go-kart, adjusting the seat and tightening some screws. By the end of that school day, the seat was bolted down and the steering wheel had been locked into place. The third student in the group, Joey, wasn't in school that morning, because he was speaking on a panel on electric cars with Hauger at Temple University.

The big takeaway from this is that the students were leading the learning experience. Nobody was giving them instructions. Nobody was interrupting them when they stumbled. Nobody was surveilling the scene. They ruled the project. It was their own.

"If the project fails, it's not a big deal," said Jesús. When they get stuck, he added, they ask their fellow students and advisers for assistance. The go-kart was finished two weeks later.

For Jesús, the experience at the Sustainability Work-shop School has been humbling. He didn't like his old high school—Benjamin Franklin High School—and "felt like that they didn't care about my education." Upon enrolling in the school, Jesús was not sure what to expect, although he did know a few of the students beforehand. What were his parents' impressions of his new school? "As long as I'm coming to school and I'm getting my work done," he says, "my parents are supporting me. They like the program. I communicate much more here than in my old school."

Dressed in a tight T-shirt and blue jeans with tattoos inked over his slender arms, Nate made a similar comment: "My mom told me, 'As long as you pass, I'm cool with you coming here.'"

The go-kart project was the fourth project the team had undertaken so far that school year. To mold the school's community, the students began the year by reading the award-winning novel *The Absolutely True Diary of a Part-Time Indian* by Sherman Alexie, which detailed the story of a young cartoonist's life on a Native American reservation. "The book taught me that you should let people into your life, because it can be pretty damn amazing," said Ada, a student. Next, as an icebreaker, everyone, including the teachers, got involved in the "Who Am I?" autobiography project. Students and teachers wrote essays detailing their past, essays predicting their future, a college essay, and a number of personal statements and missions. Then they broke off into three rooms and presented their work. The activity helped shatter the existing cliques among the students, making it easier to connect and collaborate with one another and understand the project-based learning method. For Jesús, it was a particularly sobering experience. When he was five years old, a television tipped over the stand and hit him in the head. For three straight days, he was in a coma. The project eased his painful memories of the incident, he recalled. "I found out things about my life that I didn't know and learned about my friends." Jesús became more optimistic about his future and finally began loving learning.

Culture and community building continued after that. The students split up into teams and created a sustainable living space outside. They planted herbs on the roof of a house to make a garden. The plants were growing even in the aftermath of Hurricane Sandy. From this point forward, there was a gradual progression from teacher- to student-designed projects. One of the cofounders of the school, Matthew Riggan, said, "Our beginning projects are scaled down and more academic. Over time, they get more free."

I sat down with Riggan for some time. "This school is in response to the question, What if real work was the center of a school?" he said. Real work. Real thinking. Real projects. Real world. "We learned that a lot of extra support is needed in designing and carrying out work and understood how ready students are to be a part of this kind of environment and do real work."

Boiling down their philosophy into a few words, he noted, "Students know that we respect them. We don't talk down to them. We give them a lot of freedom and latitude. We see them as people. Students get to work on things that they want to work on. We're not fighting them."

Another cofounder of the school, Michael Clapper, told me, "When you trust kids, they rarely let you down."

Riggan admitted that the school isn't always a well-oiled machine. There are challenges every day. Sometimes, students just want someone to give them the answer, he said. But "all of them would argue that they'd rather be here than elsewhere."

ADA, AN EIGHTEEN-YEAR-OLD student, was pecking away at her laptop when I wandered into the room one morning. Seated around a large table, a few students were creating an online sustainability magazine, which featured dispatches about trash, food, houses, obesity, and cars. The team nailed down a brief business plan, received feedback from other people at the school, and conducted research.

Ada loves this school. She realized that she wasn't able to express herself the way she wanted to at her former school, Benjamin Franklin High School. "I was excited to do public speaking here, research, build, and create things," she told me. "At first, my mom felt scared, because I had to take a train to get here, but after a while, she became very excited and supportive."

Another fascinating project she was involved in was the computer-aided design (CAD) project where students invented things that they could use in real life. Working on it every afternoon for three weeks, she made a binder and put her photographs and magnets in it. Other students made iPhone cases. In the process, she was learning everything from mathematics to engineering.

Suddenly, Clapper popped his head into the room. There was always some level of supervision. "I like the layout of the site, but it needs to include specific sections and links." He then asked, "What other projects would be worth writing about for your magazine?" "Maybe some of our sponsors?" one student chimed in. "FreshDirect!" Clapper replied. "So why don't you interview someone from there?" The teacher has faded into the background and simply provides feedback. Ada put it succinctly, "If you tell teens what and how to learn, they will feel like they are being locked up in a jail cell."

Before breaking for lunch, everyone congregated in the Big Room to discuss what they accomplished that morning. Patience had finished writing one of the two book reviews she planned on completing that day, and another student had done some research and learned how to use spreadsheets. Clapper then talked briefly about the rest of the schedule of the afternoon and week.

Here are two of the student projects and activities at the school:

Seventeen-year-old Michael was working with a group that was developing and transporting a self-sufficient modular home, made out of recycled shipping containers, to Haiti. His part of the project was designing a dashboard that would control and monitor the electrical systems. He said, "The goal of my project is to be able to monitor the output by the solar panels and the batteries they are charging." Earlier, he had developed an app that calculates fuel economy.

At age eighteen, Dareese was designing his own line of eco-friendly fashion. He hoped it could become the next eco-friendly brand in the United States. A "problem child" and troublemaker at his old school, he loved the vibe of doing projects rather than sitting in a classroom. Working on the brand nonstop for the twelve weeks until the end of the school year, Dareese, with his partner Elizabeth, had been testing price points, setting up the online shop, and sewing the actual bamboo clothes. "It's very fun," he said. "I love fashion. I never could have imagined doing this project, so I'm really surprised at myself." By the time they graduate, they hoped to sell a few items in the shop.

I sat down with Michael Clapper after I picked up some lunch—a plate of salad dressed in vinegar and croutons, courtesy of FreshDirect, a New York–based online grocer that furnishes the school's lunches. Clapper is bald, has rounded spectacles, and was wearing a striped blue shirt and navy slacks. After teaching at West Philadelphia High School for six years, he shifted to academia, becoming an assistant professor of education at St. Joseph's University, where he worked with preservice teachers at the undergraduate and graduate levels. But he suddenly quit his tenured position to teach at this school because he'd been "waiting his entire life for an opportunity like this." Two things separated this learning environment from most others, Clapper said: "relationships and trust." Every student I spoke with seemed to be very fond of him.

ONE AFTERNOON, MORE than half of the students had departed for Drexel University for a class. Some students remained at the school for their humanities seminar. Clapper and seven students were huddled around a big table. He threw out a question to the group: "Why do people listen to music?" The students then scribbled their responses in their journals and opened up a peppy and animated discussion. Then the lights were switched off and clips of various kinds of music, curated by Clapper, were played on a video projector. The students listened to several genres of music and discussed them for another half hour.

The seminar reminded me of the Harkness method at Phillips Exeter Academy, a prestigious private college preparatory school in New Hampshire. In April 1930, Edward Harkness, a philanthropist and oil tycoon, donated a sum of money to the school and gave some recommendations on how to spend it. "What I have in mind is [a classroom] where [students] could sit around a table with a teacher who would talk with them and instruct them by a sort of tutorial or conference method, where [each student] would feel encouraged to speak up," he wrote in a letter to Lewis Perry, Exeter's principal. "This would be a real revolution in methods."[14] Thus, the Harkness table was born. Seated around a large

oval table, twelve to fifteen students and a teacher are invited
to have an exchange of ideas and questions, ensuring that no
one is left out. Everyone is a contributor. Today, the Harkness method is still a keystone of the classes at Exeter.

ONE EVENING, I caught up with Ann Cohen, Sustainability Workshop School board member, for dinner. Later, we
stopped by a Philadelphia Student Union meeting, where I
met Azeem Hill, the former captain of the West Philadelphia
High School Hybrid X team. "We need schools that develop
leaders and problem solvers, not test takers," he said in a
talk at the PopTech 2010 conference. "That's how you solve
the dropout problem."

One exercise students at the school conducted was to
imagine their dream school. Satisfyingly, the results were
almost identical to one they were currently in. From student
after student, I kept hearing the words "There isn't anything
I don't like about this school." When you bear in mind that
most of them lived in the poorest neighborhoods of Philadelphia, it's stunning that about 80 percent of the students in
the second year of the pilot program were accepted into college. As Hauger put it, "We're trying to create a place where
we would be proud to send our own children."

IN APRIL 2013, the Philadelphia School Partnership (PSP)
announced that it would dole out $6 million in grants to three
Philadelphia schools. One was the Sustainability Workshop
School, which would receive $1.5 million over three years
and expand into a full high school with grades nine through
twelve in a new location. Meanwhile, that spring the dis-

trict also shuttered twenty-four schools, designating the Workshop School the sole new school in the city for the next school year. "There's this perfect storm that occurred," Hauger said. "Some of us believe it was divine intervention. Some of us believe it was just good timing."

In September 2013, the Workshop School ("Sustainability" was dropped from the name) opened its doors in the former annex building of West Philadelphia High School where the original automotive shop had been. Ninety-two students from ninth through twelfth grades were enrolled. Nearly all of them were African American and qualified for free or reduced lunch. Two-thirds of them were ninth graders.

On a frigid morning in January 2014, I paid a visit to the new school. Cohen picked me up from Thirtieth Street Station. As we sped through the streets of West Philadelphia, the plush University of Pennsylvania campus quickly gave way to the poorer and more diverse neighborhood of Walnut Hill.

In Michael Clapper's class, students were in a tizzy as they raced to finish their projects. It was the last day of the quarter, which is about ten weeks long. For the next two days, they would present their work in a public exhibition to teachers, parents, and community members.

A typical school day is divided into two parts. Mornings are dedicated to working on interdisciplinary projects within advisories. At the beginning of the year, the ninth graders were randomly split up into five advisories of about fifteen students each. They stay with the same teacher all year. Sometimes, there is co-teaching. Afternoons consist of electives, career and technical education (CTE), and several seminars in English and math. Here, students have some choice over what to take.

During CTE, students head downstairs to one of the

three garages: Fabrication Shop, Auto Tech Shop, or Auto Collision Shop. Each shop has its own classroom. Josh, an eleventh grader, gave me a tour. He has a goatee and was dressed in a navy sweatshirt and black pants. He hopes to work as a technician one day. On one side of the Fab Shop, there were laser cutters, 3D printers, sewing machines, computer numerical control (CNC) routers, drill presses, and saws. On the other side, there were two parked cars. One of them was a converted Ford Focus gasoline plug-in hybrid, one of the vehicles the West Philly Hybrid X team entered into the 2010 XPRIZE. The other car was a work in progress. Called the Factory Five 818 project, the students were building a car, using a donated kit, the motor of a Volkswagen Jetta, and parts from a Subaru Impreza WRX. They winded up finishing it two days before the end of the school year.

During this visit, I met Hauger in the office. "We're living the dream," he said. "We knew it was going to be a challenge." The people at the highest levels of the district have given the school "their blessing."

The new school gave off a much different vibe compared to the pilot program. It felt more like a traditional school environment. But that is not the fault of the people who run the school. It is the reflection of a system that was not built to accommodate the needs of the learners. The Workshop School is nearly the most radical model of schooling that can legally function within the public school system. It is prevented by higher authorities from being even more so.

From the outside, the school building unfortunately looks a bit like a prison. If the school could be completely redesigned, Hauger has dreamed "it would look more like an open workshop with some traditional classrooms." Inside, the students follow a structured curriculum. For the ninth graders, the overall projects and their themes are designed by the teachers, but students often have some choice over the topic of study. The goal is that over time, the students will begin to design their own projects. "Hopefully, if this is working well," said Hauger, "with the ninth graders we started with, by twelfth grade they're not only designing their own projects, but they're [also] designing their own external learning experiences." By that, he means things like internships, jobs, and college classes. Teachers give out grades—reluctantly. He says the school personally would prefer not to have grades, but it has never raised the issue with the district. The students will also need to take the Keystone Exams, the state's standardized tests, but the school does not do test preparation.

Poverty is, by far, the biggest challenge for the school. On average, the ninth-grade students are coming in at a fourth- or fifth-grade level. "So you have real academic deficits," Hauger explained. "But you also have real social and emotional deficits, too. It's just tragic . . . The kids bring that trauma in with them and there are not enough resources to deal with it. The good thing about this approach is that students are developing real relationships with adults. And this is a safe place. In many ways, they are being cared for much better than a traditional high school can.

"And there needs to be certain structures and supports in place, because they haven't had that type of freedom before. It's funny, but one of the indicators that things are working well is that kids start to behave like kids, which is annoying. When you see fourteen-year-olds, after the second or third week, become comfortable—they start to touch, grab, push, and play—then you realize that this is working. If you go to a scary high school in Philly, you won't see that behavior. Those kids are just trying to protect themselves. Safety is [their] primary concern . . . Too many of them don't have an opportunity just to be kids. They go home and have all these other responsibilities and traumas that they're dealing with."

What's most admirable about the people at the Workshop School is that they explicitly sought to work with the poorest and most disadvantaged young people in the city—the group that has the most to gain from this type of education. This school is one of the few beacons of light in the public school system.

CHAPTER 8

Enrolling in the Real World

Innovative models of education are not just limited to primary and secondary education, they are also scattered throughout higher education. There are a handful of institutions offering their students transformative, purposeful learning experiences.

For instance, Franklin W. Olin College of Engineering in Needham, Massachusetts, has a unique approach to engineering education. There are no formal academic departments. Classes are taught in a studio setting, and the curriculum is interdisciplinary and grounded in real-world projects, from designing the AutoFrost automatic cake decorator to devising a weather balloon system.

There's also Goddard College, a small liberal arts college in Vermont that shares much of its philosophy with one of the pioneers of progressive education, John Dewey. I am currently an undergraduate student there. About six hundred students are enrolled in undergraduate and graduate programs in fields like individualized studies, education, creative writing, and fine arts. The cornerstone of the institution is its unique low-residency model, where each semester students participate in an eight-day residency on campus and then spend sixteen weeks off campus working independently on their learning goals with direct communication with faculty members. The learning is based on the student's individual interests. Evaluations, instead of traditional grades, are given by the faculty. Several other colleges also offer narrative evaluations instead of grades: Evergreen State College in Washington, Hampshire College in Massachusetts, New College of Florida, and Prescott College in Arizona.

There is no college or university that serves many thousands of students and operates as radically on a large scale as these smaller schools do. There are, however, a few colleges that have started fascinating experiments to tinker with new models of learning. One of these experiments was recently launched at Lehigh University in Bethlehem, Pennsylvania. In 2013, Urban Outfitters cofounder and Lehigh alumnus Scott Belair donated $20 million to the school with the condition that the two former Bethlehem Steel research buildings sitting on South Mountain would be renovated into spaces for invention and learning. After a successful pilot run in the summer of 2013, the program, called the Mountaintop experience, returned the following summer—this time with more than a hundred students who were immersed in several hands-on projects. There was no prescribed curriculum, no credits, grades, or tests. Students worked on documentaries about race and diversity and a Nobel Prize–winning poet, conducted science experiments, and designed things like a new food waste-disposal system for the campus and a low-cost hand prosthetic.[1]

According to the 2014 National Survey of Student Engagement, only 57 percent of college seniors have taken part in an internship or field experience, 13 percent have studied abroad, and 28 percent have done research with a faculty member.[2] Those activities often end up being the most rewarding parts of college. Providing such opportunities could also be a brilliant recruitment strategy that most institutions are failing to pursue. At a time when high school students are being constantly pestered by colleges to apply, what better means of standing out from the pack than if a college tells prospective students that it will give them the freedom, time, funding, faculty support, and outside mentorship for them to be involved in some activity, project, or other pursuit of their choosing?

There are some colleges that give their students a chance to participate in an apprenticeship or cooperative education program. And as we will see shortly, apprenticeships are slowly being rekindled. On its website, the University of Waterloo in Canada claims it has the largest postsecondary co-op program in the world: 19,000 students, more than 60 percent of its undergraduate students, are enrolled in a co-op over three semesters in 122 programs. Overall, 5,200 employers have hired these students. Students can get up to two full years of work experience while enrolled in college. By the time they graduate, they will have earned on average $37,000 to $78,000.[3] It's a win-win for the students and their host companies, who often end up making job offers to the students.

The innovative colleges I've mentioned are very similar to one another in that they often have small class sizes, focus on interdisciplinary, seminar, and project-based classes, offer close contact between professors and students, and provide opportunities for students to do apprenticeships, real-world projects, or research for credit.

The real transformation in higher education will occur

when the learners become the creators of their own curriculum. We must not be fooled by iterations of conventional schooling masquerading as something revolutionary—such as the wave of propaganda for massive open online courses (MOOCs).

MOOCS SPELL THE coming of a revolution in higher education. MOOCs will lead to the demise of thousands of colleges and universities around the world. MOOCs will elevate millions of people out of poverty. MOOCs will save us all. Those are the claims that have been repeated over and over again by venture capitalists and entrepreneurs and *New York Times* columnist (and MOOC cheerleader) Thomas Friedman.[4] MOOCs are the shiny new objects in the education world. The *New York Times* even lauded 2012 as "the Year of the MOOC."[5]

Interestingly, what most people know of as a MOOC today is really a complete departure from the way the original MOOC was structured. In 2008, the Canadian academics George Siemens, Stephen Downes, and Dave Cormier offered the first MOOC (a term coined by Cormier), called "Connectivism and Connective Knowledge." Twenty-four students at the University of Manitoba took the course for credit, and 2,200 members of the general public signed up for free. There were lectures, blogs, wikis, threaded discussions, and newsletters available to the participants. The platform was open source. Spanish-speaking students had the ability to have discussions in language-specific communities.[6]

Then, between the fall of 2011 and early 2012, Udacity and Coursera, two for-profit companies that produce MOOCs, were founded by several Stanford professors. The nonprofit edX (a joint partnership between Harvard and

MIT) entered the space later in 2012. The three companies co-opted the term "MOOC" and corrupted its original features by championing the most intolerable and least effective aspects of education. They beam free online lectures by talking heads, homework assignments, and quizzes and tests into the computers of millions around the world.

These MOOCs are grounded in traditional, didactic approaches to learning. The learner is viewed as a passive vessel that must be filled with knowledge and facts by a teacher. It's patronizing and rarely leads to long-term retention of knowledge. As Georgia Tech professor and game designer Ian Bogost noted in an essay, "If the lecture was such a bad format in the industrial age, why does it suddenly get celebrated once digitized and streamed into a web browser in the information age?"[7]

Consequently, the pedagogical effectiveness of MOOCs has been called into question. Between June 2012 and June 2013, researchers at the University of Pennsylvania Graduate School of Education tracked a million students through sixteen Coursera courses. They discovered that the average course completion rate was just 4 percent. The researchers also found that only about half of those registered for a course viewed at least one lecture. There's no doubt that the numbers are a bit skewed, as many users are just curious about how MOOCs work and wish to browse through the course material without completing the assignments. But a 4 percent completion rate is a telling embarrassment.[8]

Many other studies arrive at a similar conclusion: online courses have high attrition rates, particularly for low-income and minority students.[9] Examining the data collected from more than forty thousand community and technical college students in Washington State, one study reported that "all types of students were more likely to drop out from an online course than a face-to-face course."[10] In 2013, Udacity's pilot program at San Jose State University (SJSU), in which students at SJSU, local community colleges, and area high schools were offered the opportunity to take three remedial and entry-level online college courses for credit, was suspended within six months after results showed that more than half of the students failed the final exams.[11] "It turned out," reports Katy Murphy in the *San Jose Mercury News,* that "some of the low-income teens didn't have computers and high-speed Internet connections at home that the online course required. Many needed personal attention to make it through."[12]

Near the end of that year, Sebastian Thrun, cofounder and CEO of Udacity, finally admitted in an interview with *Fast Company* that its courses were a "lousy product." But then he bizarrely proceeded to blame the students in the San Jose State pilot program for their inability to learn from his platform, even though the MOOC crusaders intended that low-income, underprivileged students would be the greatest beneficiaries from this technology. "These were students from difficult neighborhoods, without good access to computers, and with all kinds of challenges in their lives," he said. "It's a group for which this medium is not a good fit."[13] If that's the case, then Thrun and his fellow techno-utopianists should stop peddling the fiction that MOOCs are effective tools for making higher education more accessible, designed with the best interests of poor people in mind.

One of the talking points used by MOOC evangelists is that the courses are bringing an education from the elite universities to the masses. There are two problems with this assertion. First, the educational experience at these schools is not limited to lectures and homework assignments. The cultures of these schools are equally or more influential in the overall educational experience. Second, research suggests that MOOCs are reaching only the most privileged learners in the world. A survey conducted by researchers at the University of Pennsylvania of 34,779 students in more than two hundred countries enrolled in MOOCs found that 83 percent already held a two- or four-year degree and nearly half had advanced degrees. Additionally, in countries with marked educational inequities like India, Brazil, South Africa, Russia, and China—the assumed target market for these courses—roughly 80 percent of the students taking them already had a college degree.[14] You can't take online courses if you don't have a computer and Internet access, and these things are the tools that poor people often lack.

Where MOOCs are being implemented in developing countries, other serious concerns have been raised. MOOC providers are stepping on local cultures, traditions, and languages and ramming through Western, English-language online platforms with courses primarily from elite universities. Some accuse MOOCs of being a "neocolonial" force. Gianpiero Petriglieri, associate professor of organizational behavior at INSEAD, a business school, put it succinctly in the *Harvard Business Review:* "Colonialism is a particular kind of socialization. It involves educating communities into the 'superior' culture of a powerful but distant center by replacing local authorities or co-opting them as translators. A liberating education, on the other hand, makes students not just recipients of knowledge and culture but also owners, critics, and makers of it."[15]

MOOCs are a wonderful resource for many self-directed learners, but the teaching model needs to be reformed into a learner-directed and participatory model. Even so recast, they are still not a magic bullet for the problems in higher education. The higher education community needs to call out and confront techno-utopian education fantasies that only exacerbate inequality and sustain the most oppressive elements of education.

IN LATE 2012, British spoken word artist Suli Amoako launched a video, "Why I Hate School but Love Education," that made the rounds all over the Internet. He called for young people to "understand your motives and reassess your aims" and highlighted outliers in history who have done very well for themselves and society without any or much formal schooling, like Steve Jobs, Richard Branson, Oprah Winfrey, and Henry Ford. The final line of the video is: "There's more than one way in this world to be an educated man."[16] That's spot-on.

However, we need to be extremely cautious when talking about the validity of the "UnCollege" movement and whether students should drop out or forgo college altogether or not. People cite famous college dropouts like Bill Gates and Mark Zuckerberg as evidence that you don't need a degree to succeed in the world and you will be better off not going to college. Yet that's a very narrow and distorted view that does not apply to a large portion of the population. A vast majority of the people on the list of famous, successful college dropouts are white males. They have benefited tremendously from our system of white male privilege. They likely had economic stability at home, parents to support them if they failed, and a bounty of social capital, like family connections. It appears they would have succeeded with or without a degree. They are the exception rather than the norm. Meanwhile, there are millions of college dropouts and people who weren't able to attend college who are living in poverty and toiling away at minimum-wage jobs or even incarcerated.

Low-income and minority students should strongly consider going to college even when they may be saddled with enormous student loan debt and have no guarantee of financial stability. Skipping out can be detrimental to their futures. "College is a purchased loyalty oath to an imagined employer," explains anthropologist Sarah Kendzior in Al Jazeera English. "College shows you are serious enough about your life to risk ruining it early on. College is a promise the economy does not keep—but not going to college promises you will struggle to survive."[17]

Our society has a very firmly rooted system of credentialism—an obsession with credentials when it comes to hiring and social status. College is one of the few places where social capital can be amassed and premier credentials are earned. Without them, there is little shot at climbing to a higher rung of the socioeconomic ladder.

African Americans, in particular, are also forced to bear the brunt of hiring discrimination. Recent black college graduates are more than twice as likely to be unemployed as recent white graduates. What's more, a study by the nonprofit organization Young Invincibles found that a black male with an associate's degree has a similar chance of acquiring a job as a white male high school dropout. And a black male with a bachelor's degree has about the same employment chances as a white male college dropout. These enormous employment gaps are due largely to the widespread racial discrimination in the labor market, which has been documented by extensive research.[18] The deck is stacked against African Americans, so they are the ones who should least consider alternatives to college.

So who are the people who should consider skipping college and "enrolling" in the real world? Evidence suggests someone who is not low income or a minority and hopes to pursue fields such as entrepreneurship, business, technology, design, art, writing, and journalism.

In high school, students should ask themselves, What are my goals for the future? What path should I embark on that will allow me to fulfill them? When mulling over going to college, they should also ask themselves, Why should I go to college? What do I hope to achieve while I'm there? There should be a clear justification for spending tens of thousands of dollars and giving one's life over to an institution for four years. It's better to figure that out well before plunking down all that tuition and textbook money.

One major factor in the decision should be the amount of debt the student will have when he graduates. If a student knows he will be burdened financially after college and his college does not have a brand name, then that's all the more reason to consider less expensive options.

A number of highly publicized alternatives to college have emerged in recent years. Currently, they are primarily accessible to upper-middle-class and wealthy white and Asian kids, but it will only be a matter of time before they are part of the mainstream and more widely available.

Thiel Fellowship

Started in 2011 by the billionaire PayPal cofounder Peter Thiel, the Thiel Fellowship's mission is to "[bring] together some of the world's most creative and motivated young people, and help them bring their most ambitious projects to life." Since then, one hundred people under the age of twenty-three have been granted a total of $100,000 each over two years to start their own company or organization and have received access to a phenomenal pool of mentors. The only catch is that they have to stay out of college for the two years. (Full disclosure: I applied to the program in 2011 and 2012 and made it as far as the semifinalist round both times.)

The fellows have engaged in projects in a variety of fields, like energy, education, health care, software, and fashion. In a statement in 2014, Jonathan Cain, president of the Thiel Foundation, said, "By our math, about 7% of fellows have ultimately returned to school in some capacity; meanwhile, fellows have also generated more than $100 million in economic activity, created hundreds of jobs, and sold companies worth millions."[19] The fellows I've spoken with have all spoken highly of how much they've learned and progressed in refining their projects and ideas and fostering relationships with others, significantly more than if they had been in a college setting.

From its inception, critics, particularly academics, have directed stinging vitriol at the fellowship. Columbia University sociologist Shamus Khan called the program "an act of total self-indulgence."[20] Former Harvard president Larry Summers declared it "the single most misdirected bit of philanthropy in this decade."[21] Others like entrepreneur and academic Vivek Wadhwa have chastised the fellows for what he sees as their limited success.[22] Consider, though, that he and most of the general population were not doing anything remotely comparable when they were in their late teens. Those misguided attacks miss the legitimate defects of the program.

The ultimate problem with the Thiel Fellowship is that it is a mechanism for perpetuating privilege. It hands an exceptional opportunity to the very people who need it the least.

The Thiel fellows will likely succeed with or without the fellowship. Most of the past and current fellows are white or Asian males. There are an appallingly few number of women and almost no blacks or Hispanics. Plus, during the application process, students who have been accepted to or are currently enrolled in the nation's most prestigious colleges and universities are seen more favorably. If you want proof, just look at the classes of fellows. They are overflowing with students with such credentials.

If the Thiel Fellowship was awarded only to low-income and minority students, that would be groundbreaking and I would throw my support behind it. In its current form, however, it is a program largely of, by, and for the people already near or at the top of society.

Apprenticeships

First surfacing in Europe during the Middle Ages, the apprenticeship system was developed by the craft guilds. The guilds' master craftsmen employed young people starting at the age of fourteen or fifteen until about twenty-one and covered their costs for food and housing, clothing, and other essentials during the course of their indenture.[23] In return, the young men entered into a legally binding contract—an indenture—that committed them to working a certain number of years in a master's shop.[24] As apprentices, they would be taught the fundamentals of the trade. The extra hands were a cheap and productive form of labor for the master craftsmen, and the young people reaped the boons of learning a specific craft or skill—through strenuous repetition, observation, modeling, and imitation.

In his book *Mastery*, Robert Greene notes, "If one added up the time that apprentices ended up working directly on materials in those years, it would amount to more than 10,000 hours, enough to establish exceptional skill level at a craft."[25] Years later, the apprentice would hope to have accumulated enough capital to start his own shop. Some professions within this system included silversmiths, printers, painters, and sculptors.

Apprenticeship made its way to America through craft workers who immigrated to the country, and it became a very popular system in the colonies. Many illustrious figures were apprentices: Benjamin Franklin was a printer. George Washington was a mason's surveyor. And Paul Revere was a silversmith.[26]

The apprenticeship system held dominion in America for more than a century. Once the industrial revolution began and factories burgeoned in cities, apprenticeships began to vanish and the assembly line took over. They were also dealt a blow as compulsory schooling became ubiquitous, essentially eliminating alternatives to traditional schooling. According to a report by American University economist Robert Lerman, roughly 480,000 people participated in 27,000 apprenticeship programs registered with the U.S. Department of Labor in 2008. In terms of the whole American workforce, that accounts for a minuscule 0.3 percent.[27]

In countries like Switzerland, Austria, and Germany, apprenticeships never lost their luster and remain an attractive alternative to college for many young people. Compared with the grim youth unemployment numbers in the United States, where about 12 percent of young people are out of work, Germany has Europe's lowest youth unemployment rate of 7 percent. Its success can be credited to its dual training system, or *duales Ausbildungssystem,* which trains about 1.5 million people annually.[28]

After high school, 60 percent of German graduates

choose to pursue a vocational education rather than an academic course of study. Students spend two to three and a half years in such programs and are paid less than 700 euros a month, depending on the sector and region. After they complete their apprenticeships, the students are often hired by that same company.[29]

To reduce exceptionally high youth unemployment rates, the United States ought to take a lesson from the Germans. A study estimated that "the social benefits to apprenticeship were about $50,000 per apprentice, far more than minimal gains accruing to community college students and WIA [Workforce Investment Act] trainees."[30] Two things are required to create more apprenticeships: First, companies need to shift their thinking from training workers in the skills they don't have upon hiring to actually becoming the hub of the post–high school learning process. Second, the federal government must increase the budget for overseeing apprenticeship programs. Currently, only a pitiful $25 million is spent annually.[31]

One downside to apprenticeships is that it can produce a two-tiered system; in Germany, students are tracked into either vocational or academic streams as early as age ten. There is not much of an opportunity to switch over later on. Meanwhile, in American schools, the vocational path is held in contempt and only intended for the so-called less intelligent students. To get more students in what is formally known as "career and technical education," such programs need to operate within schools themselves and be intertwined with the academic programs, instead of being siloed. We also need to hold both types of education in the same esteem. Schools like the Metropolitan Regional Career and Technical Center (part of the Big Picture Learning schools network) in Providence, Rhode Island; High Tech High in San Diego, California; ACE Leadership High School in Albuquerque, New Mexico; and the Workshop School in Philadelphia are excellent models to work toward.

AN UNLIKELY DUO was trying to get apprenticeships back in vogue in the United States for "21st century careers in business, technology, design, and entrepreneurship." A few years ago, Kane Sarhan, who is in his late twenties, and Shaila Ittycheria, who is in her thirties, were colleagues on two opposite sides of the company LocalResponse, which connects advertisers with customers based on social media activity. (It has since been renamed Qualia.) Sarhan had joined the company as the apprentice to the founder. Ittycheria had risen through the corporate world. She spent some time working in Microsoft's Finance Rotation Program, graduated from Harvard Business School, and later landed a job as a hiring manager at LocalResponse.

"Shaila and I were at Lillie's in Union Square talking about life and work when the topic of higher education came up," recalls Sarhan. Ittycheria, when interviewing college graduates from the most esteemed institutions, realized that most did not have anything much as yet to contribute to the company, nor did they have many relevant skills or competencies. In contrast, Sarhan had lived through two apprenticeships in the hospitality and technology industries, finding them very valuable.[32]

That brief meeting over coffee eventually snowballed into what became known as Enstitute, a tuition-free, two-year apprenticeship program that "provides an alternative path to traditional post-secondary education." Launched in 2012, the inaugural class of eleven fellows, ranging from high school graduates to college dropouts to college graduates, worked for some of the best entrepreneurs in the New York City technology scene, like Thrillist cofounder Ben Lerer and venture capitalist Mark Peter Davis. Each received a stipend of about $800 a month and had their room and board costs covered.

In the program, as a supplement to the work experience, the fellows studied a blended curriculum that featured offline and online learning in business, technology, and design. And twice a week, guest speakers in various industries were invited to share their knowledge and expertise with them.

The first class lived under one roof in a chic loft in the Financial District. When I met a few of them in 2012, one gleefully told me that he learned more in the first week of the program than in all of his four years of college.

"What's incredible about Enstitute is that I am excited to get up every day because I am doing what I love," said Ethan Horne, then a fellow apprenticing under Jason Beckerman at Unified, a marketing cloud technology company.

Jasmine Gao, then a fellow apprenticing under Hilary Mason at Bitly, a URL shortening service, told me, "Enstitute has taught me how to learn. During every networking event, guest speaker session, and project, there was always an influx of information." "However," she added, "what determined whether or not I really learned was not the amount of information I managed to commit to memory but rather the types of conclusions I made and how I applied those to reinforce and/or change certain behaviors and beliefs for my own improvement."

Enstitute said 90 percent of the fellows in the pilot program either landed full-time offers or started their own companies. It later expanded to Washington, D.C., and Miami with companies and nonprofit organizations in digital media, advertising, and social enterprise that offer apprenticeships. Unfortunately, at the end of 2015, Enstitute shut down. "Due to limited capital, we were unable to bring on the staff needed to adequately operate at scale," according to a statement.

But the organization made clear that the apprenticeship model was very effective and transformed many lives for the better: "We've watched young people, who were previously written off after they couldn't afford to finish college, achieve wild success working at start-ups and become highly sought after employees. We've seen candidates who were already a few years into their careers come to us to reinvent themselves, discover a new suite of skills and competencies that opened new doors and accelerated their career trajectories. We've witnessed the application of self-directed learning; apprentices solved real-life problems with real-life consequences . . . Ultimately, we know the apprenticeship model works."

The movement to revive apprenticeships in this country is nowhere near over. It didn't hurt the cause when President Obama revealed on ABC's *The View* that after his presidency, he would like to help "create mentorships and apprenticeships" and give "young people the sense of possibility and opportunity."[33]

Coding Schools

Coding schools, which teach computer programming, have been popping up all over the nation. One of the more popular ones is Dev Bootcamp, a nineteen-week program that trains people to become software developers through a project-based curriculum in New York, Chicago, and San Francisco. Tuition ranges from $12,700 to $13,950 depending on the city, and 85 percent of its graduates have found jobs.[34]

The technology industry is one of the few that have challenged head-on the cult of credentialism. It's much easier to land a job in this field without a college degree, as employers often consider digital portfolios and GitHub (a platform that hosts open-source software projects) profiles in hiring. In 2013, Google (Full disclosure: I spoke at Google's Think Education conference in 2013; I did not receive compensation) made news when its senior vice president of people operations, Laszlo Bock, told *The New York Times*, "G.P.A.'s are worthless as a criteria for hiring, and test scores are worthless . . . We found that they don't predict anything."[35] As many as 14 percent of people on some teams at Google do not have a college degree. Bock, in another *Times* interview, said, "When you look at people who don't go to school and make their way in the world, those are exceptional human beings. And we should do everything we can to find those people."[36]

Autodidacticism

In the fields of writing, journalism, marketing, and art, many people have succeeded by self-educating themselves with limited or no assistance from formal institutions. How did they do it? What resources and programs did they turn to? Here are the stories of a few of these people and the lessons we can learn from them.

WRITING

Ray Bradbury, the famous science-fiction author, passed away in 2012 at the age of ninety-one. The *New York Times* obituary reported, "More than eight million copies of his books have been sold in 36 languages."[37] His most famous work is *Fahrenheit 451*, a dystopian novel envisioning a world with unchecked government control and censorship. He wrote an early draft of it in UCLA's library on a typewriter that he rented for ten cents per half hour. He spent a total of $9.80.[38] The library was his classroom and his workspace.

Born in the small city of Waukegan, Illinois, in 1920, Bradbury was hooked on popular culture very early on. He often went to the cinema and traveling circuses and regularly consumed comic strips. His parents taught him how to read at a very young age.[39]

In the thick of the Great Depression, the family moved between Waukegan and Tucson, Arizona, before eventually settling in an apartment in the middle of Hollywood, California. Bradbury's father got a job at a cable company as a utility lineman for fourteen dollars a week. For the young boy, Hollywood was the ideal city. Living just four blocks from the flagship Uptown Theatre, every week he would sneak into the movies. Then he "skated all over town, hellbent on getting autographs from glamorous stars," he told *Playboy.* "It was glorious."[40]

At age twelve, Bradbury decided to pursue writing and began scribbling stories on a roll of butcher paper.[41] His inspiration came from an unlikely encounter with a magician named Mr. Electrico. According to a blog post dated December 2001, Mr. Electrico told him to "live forever" and also said he'd met him before, explaining that Bradbury was his "best friend in the great war in France in 1918," who was wounded in a battle and died in his arms. Bradbury credited the magician for giving him a future as a writer, noting, "All I know is that he said, 'Live forever' and gave me a future and in doing so, gave me a past many years before, when his friend died in France . . . I went home and the next day traveled to Arizona with my folks. When we arrived there a few days later I began to write, full-time. I have written every single day of my life since that day 69 years ago."[42] One of Bradbury's dreams was to one day see his books on the shelves alongside his literary heroes, like Edgar Allan Poe and L. Frank Baum.

In elementary school in Illinois, he had been impaired by a number of vision problems. At Los Angeles High School, he did well in his English and art classes but failed mathematics. He also failed socially. In *The Bradbury Chronicles*, Sam Weller wrote, "Unlike the popular kids who drove cars, played sports, and dated, Ray roller-skated, wrote stories . . . Complicating matters, Ray was writing mostly science fiction, a genre with little literary credibility, as he soon discovered."[43] Fortunately, two wonderful teachers saw something in him. Snow Longley Housh, his poetry teacher and club adviser, and Jennet Johnson, his short-story class teacher, encouraged him to continue writing. On one of Bradbury's early science fiction stories, Johnson wrote, "I don't know what it is you're doing, but don't stop." During his lunch periods, Bradbury would go to the typing room and write stories. He wrote, on average, one short story each week. In addition, he sometimes contributed movie reviews and columns to the school newspaper and joined the school drama club.[44]

Bradbury was now very serious about becoming a writer, and possibly acting as well. After high school, cherishing his freedom, he weighed the prospect of going to college. After he was accepted into Los Angeles City College, he realized that he didn't have the money for tuition and really hated school, especially "the grind of classes and the early mornings."[45] (I feel you, Ray.) So instead, he educated himself by going to the library three days a week for the next ten years. He sold newspapers on the streets of Los Angeles during the day.[46]

According to Jonathan R. Eller's *Becoming Ray Bradbury,* Bradbury recounted his learning path in an unpublished 2002 interview: "And so I went to the library (I couldn't afford to buy the books) and I read all the short stories by all the great American writers, a lot of the Europeans, so that it all goes into your bloodstream. And then I read all the great essays over a period of time, and I read all the great poetry, starting back 200–300 years. So all these things go into your bloodstream and they shouldn't be thought about, they should be part of the ambience of your character. And you learn from them secretly, then, when you write, the secrets they give you come out automatically in your writing."[47]

In a short-story titled "Bright Phoenix," he writes in meticulous detail of his fondness for libraries: "Now, as always, I considered my library as a cool cavern or fresh, ever growing forest into which men passed from the heat of the day and the fever of motion to refresh their limbs and bathe their minds an hour in the grass-shade illumination . . . I had seen thousands careen into my library starved, and leave well-fed. I had watched lost people find themselves. I had known realists to dream and dreamers to come awake in this marble sanctuary where silence was a marker in each book."[48]

About a decade later, around the time he got married, Bradbury "graduated" from the library, having read every book on the shelves and written a thousand-plus stories. He told *The New York Times,* "I don't believe in colleges and universities. I believe in libraries because most students don't have any money."[49] Bradbury went on to produce some of the greatest classics of science fiction.

Libraries are the temples of self-education. In the biographies of famous and successful people, you will find that many of them spent their childhoods browsing the shelves of their local library. Reading books was their vehicle for interacting with the world around them and, for some, breaking out of the cycle of poverty. Libraries are also the anchors of our communities. They bring together a confluence of people from far-flung socioeconomic backgrounds, ethnicities, religions, genders, and ages that would probably never have a chance to interact with one another anywhere else. You'll see everyone from the homeless to immigrants to the unemployed to senior citizens to parents and children. Most of us underestimate libraries' importance. They are the place the homeless go for shelter during the day. They are the place the unemployed go to for job-training classes. They are the place low-income people go to get access to books and computers.

Apart from the books, videos, magazines, and computers that are free and widely available, libraries regularly hold classes, job search workshops, book discussions, and movie nights, which are free or very inexpensive. A 2013 study found that for every tax dollar spent on public libraries in Florida, there was a $10.18 return on investment in terms of more jobs, greater economic output, and higher incomes.[50] In short, they are indispensable to the public good.

It was the nineteenth-century steel tycoon and onetime wealthiest man in the world Andrew Carnegie who became the force behind the massive expansion of libraries across the country. A dirt-poor immigrant from Scotland, he was a largely self-taught man with only five years of formal schooling.[51] Colonel James Anderson, a retired businessman in Allegheny City, Pennsylvania, graciously opened his library of four hundred books to some boys every Saturday afternoon. Carnegie would borrow many of them to read.[52] He wrote in his autobiography, "The windows were opened in the walls of my dungeon through which the light of knowledge streamed in. Every day's toil and even the long hours of night service were lightened by the book which I carried about with me and read in the intervals that could be snatched from duty." With a few friends, he also launched the Webster Literary Society, where he learned the art of speech and debate.[53]

Decades later, after making hundreds of millions of dollars in the steel industry, in the course of which he ruthlessly exploited his workers, Carnegie decided to give much of his wealth away to philanthropic causes. With a contribution of $55 million, he helped build a total of 2,509 libraries, 1,679 of them in the United States. That is why some consider him the "Patron Saint of Libraries."[54]

Today, there are more than one hundred thousand libraries in the nation. Many are vulnerable to being shut down as increasing numbers of city and local budgets are being cut. We need libraries more than ever before—self-directed, informal learning cannot thrive without them. They are the places that can help produce future Ray Bradburys.

JOURNALISM

In the past, a bachelor's degree was not required to get a job in journalism. Many people broke into the industry through internships and training programs at the networks, newspapers, and magazines themselves. A survey from Indiana University observed that in 1971 only 58.2 percent of journalists were college graduates.[55] Some of the greatest journalists in history, like Walter Cronkite, Peter Jennings, William Safire, and Carl Bernstein, never formally studied journalism or completed college, yet today it is rare to come across a journalist who hasn't done one or the other. In 2013, the percentage of journalists who were college graduates shot up to 92.1 percent. Just to land most internships and jobs in journalism today requires college enrollment or a college degree, usually from an elite institution. College student and journalist Sarah Harvard has personally experienced these irrational hiring policies.[56] She has found her internships to be so much more valuable and worthwhile than all the time she has spent in college, so she dropped out. But she remains worried that future employers will require a degree.

From her junior year of high school until the summer before her freshmen year of college, Harvard was a student reporter for The Mash, the *Chicago Tribune*'s teen edition. A few times a month after school, she learned the nuts and bolts of journalism: critical thinking, collaboration, copy-editing, fact checking, interviewing, and working on a dead-line. She wrote stories and interviewed people like Chicago mayor Rahm Emanuel and rapper T. I. One of her pieces won first place in the 2011 Newspaper Association of America Foundation Youth Content Awards: Sports Story. Harvard studied at George Mason University for her freshmen year and American University for her sophomore and junior years. In college, she interned at the office of U.S. senator Rand Paul, Students for Liberty, and Al Jazeera English and contributed freelance pieces to *Salon* and *VICE*—an amazing range of experiences. "Internships," she said, "give me the best opportunity to test out what I would like to do and what company culture speaks out to me."

Andrew Ross Sorkin, the famed author and financial journalist for *The New York Times*, took a quite unorthodox path to breaking into journalism. In an interview with *Business Insider,* he explained that during his senior year of high school in the 1990s, he persuaded *Times* advertising columnist Stuart Elliott, whom he read "so religiously that I wanted to work for him before I died," to take him under his wing and allow him to observe him for five weeks, with the understanding that Sorkin would be stapling and making copies most of the time.[57] Every morning, he would have to linger outside the building waiting for Elliott to arrive so that he could get a visitor's pass. He didn't even have a desk.[58]

One day, a few weeks into the "unofficial internship," an editor overheard him by the fax machine talking about the Internet. He was dressed professionally, and the editor mistakenly thought Sorkin was a reporter and assigned him a story. He got his first byline in the paper and the rest is history. Sorkin calls it "the best education I ever had."[59] He later went off to study at Cornell; he wrote seventy-one articles for the *Times* before graduating.[60]

Some publications like *BuzzFeed* and *Slate* have been publicly more receptive to hiring people without degrees or at least degrees from elite colleges. Jon Steinberg, former president and COO of *BuzzFeed,* told the *Daily Princetonian,* Princeton University's student newspaper, "When people apply to come work at BuzzFeed right now, I don't really care where they went to college. It doesn't really indicate anything to me. I care about what are their passions, what have they done, what have they written, what have they created?"[61]

"In general, I don't care about your GPA or whether you went to an Ivy League school," wrote Katherine Goldstein in *Slate,* who formerly worked at the online magazine, "so definitely don't expect this alone to swing open any doors for you. Of all the entry-level people I've hired, the one that went on to have the most successful career in media never finished college. If you are still in college, you should mention where you go and what you study. But the further out of college you are, the less I want to hear about where you went or how you did there."[62]

While real hurdles indeed exist, there are still some effective ways to launch a career in journalism without formal credentials.

MARKETING

Meet Ryan Holiday, former director of marketing for American Apparel; editor-at-large of Betabeat, the *New York Observer*'s Innovation section; and author of two books, one a bestseller titled *Trust Me, I'm Lying: Confessions of a Media Manipulator*—all before the age of thirty. After graduating from high school in Northern California, he went on a near-full-ride scholarship to the University of California, Riverside. Disappointed by high school, he was expecting Riverside to be a place where real learning was finally going to happen. But shortly into it, he found college to be "very understimulating."[63]

Working for the college's newspaper, Holiday penned a review of the infamous ex–frat boy and author Tucker Max's site and e-mailed Max the piece. He loved it. A year later, in a meeting in New York, Holiday gave Max some suggestions on how he could contribute to his company, Rudius Media. Max, in response, offered him an internship, which turned into a job months later. This was during Holiday's sophomore year of college.

During the following summer, the nineteen-year-old moved to Los Angeles and slept on Max's floor. While working for Max, he simultaneously started an internship at a talent management company. When the summer began to fade, Holiday was ready to head back to school for his final year of college. Then one Monday, the company signed a multi-

platinum rock band—a signing he had a large part in landing. Holiday's boss asked him, "Why are you going back to
school? What would happen if you didn't?"

"It was the first time I seriously considered not going
back," he recalled to me. With only a year to go until graduating early with honors, Holiday walked into the registrar's
office and filled out the paperwork to leave college. He wrote
in a blog post, "I'd just helped sign my first multi-platinum
rock act and I wasn't about to go back to the dorms and tol-
erate reading in the newspaper about other people doing my
work."[64] He adds that he believes his real education began
the first day he dropped out of school.

One day, Max, Holiday, and renowned author Robert
Greene had lunch in Los Angeles. Greene was searching for
a research assistant to help out with his new book *The 50th
Law*. Having already read all of his books, Holiday asked
Greene to give him the position, which Greene did. Now
Holiday was juggling three jobs at the same time—managing
the rock bands, doing marketing for Tucker Max, and conducting research for Robert Greene. Holiday did that nonstop for a whole year. As Greene's assistant, he tirelessly read
scores of books, marking key passages and stories.

Then Holiday met Dov Charney, founder and former
CEO of American Apparel (he was finally fired in 2014
amid many lawsuits alleging sexual harassment), through
an introduction from Greene, who was on the company's
board. Charney needed some marketing done and hired
Holiday for the position of director of marketing.

"I taught myself how to do that kind of marketing
through the books I read, the apprenticeships I had, and
the mentoring I received," he told me. No formal education
required.

At age twenty-four, Holiday said he decided to, in his

words, "drop out again." He moved from Los Angeles to New Orleans to work on *Trust Me, I'm Lying*, a book that spilled the secrets of media manipulation. It was eventually sold to Penguin for a six-figure advance.

He wrote in a blog post, "I've worked as a Hollywood executive, researched for and promoted multiple NYT best-sellers, and was the Director of Marketing for one of the most provocative companies on the planet. I had achieved more than I ever could have dreamed of—the scared, over-whelmed me of 19 could have never conceived of having done all that."[65]

ART

As a child growing up on Long Island, Molly Crabapple struggled to pay attention in class. She would doodle inces-santly, to the irritation of her teachers.[66] When she was twelve, her school singled her out and a school psychiatrist diagnosed her with oppositional defiant disorder. "I rebelled because I was a child and I wanted to be human," she later wrote in *VICE*.[67] It wasn't long before she was expelled from the school. In high school, she failed a few classes but ended up graduating early by doubling up on credits.

With a few hundred dollars to her name, Crabapple, at age seventeen, departed for Europe. One morning in Paris, she came across the English-language bookstore Shake-speare and Company and met the proprietor, George Whit-man. He invited her to live there in exchange for working the cash register for a few hours a day. (In 2005, he told *The Guardian* that more than 40,000 people have slept in the bookstore's thirteen beds since its opening in 1951.)[68] That's where Crabapple began her true education, spending hours filling a leather-bound notebook with drawings. "Here was this place created in complete defiance of everything I had thought I had known about life," she told me. "We didn't have to pay for things. People could just come and go. It was beautiful. It was based on books. It had been around for fifty years, so it wasn't some like fly-by-night experiment." She also called Whitman "one of the most influential people in my life."

In 2001, shortly after her eighteenth birthday, Crabapple began studying at the Fashion Institute of Technology, a public college in Manhattan. In her words, it was "an embarrassment to the education system." She said some teachers were subpar and many of the skills and techniques she was taught were obsolete. Her critique extended further to question the notion of art schools themselves. "Art is a really hard thing to make a living in," Crabapple said. "Art schools deliberately churn out thousands of times more artists that can never be accommodated." While in college, she was modeling on the side. After three years of being fed up with her schooling, she dropped out.

In 2005, she cofounded Dr. Sketchy's Anti-Art School, an alternative drawing program that uses underground performers as subjects of drawings. There are now branches in 140 cities around the world. For four years Crabapple was the staff artist for the Box, a New York City nightclub. Since then, her art and journalism have had an international reach, appearing in many publications, in exhibitions, on the cover of Matt Taibbi's *New York Times* bestselling book *The Divide,* in the permanent collection of the Museum of Modern Art, and in other places.

Crabapple's advice to young people who are interested in pursuing a career in art? First, she says, you need to be drawing during all of your free time. "If you have a problem motivating yourself to do it, then you shouldn't be doing it. Get a stable job [instead]." Then she recommends moving to a city with a good art scene, buying drawing books, seeking out professional artists to be mentors, and making a close examination of your weaknesses—all of which can be done cheaply. For your art itself, she explains, "When your art comes from love and expression, it's fucking real. I suggest doing the style that you love and then attacking it with merciless rigor, so you can be fucking brilliant at it . . . I always think that mercenary grit actually enables people to achieve their dreams and do the passionate projects that they love, whereas if they approached the world with this naïveté, they end up drawing other people's projects that they hate until they're burnt out and end up hating art and not doing anything."

When it comes to deciding whether to go to art school or not, Crabapple believes you need to be clear about the real reason you might choose to attend an elite school. "The reason you're going to an Ivy is not because you're going to get some great education. The reason people go to Ivies is that it's networking with the future lords of the universe."

Because she hasn't spent much time in formal institutions, she finds that she has an extremely different outlook on how the world operates from many people who have. "They maintain this very hierarchical view of the world, where they know their place in it. They have this idea that people are chosen for things and that there's a fair choosing mechanism. That's just not the way the world runs. The world has never run like that."

Not being raised through institutions, Crabapple observes, has given her a "much more skeptical view of how power and power relations . . . and how the so-called meritocracy works." She continues, "I don't think I ever would have had a career if I had just obediently gone along with how things should have been."

. . .

TOO MUCH PRECIOUS time of young people's lives has
been wasted by participating in the race to acquire more credentials. The primary function of credentials is signaling—
indicating to employers and the general population an
individual's level of intelligence and competency. As flawed
as it is, it has worked for employers for the most part, but far
less well for employees.

Credentialism has gone virtually unquestioned, because
until recently there haven't been effective alternative methods
available to screen job candidates and distinguish between
people beyond looking at their academic credentials. The
belief that an individual who graduated from Harvard,
Yale, or Princeton is almost always more intelligent and
competent than an individual who graduated from a state
or community college remains strong. In 2013, *The New
York Times* reported on a phenomenon known as "degree
inflation," where "the college degree is becoming the new
high school diploma."[69] Some employers are now requiring
at least a bachelor's degree for jobs that traditionally did not
require more than a high school education.

In 1971, Austrian philosopher Ivan Illich in *Deschooling Society* took a radical stance on this issue: "We need a
law forbidding discrimination in hiring, voting, or admission to centers of learning based on previous attendance at
some curriculum. This guarantee would not exclude performance tests of competence for a function or role, but would
remove the present absurd discrimination in favor of the
person who learns a given skill with the largest expenditure
of public funds or what is equally likely has been able to
obtain a diploma which has no relation to any useful skill or
job. Only by protecting the citizen from being disqualified

by anything in his career in school can a constitutional dis-establishment of school become psychologically effective."[70]

Unfortunately, I doubt such a law will ever be seri-ously considered, let alone enacted. Today, as we are see-ing an increase in degree inflation, there are nevertheless more employers who are ditching the college degree require-ment and allowing prospective employees to present portfo-lios, badges, and GitHub profiles for evaluation. That's an encouraging sign and makes me hopeful. Self-taught people, dropouts, or the ones who didn't go to college—many of whom are just as, or more, brilliant and capable than college graduates—have the most to benefit from the eradication of these discriminatory and close-minded hiring practices.

CHAPTER 9

School Without Walls

Is it likely that public schools will be reformed from within to realize even part of the vision that informs this book? Unfortunately, no. And here's why: To even have a chance at fulfilling a revolution in education, Congress would have to repeal the No Child Left Behind Act—and the Race to the Top program would need to be terminated. You'd have to dismantle the entire corporate education reform project. You'd have to get rid of state graduation requirements, standardized testing, standards, and grades. You'd have to transform colleges of education. But perhaps the largest barrier to change is the mind-set of the people who work in the system. They are generally very opposed to the idea of relinquishing even a scintilla of power to the students in the learning or governing process.

Don't get me wrong. I've met countless people in public schools who share similar perspectives and are trying their best to provide meaningful learning experiences to their students given the enormous restrictions put on them. But they often get so beaten down by the system that they end up leaving in frustration.

There are amazing public schools throughout the country. The problem is that put together they make up less than 5 percent of all schools and they are increasingly under pressure to raise their test scores. Many districts have terrific alternative education programs, but those are often very small and only open to kids with learning disabilities, poor grades, or behavioral issues. One excellent example of an alternative school is the Village School in the Great Neck School District in New York. It serves fewer than fifty students in grades nine through twelve. Classes are small and students are evaluated instead of being graded by teachers.

What John Holt wrote in his 1976 book *Instead of Education* could not be more relevant: "Do not waste your energy trying to reform all these schools. They cannot be reformed. It may be possible for a few of you, in a few places, to make a place called a school which will be a humane and useful doing place for the young. If so, by all means do it. In most places, not even this much will be possible. The most we will be able to do may be to find ways to help some children escape education and schooling, and to help some others, who cannot escape, to be less damaged by it than they are now."[1]

The revolution in education is already beginning to happen outside of the system in free and democratic schools, the maker movement, and community learning spaces.

A few decades ago, philosopher Ivan Illich published his landmark book *Deschooling Society*, in which he argued that we should not abolish schooling, but as we've done with the church, "disestablish" it—in other words, strip schooling of its esteemed status and the privileges gained from participating in it. He wrote, "We need research on the possible use of technology to create institutions which serve personal, creative, and autonomous interaction and the emergence of values which cannot be substantially controlled by techno-crats." For real learning to occur, he proposed the creation of "learning webs" and noted that people need to gain access to four sets of educational resources:

> 1. Reference Services to Educational Objects—which facilitate access to things or processes used for formal learning . . .
> 2. Skill Exchanges—which permit persons to list their skills, the conditions under which they are willing to serve as models for others who want to learn these skills, and the addresses at which they can be reached.
> 3. Peer-Matching—a communications network which permits persons to describe the learning activity in which they wish to engage, in the hope of finding a partner for the inquiry.
> 4. Reference Services to Educators-at-Large—who can be listed in a directory giving the addresses and self-descriptions of professionals, paraprofessionals and freelancers, along with conditions of access to their services.[2]

Illich was obviously well ahead of his time. The Internet has provided many of those very resources he called for, but we haven't harnessed its full potential yet.

The ultimate dream is for the city and community to be reimagined as the school itself. We need to shore up public education and create noncompulsory, noncoercive, free, and accessible learning spaces for young people and adults alike.

Currently, we have what are described as "third places," like makerspaces, libraries, museums, and community centers. We also need to create more publicly funded spaces outside of formal institutions for curiosity and self-directed learning to flourish.

The history of coffeehouses could offer some direction. Imported into Europe from the Arab world in the seventeenth century, coffeehouses became centers of informal learning, hobnobbing, debate, news, politics, and innovation. The first one was opened by a Greek servant named Pasqua Rosée in St. Michael's Alley in London in 1652. In just a few decades, hundreds of coffeehouses were in operation across the city.[3]

Apart from being a place to get a cup of coffee, coffeehouses were places to gather and make conversation. In the numerous ongoing debates throughout the day, it didn't matter whether you were of elite or poor status, whether you had a title before your name or not, whether you were a clerk or a member of Parliament. Nobody was barred from participating. Markman Ellis, professor of eighteenth-century studies at Queen Mary University of London, observes in *The Coffee House,* "All speakers are considered equal and within the collective fiction of the coffee-house hierarchy is erased."[4] (However, it's important to note that women were generally prohibited from entering coffeehouses, so they were definitely gender-segregated places.)

Coffeehouses were also the go-to place to get the latest news and gossip. Newspapers, gazettes, literature, and pamphlets were given out, and journalists would often announce breaking news at the coffeehouse. Some people even received their mail there.

Between swigs of coffee, intellectuals, scientists, artists, businessmen, journalists, students, writers, and politicians would fraternize, a fecund scene that couldn't be found anywhere else in English society. The mixing of people who worked in a diverse set of disciplines and fields made coffee-houses the hub of creativity and ideation. Many scientists from the Royal Society delivered eminent lectures there. The seeds of the insurance company Lloyd's of London were planted in Edward Lloyd's coffeehouse on Tower Street. Isaac Newton was reported to have dissected a dolphin at the Grecian Coffee House.[5] Adam Smith wrote *The Wealth of Nations* at the British Coffee House on Cockspur Street, and handed out chapters for people to critique.[6]

With an admission fee of a mere penny, they were nick-named "penny universities." One observer noted that in a coffeehouse, a man could "pick up more useful knowledge than by applying himself to his books for a whole month."[7] They were spectacularly cheap forums of education.

Today, the number of public spaces for learning, net-working, and debating is lagging, but in more cities, spaces that offer a host of resources, from classes to mentors to teachers, are emerging. The one downside is that they are not very accessible to children. In New York City, there are places like General Assembly, a start-up school that offers classes in business, design, and programming and work-spaces for entrepreneurs (it also has campuses in Austin, Boston, Chicago, Los Angeles, San Francisco, Berlin, Lon-don, Hong Kong, and Sydney); the Brooklyn Brainery, a space that offers inexpensive classes in a variety of topics; Trade School, a nontraditional learning space that runs on barter; Anhoek School, an "experimental all-women's grad-uate school" with a "curriculum based on cultural produc-tion (political, aesthetic, and theoretical)"; the Public School, a school with no formal curriculum that holds classes and meetings in Los Angeles, San Francisco, and Berlin; Recurse Center, a free three-month, full-time school for program-ming; and many more.

In San Francisco, in addition to General Assembly and the Public School, there's [freespace], a pop-up community center devoted to hacking the civic experience. A few years ago, for a hundred days, there was One Hundred Days of Spring. A former boutique clothing shop was transformed into a "gypsy-tent-circus-wagon-theater-gallery-cum-classroom, the storefront, reborn as the Schoolhouse," as the *San Francisco Bay Guardian* put it, where people signed up and taught classes.[8] Their motto was "Teach something. Learn something. Create something."

DURING THE 1970S, a few "school without walls" experiments cropped up in several cities. The most famous one was Philadelphia's Parkway Program, an alternative public high school. In its May 16, 1969, issue, *Life* magazine called Parkway "probably the most radical of all current high school experiments."[9] The following year, *Time* magazine dubbed it "the most interesting high school in the U.S. today."[10]

In the program, hundreds of students used the city of Philadelphia as their school. Besides a loft to store their belongings and participate in weekly "town meetings" to discuss community issues, there weren't any formal classrooms. As the founder John Bremer once put it in a speech, "Let us suppose that students in the future will learn about government in City Hall, about biology in the zoo, about art in the city and in art museums, about labor relations on the waterfront. Why can we not get students to use the city as the campus?"[11] The student body was split into a few "units." Courses and independent study opportunities were offered, but the only compulsory part of the program was tutorials, which were meetings a few times a week with about fifteen students and two faculty members. This is when basic skills were cultivated. And instead of grades, teachers gave evaluations.

Today, one initiative brewing in a few cities across America, channeling some of the ethos of the "school without walls" movement, looks incredibly promising. After succeeding in lengthening the school day in Chicago in the summer of 2012, Chicago mayor Rahm Emanuel wanted next to address the "summer slide"—the so-called loss in knowledge and skills during summer vacation for largely low-income youth. He and his team began noticing the enormous amount of learning that occurred outside the walls of the classroom, especially during the summer months, and wanted to see how the city could expand those opportunities to reach more people. At the end of the year, the mayor's office got in touch with the MacArthur Foundation, which is based in the city and had been involved in funding and supporting many education programs.

Beth Swanson, formerly the mayor's deputy chief of staff for education and now vice president of strategy and programs at the Joyce Foundation, told me their conversation revolved around two questions: "How do we start to track it? How do we capture that learning?"[12] MacArthur saw digital badges, similar to Boy Scout merit badges, as a way to measure, identify, and document the specific learning that takes place in nonformal education settings. For several years, they had been investing into the research and development of badge systems, like Mozilla's Open Badges project. Eventually, a partnership between the City of Chicago, the MacArthur Foundation, and Mozilla was established.

In January 2013, Emanuel publicly announced the "Summer of Learning" program to be launched the upcoming summer. Libraries, museums, parks, universities, and organizations would offer a constellation of free or low-cost learning activities, internships, and volunteer opportunities, and students, upon completion, could earn a digital badge that exhibited the knowledge and skills obtained. As the motto of Mozilla's Open Badges project goes, "Get recognition for skills you learn anywhere." Within a few months, youth-serving city agencies and more than a hundred organizations climbed on board. Meanwhile, with the help of DePaul University's Digital Youth Network (DYN), which is funded by MacArthur and the National Science Foundation, the city's partners were engaged in building and designing the Summer of Learning site and the badge infrastructure, recruiting students, and training staff at youth organizations. Megan Cole, director of marketing and operations at the Badge Alliance, said, "Having the mayor buy in served as a catalyst for the program."[13] It greatly helped in getting the word out and adding credibility.

The pilot run during the summer of 2013 was a huge success. More than 230,000 young people across Chicago participated in the Summer of Learning.[14] More than 150,000 badges were awarded by more than one hundred organizations. Some badges included the Summer Service badge through the Academic and Enrichment Summer Camp at the Gary Comer Youth Center, the Cryptographer badge through University of Chicago's Game Changer Chicago Design Lab, and the Urban Ecologist badge through the Peggy Notebaert Nature Museum. Fifty-six percent of the badges were issued to African Americans and 29 percent to Latinos.[15] Swanson said the experiment gave them an excellent data set of students' interests and activities, information they did not have before.

A few people told me that it's still unclear to students, teachers, and employers what the value and significance of badges are and how to evaluate them appropriately. That's what the team in Chicago is trying to figure out themselves. In Chicago public schools, teachers can see in the badges their students' talents and passions, things that may not be evident in the classroom. In the near future, badges could be included on an internship, college, or job application. DePaul University is now considering badges as part of its admissions process. Most of all, badges are a godsend to self-directed and nontraditional learners, who have few other ways to demonstrate their competencies.

One concern often raised about badges is that they will cause a decrease in students' intrinsic motivation, encouraging them to complete activities for the sole purpose of amassing badges. Sybil Madison-Boyd, director of the learning pathways program at the Digital Youth Network, told me, "Our anecdotal experience is that it's rarely about the badge."[16] She noted that among the younger kids, there is sometimes an urge to collect, but among the teenagers, that's not the case. Cole also explained that after a student receives a badge, the system is designed in a way so that it will suggest activities in a similar domain. It will "help you discover pathways and what you might be really good at [that] you don't know about."

As news spread, the Summer of Learning initiative began attracting attention from other cities. The MacArthur Foundation invited mayors, representatives, and stakeholders to a two-day meeting in December 2013 in Chicago to learn more about the city's program, its results, and how they could get a similar program up and running in their own city. Representatives from eleven cities were present at the event. Swanson explained that a lot of cities are trying to see "how they can provide learning opportunities to [their] youth that are not necessarily directly tied to formal education."

The people in Chicago realized that the activities and opportunities offered during the Summer of Learning didn't need to be limited to the summer months; it could be year-round. So the program was expanded and renamed the City of Learning. In 2014, four cities, including Dallas, Los Angeles, Pittsburgh, and Washington, D.C, launched their own City of Learning programs.

Ideally, the City of Learning initiative wouldn't just supplement what happens in school, but would serve as a partial replacement of school itself. A few tweaks and additions would help. Abandoned and underutilized buildings could be turned into public spaces. Schools could open up year-round for the entire community to use. Classes, seminars, and workshops could be held there.

We'll always need physical spaces for students to be in. Not everyone, needless to say, has a parent able to stay at home; a safe, stable, and nurturing home environment; and consistent access to food. Once the city and community becomes the school, then children can learn however, whenever, whatever, and with whomever they choose. They can spend their time in museums, parks, makerspaces, libraries, community centers, and stores. They can tap into networks and databases of classes, mentors, teachers, apprenticeships, internships, and volunteer opportunities. Just like Philadelphia's Parkway Program, students could be put into small groups with an educator, who would be on hand to supervise, guide, and mentor. Older, more experienced children would be able to venture into the community on their own or with peers.

One day, as John Holt once put it, living and learning will become indistinguishable from each other.

·   ·   ·

IF WE WERE to successfully pull off a full-blooded transformation of our education system, what would our society look like? It would have human beings who are generally more curious, creative, freethinking, socially conscious, and skeptical of power and authority. But people's economic situation would largely remain the same. As historian Michael Katz notes in his book *Class, Bureaucracy, and Schools,* rich kids will generally end up rich adults and poor kids will generally end up poor adults no matter whether they attended a free or democratic school or a traditional school.[17] Schools are powerful institutions in terms of shaping and molding future generations, but at the same time, we need to acknowledge that they are extremely limited as drivers of social transformation. In addition to restructuring schooling, we need systemic changes to our economic, political, and social systems as well, because racism, sexism, militarism, and extreme inequality will not suddenly cease to exist. "My firm view," educator Allen Graubard laments in his book *Free the Children,* "is that attempts at truly humanizing the public schools must run up against the fundamental social realities—the sickness of American society."[18] But just because the task is immensely difficult is no reason not to take a shot.

Conclusion

We have not been in a better position in decades to radi-cally reimagine and transform our education systems. From progressive and democratic schools to innovations in higher education to the maker movement, there is incredible prog-ress being made, and it should be acknowledged. There is a surge of interest in alternative models of education outside of the traditional education-industrial complex. Millions of people are questioning the benefits and tenets of conven-tional schooling. We can see this in the growing number of parents who are choosing to homeschool or unschool their children. We can see this in the nationwide rebellion led by students, teachers, and parents against standardized testing and corporate education reforms through protests, civil dis-obedience, and opting out of testing. Parents, especially, are slowly beginning to say no to incessant testing, the Common Core standards, and budget cuts. They don't support every principle of freer, experiential, and democratic education, but at the very least they see something inherently wrong with the amount and quality of homework their children receive daily, the standardized tests that children have to take each year, the students' rote instruction in the classroom, and overall unhappiness in school.

Of course, there is still much more to be done. This is not a divisive and high-profile culture war issue like climate change, gun control, or same-sex marriage. There is not as yet widespread understanding of the underlying problems, nor is there majority support for the proposals I've outlined. And this is not an issue that can be solved alone through legislation and politics. As Indian philosopher Jiddu Krishnamurti once wrote, "Systems, whether educational or political, are not changed mysteriously; they are transformed when there is a fundamental change in ourselves."[1] It's up to us to organize, to let people know that this system doesn't have to be this way, and to show them that a new paradigm of education is possible. Democratic education needs to become so irresistibly attractive that the public has little choice but to join this movement. We should look to our forebears—John Dewey, Maria Montessori, A. S. Neill, John Holt, Paul Goodman, Ivan Illich, Jonathan Kozol, Paulo Freire, and many others—and understand where they succeeded and faltered. And with that understanding, we should stop pinning our hopes on a secretary of education, chancellor, or superintendent swooping in and making the changes we desire. If there's anything the history of schooling tells us, it's that the people in power are the ones who have resisted even an iota of authentic reform and have cemented and exacerbated the most draconian features of the system.

After my visits to democratic and progressive schools, I often think, What if all children could have such an educational experience? We have an opportunity to create a system that values and upholds children's rights, opinions, and interests, allows the learner to have autonomy and freedom, refuses to distinguish between learning and living, ingrains the community and surrounding world in the life of the child, and does not allow corporations to dictate education policy. We need to empower young people to not be afraid to speak up and to have an active role in shaping their schools and communities. It's not impossible.

I distinctly remember a conversation I had with Simon Hauger, cofounder and principal of the Workshop School. He was telling me that when the superintendent of Philadelphia schools went on a tour of the school when it was located at the Navy Yard, one of the first things he told Hauger was, "The kids are happy." Hauger told me, "Then you realize, oh shit, he walks into schools every day, and the kids aren't happy." One of the most influential tools we have is reminding adults what it is like to be a student in school: how much of a dehumanizing, dull, and mentally and physically exhausting experience it can be. That is why I urge parents, teachers, and concerned citizens to experience what it's like to be a student in school again by shadowing a young person for a day or two in a traditional school and then publicly report their observations.

One day, I hope we will find ourselves horrified by what we once made children go through for six to seven hours a day, five days a week, 180 days a year, and thirteen years. Until then, we must not stop rallying and fighting for children and their rights and democratic, experiential, progressive, and noncoercive education for all.

My parting words are for my generation—young people: You are more than some arbitrary test score or grade. You are human beings. You have rights. You have a voice. And, most important, you have power. So go out there and use them all.

ACKNOWLEDGMENTS

I would be remiss not to mention some of my heroes—the educators, writers, and activists who have paved the path before me: John Dewey, Maria Montessori, Paulo Freire, Alexander Sutherland Neill, John Holt, George Dennison, Herbert Kohl, Jonathan Kozol, Ivan Illich, Paul Goodman, Peter Gray, and John Taylor Gatto. I plan to do my part in helping to keep their legacies and ideas alive.

I am indebted to all the young people, educators, parents, activists, scholars, and writers who shared their stories and expertise with me. I am also much appreciative of all the schools and programs that welcomed me in to visit and conduct reporting.

I am very grateful to everyone who read early drafts and offered their comments and feedback: Pat Thompson, Victoria Cochran, James Cersonsky, Michael Crawford, Patrick St. John, Tomis Parker, Daniel Kao, Tim Cook, and Louis Anslow.

A special thanks to Bobby Buchanan, my adviser at

Goddard College, who pored over several drafts and always provided thoughtful and helpful responses.

I want to especially thank my agent, Betsy Lerner. We immediately bonded over our mutual love for the New York Yankees. She believed in this book from the beginning, and I am tremendously grateful for all her work in making this book happen.

I was fortunate to have an extraordinary editor, Gerry Howard. He shepherded this book into existence and never failed to challenge and push my thinking and arguments. I also want to thank the rest of the indefatigable team at Doubleday and Random House: Nora Reichard, Michael Goldsmith, Jeremy Medina, and Kim Thornton Ingenito.

Finally, my deepest gratitude lies with my parents for their unending love and support. This book is dedicated to both of you.

NOTES

The names of some children have been changed. Some identifying details have also been changed to protect the privacy of individuals. Some of the ages of the individuals are based on when I met them and are not up-to-date. I have cited the interviews I personally conducted with individuals but not the ones conducted in the context of in-person reporting, like school visits.

INTRODUCTION

1. I was inspired by a speech the late activist Aaron Swartz gave when he was in school:

    Every day, millions of innocent children are unwillingly part of a terrible dictatorship. The government takes them away from their families and brings them to cramped, crowded buildings where they are treated as slaves in terrible conditions. For seven hours a day, they are indoctrinated to love their current conditions and support their government and society. As if this was not enough, they are often held for another two hours to exert themselves almost to the point of physical exhaustion, and sometimes injury. Then, when at home, during the short few hours which they are permitted to see their families they are forced to do additional mind-numbing work which they finish and return the following day. *This isn't some repressive gov-*

ernment in some far-off country. It's happening right here: we call it school.

Aaron Swartz, "The Final Days," *Schoolyard Subversion,* June 3, 2001, http://web.archive.org/web/20010614074720/http:/swartz fam.com/aaron/school/.

2. Charles Basch, et al., "Prevalence of Sleep Duration on an Average School Night Among 4 Nationally Representative Successive Samples of American High School Students, 2007–2013," *Preventing Chronic Disease* 11 (December 2014).

3. Alfie Kohn, *Feel-Bad Education: And Other Contrarian Essays on Children & Schooling* (Boston: Beacon Press, 2011), 131.

4. Denise Pope, *Doing School: How We Are Creating a Generation of Stressed-Out, Materialistic, and Miseducated Students* (New Haven, CT: Yale University Press, 2003), 4.

5. Jiddu Krishnamurti, *Education and the Significance of Life* (New York: Harper & Row, 1953), 15.

6. Laurie A. Couture, *Instead of Medicating and Punishing: Healing the Causes of Our Children's Acting-Out Behavior by Parenting and Educating the Way Nature Intended* (Deadwood, OR: Wyatt-MacKenzie Publishing, 2008), 190.

CHAPTER 1

1. John Holt, *Instead of Education: Ways to Help People Do Things Better* (New York: Dutton, 1976), 222.

2. Statistics on the number of students in public and private schools in the United States: http://nces.ed.gov/fastfacts/display.asp?id=372.

3. "The High Cost of High School Dropouts: What the Nation Pays for Inadequate High Schools," Alliance for Excellent Education, November 2011.

4. John M. Bridgeland, John J. DiIulio Jr., and Karen Burke Morison, "The Silent Epidemic: Perspectives of High School Dropouts," Bill & Melinda Gates Foundation, March 2006.

5. John Taylor Gatto, *Weapons of Mass Instruction: A Schoolteacher's Journey Through the Dark World of Compulsory Schooling* (Gabriola Island, BC, Canada: New Society Publishers, 2010), 37.

6. Helen M. Todd, "Why Children Work: The Children's Answer," *McClure's Magazine* 40 (April 1913), via David B. Tyack, *The One Best System: A History of American Urban Education* (Cambridge, MA: Harvard University Press, 1974), 177–78.

7. "U.S. Teens in Our World: Understanding the Health of U.S. Youth in Comparison to Youth in Other Countries," U.S. Department of Health and Human Services, 2003.

8. Mihaly Csikszentmihalyi and Jeremy Hunter, "Happiness in Everyday Life: The Uses of Experience Sampling," *Journal of Happiness Studies* 4, no. 2 (2003), via Peter Gray, *Free to Learn: Why Unleashing the Instinct to Play Will Make Our Children Happier, More Self-Reliant, and Better Students for Life* (New York: Basic Books, 2013), 18–19.

9. Donald W. Felker, *Building Positive Self-Concepts* (Minneapolis: Burgess Publishing, 1974).

10. Brandon Busteed, "The School Cliff: Student Engagement Drops with Each School Year," *The Gallup Blog,* http://thegallupblog .gallup.com/2013/01/the-school-cliff-student-engagement.html.

11. Robert Epstein, *Teen 2.0: Saving Our Children and Families from the Torment of Adolescence* (Sanger, CA: Quill Driver Books/ Word Dancer Press, 2010), 399.

12. Neil Postman and Charles Weingartner, *Teaching as a Subversive Activity* (New York: Delacorte, 1969), 20–21.

13. Geneva Convention (IIII) Relative to the Treatment of Prisoners of War, August 12, 1949; credit to Cevin Soling for compiling some of these.

14. Cevin Soling, Talk at the Conference on Alternatives to Education, Harvard Graduate School of Education, April 27, 2013, https:// www.youtube.com/watch?v=c1nJ-tI-vew.

15. Author interviews with Sam.

16. Dan Olweus, *Bullying at School: What We Know and What We Can Do* (Malden, MA: Blackwell, 1993), 9.

17. Andrea Cohn and Andrea Canter, "Bullying: Facts for Schools and Parents," National Association of School Psychologists, October 7, 2003, http://www.nasponline.org/resources/factsheets/bullying _fs.aspx.

18. "President and First Lady Call for a United Effort to Address Bullying," U.S. Department of Education, March 10, 2011, http://www .ed.gov/news/press-releases/president-and-first-lady-call-united-effort-address-bullying.

19. Emily Bazelon, *Sticks and Stones: Defeating the Culture of Bullying and Rediscovering the Power of Character and Empathy* (New York: Random House, 2013), 10.

20. Victoria Stuart-Cassel, "Analysis of State Bullying Laws and Policies," U.S. Department of Education, December 2011, http://

www2.ed.gov/rschstat/eval/bullying/state-bullying-laws/state
-bullying-laws.pdf.

21. Seokjin Jeong and Byung Hyun Lee, "A Multilevel Examination of
Peer Victimization and Bullying Preventions in Schools," *Journal of
Criminology* (2013).

22. Author interview with Gever Tulley.

23. Alina Tugend, "Peeking at the Negative Side of High School Popularity," *New York Times,* June 18, 2010.

24. Robert Faris and Diane Felmlee, "Status Struggles: Network Cen-
trality and Gender Segregation in Same- and Cross-Gender Aggression," *American Sociological Review* 76, no. 1 (February 2011).

25. Peter Gray, *Free to Learn,* 78.

26. Adam Fletcher, "Dangers Within the Student Voice Movement,"
Cooperative Catalyst, February 15, 2013, http://coopcatalyst
.wordpress.com/2013/02/15/dangers-within-the-student-voice
-movement/.

27. Dennis Littky with Samantha Grabelle, "Voting for Homecoming
Queen Does Not Prepare Students for Democracy," *Horace* 21, no.
1 (Late Fall 2004).

28. Jennifer Senior, "Why You Will Truly Never Leave High School,"
New York, January 28, 2013.

29. "Suicide Prevention," Centers for Disease Control and Prevention,
http://www.cdc.gov/violenceprevention/pub/youth_suicide.html.

30. "Youth Risk Behavior Surveillance—United States, 2011," Centers
for Disease Control and Prevention, 2012, via Meghan Neal, "1 in
12 Teens Have Attempted Suicide: Report," *New York Daily News,*
June 9, 2012.

31. Benjamin Hansen and Matthew Lang, "Back to School Blues: Seasonality of Youth Suicide and the Academic Calendar," *Economics
of Education Review* 30, no. 5 (2011): 850–61.

32. Young Shin Kim and Bennett Leventhal, "Bullying and Suicide.
A Review," *International Journal of Adolescent Medicine and
Health* 20, no. 2 (2008); "Bullying-Suicide Link Explored in New
Study by Researchers at Yale," *YaleNews,* July 16, 2008, http://
news.yale.edu/2008/07/16/bullying-suicide-link-explored-new
-study-researchers-yale.

33. William E. Copeland, Dieter Wolke, Adrian Angold, and E. Jane
Costello, "Adult Psychiatric Outcomes of Bullying and Being Bullied by Peers in Childhood and Adolescence," *JAMA Psychiatry* 70,
no. 4 (2013): 419–26.

34. Catherine Saint Louis, "Effects of Bullying Last into Adulthood, Study Finds," *New York Times,* February 20, 2013, http://well .blogs.nytimes.com/2013/02/20/effects-of-bullying-last-into-adult hood-study-finds/.

CHAPTER 2

1. Alexis de Tocqueville, *Democracy in America* (New York: Pratt, Woodford, 1848), 345–46.

2. Ibid, 271.

3. "Benjamin Franklin: Citizen Ben," PBS, http://www.pbs.org/ben franklin/l3_citizen_networker.html.

4. Benjamin Franklin, *The Autobiography of Benjamin Franklin* (Mineola, NY: Dover Publications, 1996), 45.

5. David Labaree, *Someone Has to Fail: The Zero-Sum Game of Public Schooling* (Cambridge, MA: Harvard University Press, 2010), 43–44.

6. Daniel J. Boorstin, *The Americans: The Colonial Experience* (New York: Random House, 1958), 315.

7. Carl Kaestle, *Pillars of the Republic: Common Schools and American Society, 1780–1860* (New York: Hill and Wang, 1983), 65.

8. James W. Stockard Jr., *Handbook for Teaching Secondary School Social Studies* (Long Grove, IL: Waveland Press, 2006), 13.

9. John Taylor Gatto, *Dumbing Us Down: The Hidden Curriculum of Compulsory Schooling* (Gabriola Island, BC, Canada: New Society Publishers, 2002), 12.

10. Jack Lynch, "Literacy in Early America," *Colonial Williamsburg* (Winter 2011), http://www.history.org/Foundation/journal Winter11/literacy.cfm.

11. Pierre Samuel du Pont de Nemours, *National Education in the United States of America,* trans. from the 2nd French ed., 1812 (Newark: University of Delaware Press, 1923), 3.

12. Harvey J. Graff, *The Legacies of Literacy: Continuities and Contradictions in Western Culture and Society* (Bloomington: Indiana University Press, 1987), 343.

13. "2003 National Assessment of Adult Literacy," U.S. Department of Education, National Center for Education Statistics, 2003.

14. James Grant Wilson and John Fiske, *Appletons' Cyclopædia of American Biography* (New York: D. Appleton and Company, 1888), 190.

15. Ibid.
16. Jonathan Messerli, *Horace Mann: A Biography* (New York: Knopf, 1972), 12.
17. Ibid; Charles Morris, "Horace Mann, the Promoter of Public Education," Heritage History, http://www.heritage-history.com/?c =read&author=morris&book=progress&story=mann.
18. Johann Gottlieb Fichte, *Addresses to the German Nation* [1807–1808] (Chicago and London: Open Court Publishing Company, 1922), 20–21.
19. John Taylor Gatto, *The Underground History of American Education: A Schoolteacher's Intimate Investigation Into the Problem of Modern Schooling* (New York: Odysseus Group, 2000).
20. Martin van Creveld, *The Rise and Decline of the State* (Cambridge, UK: Cambridge University Press, 1999), 213.
21. Thomas Alexander, *The Prussian Elementary Schools* (New York: Macmillan, 1919), v.
22. Horace Mann, *Mr. Mann's Seventh Annual Report: Education in Europe* (Boston: Massachusetts Board of Education, 1844), 84, 160–61.
23. Labaree, *Someone Has to Fail*, 73–74.
24. Patricia Albjerg Graham, *Schooling America: How the Public Schools Meet the Nation's Changing Needs* (New York: Oxford University Press, 2005), 11.
25. Ellwood P. Cubberley, *Changing Conceptualizations of Education* (Boston: Houghton Mifflin, 1909), 15–16.
26. Michael Katz, *The Irony of Early School Reform: Educational Innovation in Mid-Nineteenth Century Massachusetts* (Cambridge, MA: Harvard University Press, 1968), 85.
27. Orestes Augustus Brownson, "Second Annual Report of the Board of Education, together with the Second Annual Report of the Secretary at the Board," *Boston Quarterly Review* 2 (1839): 406, 408.
28. Christopher Lasch, *The World of Nations: Reflections on American History, Politics, and Culture* (New York: Knopf, 1973).
29. Brownson, "Second Annual Report of the Board of Education," 39.
30. Karen Clay, Jeff Lingwall, and Melvin Stephens Jr., "Do Schooling Laws Matter? Evidence from the Introduction of Compulsory Attendance Laws in the United States," NBER Working Paper no. 18477, National Bureau of Economic Research, October 2012.
31. Michael Katz, *In the Shadow of the Poorhouse: A Social History of Welfare in America* (New York: Basic Books, 1996), 135.
32. Ellwood P. Cubberley, *Public Education in the United States: A*

Study and Interpretation of American Educational History (Boston: Houghton Mifflin, 1919), 564.

33. Gatto, *The Underground History of American Education.*

34. Frederick T. Gates, *The Country School of To-Morrow,* Occasional Papers, no. 1 (New York: General Education Board, 1913).

35. Myron Lieberman, *Public Education: An Autopsy* (Cambridge, MA: Harvard University Press, 1993), 55, 220.

36. "Child Labor," History.com, 2009, http://www.history.com /topics/child-labor; "Keating-Owen Child Labor Act of 1916," U.S. National Archives and Records Administration, http://www.our documents.gov/doc.php?doc=59.

37. Samuel Bowles and Herbert Gintis, *Schooling in Capitalist America: Educational Reform and the Contradictions of Economic Life* (New York: Basic Books, 1976); William L. Ewens, *Becoming Free: The Struggle for Human Development* (Wilmington, DE: Scholarly Resources, 1984), 159.

38. Paul Violas, *The Training of the Urban Working Class: A History of Twentieth Century American Education* (Chicago: Rand McNally, 1978), 142.

39. William T. Harris, Annual Report of the Superintendent, "Seventeenth Annual Report of the Board of Directors of the St. Louis Public Schools for the Year Ending August 1, 1871," St. Louis Board of Education, 1872.

40. Violas, *The Training of the Urban Working Class,* 12.

41. Michael Katz, *Class, Bureaucracy, and Schools: The Illusion of Educational Change in America* (New York: Praeger, 1971), 164.

42. John Holt, "Deschooling Society," *Reason,* April 1971.

43. Amy Byrnes, "November Is the Cruelest Month for Moms," *My Name Is Amy,* November 4, 2013, http://amynameisamy.com /november-is-the-cruelest-month-for-moms/.

44. John Holt, *Escape from Childhood: The Needs and Rights of Children* (New York: Dutton, 1974), 241–42.

45. Keith Farnish, *Underminers: A Guide to Subverting the Machine* (Gabriola Island, BC, Canada: New Society Publishers, 2013), 42.

46. George Dennison, *The Lives of Children: The Story of the First Street School* (New York: Random House, 1969).

47. Cevin Soling, "Santorum and Harvard Anarchist Agree: Public Schools Must Be Abolished," *Forbes,* February 27, 2012, http:// www.forbes.com/sites/jamesmarshallcrotty/2012/02/27/why-public -schools-must-be-abolished/.

48. Dennison, *The Lives of Children.*

49. Brian Jacob and Lars Lefgren, "Are Idle Hands the Devil's Work-shop? Incapacitation, Concentration and Juvenile Crime," NBER Working Paper no. 9653, National Bureau of Economic Research, April 2003.

50. Zachariah Montgomery, *Poison Drops in the Federal Senate: The School Question from a Parental and Non-Sectarian Stand-Point* (Washington, D.C.: Gibson Bros, 1885), 30.

51. Matt Hern, *Field Day: Getting Society Out of School* (Vancouver: New Star Books, 2003), 205.

CHAPTER 3

1. Carol Black, "Occupy Your Brain," *Schooling the World,* http://schoolingtheworld.org/occupy-your-brain/.

2. "Bush Signs Education Bill," CBS News, January 8, 2002; Steve Kemme and Sue Kiesewetter, "Bush Signs School Bill in Hamilton," *Cincinnati Enquirer,* January 9, 2002; George W. Bush, "Remarks on Signing the No Child Left Behind Act of 2001 in Hamilton, Ohio," January 8, 2002, in *Public Papers of the President of the United States, George W. Bush, January 1 to June 30, 2002, Book 1* (Washington, D.C.: U.S. Government Printing Office, 2005), 23–26; "Promise of No Child Left Behind Falls Short After 10 Years," *USA Today,* January 7, 2012.

3. Jason Stanford, "Bush's 'Texas Miracle' Debunked, Lone Star State Sparks Anti-Testing Revolution," MSNBC, February 18, 2013, http://www.msnbc.com/msnbc/bushs-texas-miracle-debunked-lone-star-st; Diana Jean Schemo and Ford Fessenden, "A Miracle Revisited: Measuring Success; Gains in Houston Schools: How Real Are They?" *New York Times,* December 3, 2003; Rebecca Leung, "The 'Texas Miracle,'" CBS News, January 6, 2004.

4. Sam Dillon, "Failure Rate of Schools Overstated, Study Says," *New York Times,* December 15, 2011.

5. Claudia Wallis and Sonja Steptoe, "How to Fix No Child Left Behind," *Time,* May 24, 2007.

6. Alexis de Tocqueville, *Democracy in America* (New York: Pratt, Woodford, 1848), 323–25, via: Williamson Evers, "Obama Should Heed Tocqueville on Schools," *Education Next,* October 20, 2011.

7. Cevin Soling, Talk at the Conference on Alternatives to Education, Harvard Graduate School of Education, April 27, 2013, https://www.youtube.com/watch?v=c1nJ-tI-vew.

8. Author interview with Simon Hauger.

9. Caroline Porter, "Group Will Rethink School Testing," *Wall Street Journal*, October 15, 2014.

10. Alfie Kohn, "Standardized Testing and Its Victims," *Education Week*, September 27, 2000.

11. Andrew Ujifusa, "Standardized Testing Costs States $1.7 Billion a Year, Study Says," *Education Week*, November 29, 2012.

12. Laura McKenna, "What Happens When Students Boycott a Standardized Test?" *The Atlantic*, April 9, 2015; Elizabeth A. Harris, "20% of New York State Students Opt Out of Standardized Tests This Year," *New York Times*, August 12, 2015.

13. John Taylor Gatto, "Against School," *Harper's Magazine*, September 2003.

14. Nikhil Goyal, "Sunday Dialogue: Transforming Our Schools," *New York Times*, October 13, 2012.

15. "Educating for the 21st Century: Data Report on the New York Performance Standards Consortium," New York Performance Standards Consortium (2012).

16. I was introduced to scientific management by this article: Shawn Gude, "The Industrial Classroom," *Jacobin*, April 2013.

17. James Hoopes, *False Prophets: The Gurus Who Created Modern Management and Why Their Ideas Are Bad for Business Today* (New York: Basic Books, 2003), 58; Raymond E. Callahan, *Education and the Cult of Efficiency: A Study of the Social Forces That Have Shaped the Administration of the Public Schools* (Chicago: University of Chicago Press, 1962), 20.

18. Robert Kanigel, *The One Best Way: Frederick Winslow Taylor and the Enigma of Efficiency* (New York: Viking Penguin, 1997), 377.

19. Frederick Winslow Taylor, *The Principles of Scientific Management* (New York: Harper & Brothers, 1911), 7.

20. Ibid, 36–37.

21. Neil Postman, *Technopoly: The Surrender of Culture to Technology* (New York: Vintage, 1993), 51.

22. Matthew Stewart, "The Management Myth," *Atlantic Monthly*, June 2006.

23. Jill Lepore, "The History of Management Consulting," *New Yorker*, October 12, 2009.

24. Taylor, *The Principles of Scientific Management*, 44–45.

25. Lepore, "The History of Management Consulting."

26. Taylor, *The Principles of Scientific Management*, 62.

27. C. B. Thompson, *The Theory and Practice of Scientific Management* (Boston: Houghton Mifflin, 1917), 37.

28. Alan M. Ball, *Imagining America: Influence and Images in Twentieth-Century Russia* (Lanham, MD: Roman & Littlefield, 2003), 27.

29. Christopher Lehmann-Haupt, "The Man Who Invented American Efficiency," *New York Times,* August 11, 1997.

30. Callahan, *Education and the Cult of Efficiency,* 244.

31. Ibid, 246.

32. Callahan, *Education and the Cult of Efficiency,* 54–55.

33. Ibid, 69.

34. Ibid, 91.

35. Ellwood P. Cubberley, *Public School Administration: A Statement of the Fundamental Principles Underlying the Organization and Administration of Public Education* (Boston: Houghton Mifflin, 1916), 338.

36. The Broad Foundation, "The Broad Foundation 2009–2010 Annual Report."

37. Nikhil Goyal, "American Students Deserve Better Than Arne Duncan," MSNBC, November 22, 2012, http://www.msnbc.com/melissa-harris-perry/american-students-deserve-better-arne-du.

38. Michael A. Fletcher and Nick Anderson, "Obama Angers Union Officials with Remarks in Support of R.I. Teacher Firings," *Washington Post,* March 2, 2010.

39. Amanda Paulson and Stacy Teicher Khadaroo, "Education Secretary Arne Duncan: Headmaster of US School Reform," *Christian Science Monitor,* August 30, 2010.

40. Sam Dillon, "Report Questions Duncan's Policy of Closing Failing Schools," *New York Times,* October 28, 2009.

41. Bob Simpson, "Why Is Corporate America Fanning the Flames of Violence in Chicago?" *Daily Kos,* May 7, 2013, http://www.dailykos.com/story/2013/05/07/1207479/-Why-is-Corporate-America-fanning-the-flames-of-violence-in-Chicago.

42. Juan Gonzalez, "Albany Charter Cash Cow: Big Banks Making a Bundle on New Construction as Schools Bear the Cost," *New York Daily News,* May 6, 2010.

43. Joanne Barkan, "Got Dough? How Billionaires Rule Our Schools," *Dissent Magazine,* Winter 2011.

44. Dan Goldhaber, "The Mystery of Good Teaching," *Education Next* 2, no. 1 (Spring 2002).

45. UNICEF Office of Research, "Child Well-Being in Rich Countries: A Comparative Overview," *Innocenti Report Card* 11 (2013).

46. Michael Harrington, *The Other America: Poverty in the United States* (New York: Macmillan, 1962), 14–15.

47. Brady Dennis, "Poverty Strains Cognitive Abilities, Opening Door for Bad Decision-Making, New Study Finds," *Washington Post*, August 29, 2013.

48. Javier C. Hernandez, "Mayoral Candidates See Cincinnati as a Model for New York Schools," *New York Times*, August 11, 2013.

49. Harrington, *The Other America*, 17.

50. Naomi Klein, *The Shock Doctrine: The Rise of Disaster Capitalism* (New York: Picador, 2008), 7.

51. Jon Hurdle, "Philadelphia Officials Vote to Close 23 Schools," *New York Times*, March 7, 2013; Dale Mezzacappa, "District Lays Off More Than 3,700 Employees," *Philadelphia Public School Notebook*, June 7, 2013.

52. Paul Socolar, "Proposed Closings Hit Black Students Most," *Philadelphia Public School Notebook*, January 10, 2013; Rania Khalek, "The 'Systematic Murder' of Philadelphia Public Schools," *Truthout*, September 12, 2013.

53. Benjamin Herold, "$139 Million: Cost of Charter Expansion So Far," *Philadelphia Public School Notebook*, July 19, 2012.

54. Benjamin Herold, "Across Philadelphia, Strong Reactions to School-Closing Plan," *Philadelphia Public School Notebook*, December 13, 2012.

55. "Investigating Charter Schools Fraud in Philadelphia," *Fresh Air*, NPR, June 27, 2011.

56. Lauren FitzPatrick, "Audit Shows CPS with Unexpected $344 Million—Union Calls It Surplus, CPS Says It's Not," *Chicago Sun-Times*, January 28, 2013.

57. Fran Spielman, "DePaul Arena Plan Advances with a Change to Keep Alderman Happy," *Chicago Sun-Times*, March 4, 2014; Ben Joravsky, "Who Wins and Loses in Rahm's TIF Game?" *Chicago Reader*, March 26, 2015.

58. Michael Tarm, "Expert: Chicago School Closings Will Endanger Kids," Associated Press, July 17, 2013.

59. Becky Vevea and Linda Lutton, "Fact Check: Chicago School Closings," WBEZ, May 16, 2013.

60. Lauren FitzPatrick and Art Golab, "Black Students Most Likely to Have Their School on CPS Closure List," *Chicago Sun-Times*, March 6, 2013.

61. Lauren FitzPatrick, "CPS Calls Teacher's Mom to Tell Him He's Getting Laid Off," *Chicago Sun-Times*, July 19, 2013.

62. Rick Perlstein, "Chicago Rising!" *The Nation*, July 22–29, 2013.

63. Elaine Weiss and Don Long, "Market-Oriented Education Reforms'

Rhetoric Trumps Reality," Broader, Bolder Approach to Education (April 18, 2013).

64. Diane Ravitch, *Reign of Error: The Hoax of the Privatization Movement and the Danger to America's Public Schools* (New York: Knopf, 2013), 31.

65. Jack Whelan, "Can Humanism Prevail Over the Technocracy?" *Education Week,* April 27, 2013, http://blogs.edweek.org/teachers/living -in-dialogue/2013/04/jack_whelan_can_humanism_preva.html.

66. Paulo Freire, *Pedagogy of the Oppressed* (New York: Herder & Herder, 1970).

CHAPTER 4

1. "New Study Reveals Most Children Unrepentant Sociopaths," *The Onion,* December 7, 2009, http://www.theonion.com/articles/new -study-reveals-most-children-unrepentant-sociop,2870/.

2. Paul Bloom, "The Moral Life of Babies," *New York Times Magazine,* May 5, 2010.

3. Ibid.

4. Alison Gopnik, *The Philosophical Baby: What Children's Minds Tell Us About Truth, Love, and the Meaning of Life* (New York: Farrar, Straus and Giroux, 2009), 5, 125.

5. Valentina Doria et al., "Emergence of Resting State Networks in the Preterm Human Brain," *Proceedings of the National Academy of Sciences* 107, no. 46 (2010); Francisca Ortega, "Babies' Brains May Be Capable of Introspection and Daydreams," *Houston Chronicle,* November 2, 2010.

6. Andrew N. Meltzoff and M. Keith Moore, "Imitation of Facial and Manual Gestures by Human Neonates," *Science* 198, no. 4312 (October 1977): 75–78.

7. Faraz Farzin, Chuan Hou, and Anthony Norcia, "Piecing It Together: Infants' Neural Responses to Face and Object Structure," *Journal of Vision* 12, no. 13 (2012).

8. Olivier Pascalis, Michelle de Haan, and Charles A. Nelson, "Is Face Processing Species-Specific During the First Year of Life?" *Science* 296, no. 5571 (2002); Jason Goldman, " 'Blooming, Buzzing Confusion'—But Who Is Confused?" *Scientific American,* July 26, 2012.

9. "Babies' Brains Tuned to Sharing Attention with Others," *ScienceDaily,* January 27, 2010, http://www.sciencedaily.com /releases/2010/01/100126220331.htm.

10. Fei Xu and Vashti Garcia, "Intuitive Statistics by 8-Month-Old Infants," *Proceedings of the National Academy of Sciences* 105, no. 13 (2008): 5012–15; Alison Gopnik, "Your Baby Is Smarter Than You Think," *New York Times,* August 15, 2009.

11. "Language Learning Begins in Utero, Study Finds; Newborn Memories of Oohs and Ahs Heard in the Womb," *Science-Daily,* January 2, 2013, http://www.sciencedaily.com/releases/2013/01/130102083615.htm.

12. Gary Marcus, "How Birds and Babies Learn to Talk," *New Yorker,* March 29, 2013.

13. John Holt, *How Children Fail* (New York: Pitman, 1964), 167.

14. George Dennison, *The Lives of Children: The Story of the First Street School* (New York: Random House, 1969), 83–84.

15. Quoting Gopnik's phrasing of the quote in *The Philosophical Baby,* 106.

16. Author interview with Gever Tulley.

17. Gever Tulley, "The Path to Brightworks," TEDxBloomington, May 14, 2011, https://www.youtube.com/watch?v=N4glAzO1sD4.

18. Ellen Key, *The Century of the Child* (New York: Putnam, 1909), 203–204.

19. Wendy Priesnitz, *Beyond School: Living as if School Doesn't Exist* (Toronto: Natural Life Books, 2012), 59.

20. Daniel Greenberg, *The Crisis in American Education: An Analysis and a Proposal* (Framingham, MA: Sudbury Valley School Press, 1970), 57, 61–62.

21. National Education Association, *Report of the Committee of Ten on Secondary School Studies with the Reports of the Conferences Arranged by the Committee* (New York: American Book Company, 1894); Diane Ravitch, *Left Back: A Century of Failed School Reforms* (New York: Simon & Schuster, 2000), 41–50.

22. William Upski Wimsatt, *No More Prisons: Urban Life, Home-schooling, Hip-Hop Leadership, the Cool Rich Kids Movement, a Hitchhiker's Guide to Community Organizing, and Why Philanthropy Is the Greatest Art Form of the 21st Century!* (New York: Soft Skull Press, 1999), 60.

23. John Holt, "Deschooling Society," *Reason,* April 1971.

24. Josh Mitchell, "Remedial Courses in College Stir Questions Over Cost, Effectiveness," *Wall Street Journal,* November 17, 2014.

25. "Bloom's Taxonomy," Whitman School of Management at Syracuse University, http://whitman.syr.edu/wsmhelp/faculty-resources/instructional-design-delivery/teaching-pedagogy/blooms

-taxonomy.aspx; "Bloom's Digital Taxonomy," Educational Origami, http://edorigami.wikispaces.com/Bloom%27s+Digital + Taxonomy; Lorin W. Anderson, David R. Krathwohl, et al., eds., *A Taxonomy for Learning, Teaching, and Assessing: A Revision of Bloom's Taxonomy of Educational Objectives* (New York: Longman, 2001).

26. John Holt, *Escape from Childhood: The Needs and Rights of Children* (Boston: Dutton, 1974), 240.

27. Edward L. Deci, Allan J. Schwartz, Louise Sheinman, and Richard M. Ryan, "An Instrument to Assess Adults' Orientations Toward Control Versus Autonomy with Children: Reflections on Intrinsic Motivation and Perceived Competence," *Journal of Educational Psychology* 73, no. 5 (October 1981): 642–50; Todd M. Gureckis and Douglas B. Markant, "Self-Directed Learning: A Cognitive and Computational Perspective," *Perspectives on Psychological Science* 7, no. 5 (2012).

28. Herbert D. Williams, "Experiment in Self-Directed Education," *School and Society* 31 (1930): 715–18; Carl Rogers, *Freedom to Learn* (Columbus, OH: Charles E. Merrill, 1969).

29. Alfie Kohn, "Choices for Children: Why and How to Let Students Decide," *Phi Delta Kappan,* September 1993.

30. Alexander Sutherland Neill, *Summerhill: A Radical Approach to Child Rearing* (New York: Hart Publishing, 1960), 123.

CHAPTER 5

1. Michelle M. Chouinard, "Children's Questions: A Mechanism for Cognitive Development," *Monographs of the Society for Research in Child Development* 72, no. 1 (2007).

2. "Capitalizing on Complexity: Insights from the 2010 IBM Global CEO Study," IBM (2010).

3. George Land and Beth Jarman, *Breakpoint and Beyond: Mastering the Future Today* (New York: Harper Business, 1992).

4. Beth Hennessey and Teresa Amabile, *Creativity and Learning* (Washington, D.C.: National Education Association, 1987), via Chris Mercogliano, *In Defense of Childhood: Protecting Kids' Inner Wildness* (Boston: Beacon Press, 2007), 68–69.

5. Erik L. Westby and V. L. Dawson, "Creativity: Asset or Burden in the Classroom?" *Creativity Research Journal* 8, no. 1 (1995).

6. Andrew Reiner, "Believing Self-Control Predicts Success, Schools Teach Coping," *Washington Post Magazine,* April 11, 2013.

7. Kate Taylor, "At Success Academy Charter Schools, High Scores and Polarizing Tactics," *New York Times*, April 6, 2015.

8. John Holt, *How Children Fail* (New York: Pitman, 1964), 136.

9. Alfie Kohn, "How Not to Teach Values," *Phi Delta Kappan*, February 1997.

10. Bruno Bettelheim, "The Importance of Play," *Atlantic Monthly*, March 1987.

11. Stuart Brown, *Play: How It Shapes the Brain, Opens the Imagination, and Invigorates the Soul* (New York: Avery, 2009), 60.

12. J. Madeleine Nash, "Fertile Minds," *Time*, February 3, 1997.

13. Brown, *Play*, 89.

14. Jerome Bruner, "Play, Thought, and Language," *Peabody Journal of Education* 60, no. 3 (1983): 60–69.

15. Lawrence J. Schweinhart and David P. Weikart, "The HighScope Preschool Curriculum Comparison Study Through Age 23," *Early Childhood Research Quarterly* 12 (1997): 117–43.

16. Brown, *Play*, 108.

17. James Herndon, *How to Survive in Your Native Land* (New York: Simon & Schuster, 1971), 116.

18. Lenore Skenazy, "Why I Let My 9-Year-Old Ride the Subway Alone," *New York Sun*, April 1, 2008.

19. Howard P. Chudacoff, *Children at Play: An American History* (New York: New York University Press, 2008), 18.

20. Michael Chabon, "Manhood for Amateurs: The Wilderness of Childhood," *New York Review of Books*, July 16, 2009.

21. Jennifer Senior, "Little Grown-ups and Their Progeny," *New York Magazine*, March 31, 2013.

22. Dorothy G. Singer, Jerome L. Singer, Heidi D'Agostino, and Raeka DeLong, "Children's Pastimes and Play in Sixteen Nations: Is Free-Play Declining?" *American Journal of Play* 1, no. 3 (2009).

23. Hillary L. Burdette and Robert C. Whitaker, "Resurrecting Free Play in Young Children: Looking Beyond Fitness and Fatness to Attention, Affiliation, and Affect," *Archives of Pediatrics & Adolescent Medicine* 159, no. 1 (2005).

24. David Elkind, *The Power of Play: Learning What Comes Naturally* (Cambridge, MA: De Capo Press, 2007), ix.

25. Peter Gray, *Free to Learn: Why Unleashing the Instinct to Play Will Make Our Children Happier, More Self-Reliant, and Better Students for Life* (New York: Basic Books, 2013), 7.

26. Mary Ann Pulaski, "Toys and Imaginative Play," in Jerome Singer,

The Child's World of Make-Believe (New York: Academic Press, 1973), 84.

27. Martin DiCaro, "Why So Few Walk or Bike to School," WAMU, May 11, 2012.

28. Pooja S. Tandon, Chuan Zhou, and Dimitri A. Christakis, "Frequency of Parent-Supervised Outdoor Play of US Preschool-Aged Children," *Archives of Pediatrics & Adolescent Medicine* 166, no. 8 (2012): 707–12.

29. Richard Louv, "Leave No Child Inside," *Orion Magazine*, March/April 2007.

30. "Childhood and Nature: A Survey on Changing Relationships with Nature Across Generations," Natural England, March 2009.

31. "Over-Cautious Parents Stop Play," BBC News, August 4, 2008.

32. Katherine Ozment, "Welcome to the Age of Overparenting," *Boston Magazine,* December 2011.

33. Roger Mackett, "Children's Independent Movement in the Local Environment," *Built Environment* 33, no. 4 (2007).

34. Scott Stossel, "The Man Who Counts the Killings," *Atlantic Monthly,* May 1997.

35. Myrna Oliver, "George Gerbner, 86; Educator Researched the Influence of TV Viewing on Perceptions," *Los Angeles Times,* December 29, 2005.

36. Daniel B. Wood, "US Crime Rate at Lowest Point in Decades. Why America Is Safer Now," *Christian Science Monitor,* January 9, 2012.

37. Christopher Beam, "800,000 Missing Kids? Really?" *Slate,* January 17, 2007, http://www.slate.com/articles/news_and_politics/explainer/2007/01/800000_missing_kids_really.html.

38. Warwick Cairns, *How to Live Dangerously: Why We Should All Stop Worrying and Start Living* (New York: St. Martin's Griffin, 2009), 45.

39. Chabon, "Manhood for Amateurs: The Wilderness of Childhood."

CHAPTER 6

1. Alexander Sutherland Neill, *Summerhill: A Radical Approach to Child Rearing* (New York: Hart Publishing, 1960), 8.

2. "Summerhill General Policy Statement," Summerhill School, http://www.summerhillschool.co.uk/policy-general.php.

3. Ron Miller, *Free Schools, Free People: Education and Democracy After the 1960s* (Albany: State University of New York Press, 2002), 46.

4. Ibid, 121.

5. "Progressives' Progress," *Time*, October 31, 1938.

6. David Labaree, *Someone Has to Fail: The Zero-Sum Game of Public Schooling* (Cambridge, MA: Harvard University Press, 2010), 139.

7. Eliot Fremont-Smith, "Scared-Eyed in the Classroom," *New York Times*, July 26, 1965.

8. Jonathan Kozol, *Free Schools* (Boston: Houghton Mifflin, 1972), 11.

9. George Dennison, *The Lives of Children: The Story of the First Street School* (New York: Random House, 1969), 98.

10. Daniel Greenberg, "Assuming Excellence: The Key to the Sudbury Valley Experience," Sudbury Valley School, April 2013, http://www.sudval.org/essays/042013.shtml.

11. Ibid.

12. David Ruenzel, "Classless Society," *Education Week*, January 1, 1994.

13. Daniel Greenberg, *Announcing a New School: A Personal Account of the Beginnings of the Sudbury Valley School* (Framingham, MA: The Sudbury Valley School Press, 1973), 6.

14. Ibid, 262.

15. Yaacov Hecht, *Democratic Education: A Beginning of a Story* (Roslyn Heights, NY: Alternative Education Resource Organization, 2011), 34.

16. Neill, *Summerhill*, 40.

17. "Alumni Say," Sudbury Valley School, http://www.sudval.com/01_abou_08.html.

18. Aaron Gell, "Land of the Free," *New York Times*, May 7, 2006.

19. Hecht, *Democratic Education*, 146–54.

20. Comment on Dayna Martin's Facebook post on July 20, 2014, https://www.facebook.com/DaynaMartin/posts/10152514730133070. Quoted with her permission.

21. Daniel Greenberg, *Free at Last: The Sudbury Valley School* (Framingham, MA: The Sudbury Valley School Press, 1995), 19–21.

22. Author interviews with Jeff Collins.

23. Horace Mann, *Mr. Mann's Seventh Annual Report: Education in Europe* (Boston: Massachusetts Board of Education, 1844), 115–16.

24. Catherine Reef, *Education and Learning in America* (New York: Facts on File, 2008), 35.

25. Frederic Burk, *Lock-Step Schooling and a Remedy: The Fundamental Evils and Handicaps of Class Instruction; and a Report of Progress in the Construction of an Individual System* (Sacramento,

CA: F. W. Richardson, Superintendent of State Printing, 1913), 7, 10–11.

26. Joseph Kett, *Rites of Passage: Adolescence in America, 1790 to the Present* (New York: Basic Books, 1977), 3, 36.

27. Quentin J. Schultze et al., *Dancing in the Dark: Youth, Popular Culture, and Electronic Media* (Grand Rapids, MI: William B. Eerdmans, 1991), 9.

28. Peter Gray and Jay Feldman, "Patterns of Age Mixing and Gender Mixing Among Children and Adolescents at an Ungraded Democratic School," *Merrill-Palmer Quarterly* 43, no. 1 (1997); quote from Peter Gray, "The Special Value of Children's Age-Mixed Play," *American Journal of Play* 3, no. 4 (2011).

29. Gray, "The Special Value of Children's Age-Mixed Play."

30. John Taylor Gatto, *Weapons of Mass Instruction: A School-teacher's Journey Through the Dark World of Compulsory Schooling* (Gabriola Island, BC, Canada: New Society Publishers, 2010), 152.

31. Peter Gray, "Children Teach Themselves to Read," *Psychology Today,* February 24, 2010, http://www.psychologytoday.com/blog /freedom-learn/201002/children-teach-themselves-read.

32. Paul Goodman, *New Reformation: Notes of a Neolithic Conservative* (New York: Random House, 1970), 107.

33. Daniel Schugurensky, *Paulo Freire* (London: Bloomsbury Academic, 2011), 21.

34. "Kids and Family Reading Report: 5th Edition," Scholastic (2015).

35. Greenberg, *Free at Last,* 15–17.

36. L. P. Benezet, "The Teaching of Arithmetic I: The Story of an Experiment," *Journal of the National Education Association* 24, no. 8 (1935).

37. Hecht, *Democratic Education,* 84.

38. Hanna Greenberg et al., *The Sudbury Valley Experience* (Framingham, MA: Sudbury Valley School Press, 1992), 178.

39. Peter Gray, "Children Educate Themselves IV: Lessons from Sudbury Valley," *Psychology Today,* August 13, 2008, http://www .psychologytoday.com/blog/freedom-learn/200808/children-educate -themselves-iv-lessons-sudbury-valley.

40. David Kirp, "Make School a Democracy," *New York Times,* February 28, 2015.

41. Marilyn Blight, "The Hanover High School Council," *Democracy & Education* 10, no. 3 (Spring/Summer 1996).

42. Author interview with Kelsey Smith.

43. Rick Posner, *Lives of Passion, School of Hope: How One Public School Ignites a Lifelong Love of Learning* (Boulder, CO: Sentient Publications, 2009), 63, 86.

44. Author interviews with Brooke Newman.

45. Peter Gray and David Chanoff, "Democratic Schooling: What Happens to Young People Who Have Charge of Their Own Education?" *American Journal of Education* 94, no. 2 (1986).

46. Daniel Greenberg, Mimsy Sadofsky, and Jason Lempka, *The Pursuit of Happiness: The Lives of Sudbury Valley Alumni* (Framingham, MA: Sudbury Valley School Press, 2005).

47. Corey Lee M. Keyes, "Mental Illness and/or Mental Health? Investigating Axioms of the Complete State Model of Health," *Journal of Consulting and Clinical Psychology* 73, no. 3 (2005): 539–48.

48. Tom Rath and Jim Harter, "Your Career Wellbeing and Your Identity," Gallup, July 22, 2010.

49. Neill, *Summerhill*, 100.

50. Diane Ravitch, *Left Back: A Century of Failed School Reforms* (New York: Simon & Schuster, 2000), 393.

51. R. I. M. Dunbar, "Coevolution of Neocortical Size, Group Size, and Language in Humans," *Behavioral and Brain Sciences* 16, no. 4 (Fall 1993).

52. Amber Noel, Patrick Stark, and Jeremy Redford, "Parent and Family Involvement in Education, from the National Household Education Surveys Program of 2012," U.S. Department of Education, National Center for Education Statistics, 2013.

53. Lisa Miller, "Homeschooling, City-Style," *New York*, October 14, 2012.

54. Author interview with Jude Steffers-Wilson.

55. Patrick Farenga, "What Is Unschooling?" http://www.holtgws.com/whatisunschoolin.html.

56. Lynn O'Shaughnessy, "Can Homeschoolers Do Well in College?" CBS News, July 20, 2010.

57. Beth Calvano, "Homeschoolers: Colleges and Universities are Looking for You!" *Examiner.com*, http://www.examiner.com/article/homeschoolers-colleges-and-universities-are-looking-for-you.

CHAPTER 7

1. Priya Ganapati, "March 5, 1975: A Whiff of Homebrew Excites the Valley," *Wired*, March 5, 2009.

2. Stephen Wozniak, "Homebrew and How the Apple Came to Be," AtariArchives.org, http://www.atariarchives.org/deli/homebrew _and_how_the_apple.php.

3. Here are two interesting critiques of the maker movement: Evgeny Morozov, "Making It," *New Yorker,* January 13, 2014; Andrew Leonard, "Evgeny Morozov's *New Yorker* Put-Down of the Maker Movement Misses the Point," *Salon,* January 7, 2014.

4. Chris Anderson, *Makers: The New Industrial Revolution* (New York: Crown Business, 2012), 21.

5. Noe Tanigawa, "Unleash Your Inner Maker," Hawaii Public Radio, May 10, 2013, http://www.hawaiipublicradio.org/content/unleash -your-inner-maker.

6. Author interview with Dale Dougherty.

7. "Photos: The Six Wonders of Obama's 'Maker Faire' Tour," *Wall Street Journal,* June 18, 2014, http://blogs.wsj.com/wash wire/2014/06/18/photos-the-six-wonders-of-obamas-maker-faire -tour/.

8. Author interview with Sandra Richter.

9. Author interview with Partha Unnava.

10. Katrina Schwartz, "Can the Maker Movement Infiltrate Mainstream Classrooms?" *KQED MindShift,* July 2, 2014, http://blogs .kqed.org/mindshift/2014/07/can-the-maker-movement-infiltrate -mainstream-classrooms/.

11. Author interview with Steve Davee.

12. "Maker Ed Places 108 Corps Members in Maker Movement Organizations," Maker Education Initiative, June 11, 2013, http:// makered.org/maker-ed-places-108-corps-members-in-maker -movement-organizations/.

13. "Why Teachers Should Put Students to Work," *The Next List,* CNN, July 1, 2012, http://edition.cnn.com/TRANSCRIPTS/1207/01 /nl.01.html.

14. "Harkness History," Phillips Exeter Academy, http://www.exeter .edu/admissions/109_1220_11688.aspx.

CHAPTER 8

1. Matt Assad, "Lehigh University Campus to Become 'Invention Incubator,'" *The Morning Call,* October 16, 2013; Richard Pérez-Peña, "A Classroom Leaves the Syllabus to the Students," *New York Times,* July 18, 2014.

2. National Survey of Student Engagement, "Bringing the Institution

into Focus—Annual Results 2014," Indiana University Center for Postsecondary Research (2014).

3. "About Co-operative Education," University of Waterloo, https://uwaterloo.ca/co-operative-education/about-co-operative -education.

4. Thomas Friedman, "Revolution Hits the Universities," *New York Times,* January 26, 2013.

5. Laura Pappano, "The Year of the MOOC," *New York Times,* November 2, 2012.

6. Stephen Downes, "Access2OER: The CCK08 Solution," *Half an Hour,* February 16, 2009, http://halfanhour.blogspot.com/2009/02 /access2oer-cck08-solution.html.

7. Ian Bogost, "The Rhetoric of MOOCs," July 23, 2012, http:// bogost.com/writing/blog/mooc_rhetoric/.

8. Laura Perna and Alan Ruby, "The Life Cycle of a Million MOOC Users," University of Pennsylvania Graduate School of Education, December 2013, http://www.gse.upenn.edu/pdf/ahead/perna _ruby_boruch_moocs_dec2013.pdf.

9. Editorial, "The Trouble with Online College," *New York Times,* February 18, 2013.

10. Di Xu and Shanna Smith Jaggars, "Adaptability to Online Learning: Differences Across Types of Students and Academic Subject Areas," Community College Research Center Working Paper, Teachers College, Columbia University, no. 54 (February 2013).

11. Ry Rivard, "Udacity Project on 'Pause,'" *Inside Higher Ed,* July 18, 2013, https://www.insidehighered.com/news/2013/07/18/citing -disappointing-student-outcomes-san-jose-state-pauses-work-udacity.

12. Katy Murphy, "San Jose State's Online College Course Experiment Reveals Hidden Costs," *San Jose Mercury News,* June 2, 2013.

13. Max Chafkin, "Udacity's Sebastian Thrun, Godfather of Free Online Education, Changes Course," *Fast Company,* November 14, 2013.

14. Gayle Christensen, Andrew Steinmetz, Brandon Alcorn, et al., "The MOOC Phenomenon: Who Takes Massive Open Online Courses and Why?" University of Pennsylvania (November 6, 2013), http:// papers.ssrn.com/sol3/papers.cfm?abstract_id=2350964.

15. Gianpiero Petriglieri, "Let Them Eat MOOCs," *Harvard Business Review,* October 9, 2013, http://blogs.hbr.org/2013/10/let-them -eat-moocs/.

16. Suli Breaks, "Why I Hate School But Love Education," December 2, 2012, https://www.youtube.com/watch?v=y_ZmM7zPLyI.

17. Sarah Kendzior, "College Is a Promise the Economy Does Not Keep," Al Jazeera English, May 14, 2014, http://www.aljazeera.com /indepth/opinion/2014/05/collegepromise-economy-does-no-2014 51411124734124.html.

18. Rory O'Sullivan, Konrad Mugglestone, and Tom Allison, "Closing the Race Gap: Alleviating Young African American Unemployment Through Education," Young Invincibles (June 2014).

19. Sarah Buhr, "Is the Thiel Fellowship Program Really Just a Sabbatical from College?" *TechCrunch,* July 8, 2014, http://techcrunch .com/2014/07/08/nearly-half-the-thiel-fellows-plan-on-returning-to -school/.

20. Amanda M. Fairbanks, "Peter Thiel Awards $100,000 to Entrepreneurs Under 20," *Huffington Post,* May 25, 2011, http://www .huffingtonpost.com/2011/05/25/peter-thiel-fellowship_n_867134 .html.

21. Gregory Ferenstein, "Thiel Fellows Program Is 'Most Misdirected Piece of Philanthropy,' Says Larry Summers," *TechCrunch,* October 10, 2013, http://techcrunch.com/2013/10/10/thiel-fellows -program-is-most-misdirected-piece-of-philanthropy-says-larry -summers/.

22. Vivek Wadhwa, "Peter Thiel Promised Flying Cars; We Got Caffeine Spray Instead," *VentureBeat,* September 11, 2013, http://venture beat.com/2013/09/11/peter-thiel-promised-flying-cars-instead-we -got-caffeine-spray/.

23. A. W. Cissel, "The Apprentices," *Thurmont Scrapbook,* Greater Emmitsburg Area Historical Society, http://www.emmitsburg.net /history_t/archives/people/apprentices.htm.

24. "Q & A: Colonial Apprenticeships," The Colonial Williamsburg Foundation, http://www.history.org/history/teaching/enewsletter /volume4/november05/apprenticeship.cfm.

25. Robert Greene, *Mastery* (New York: Viking, 2012), 59.

26. Nikhil Goyal, "In Defense of Skipping College and Enrolling in the Real World," *Forbes,* January 11, 2013, http://www.forbes.com /sites/carolinehoward/2013/01/11in-defense-of-skipping-college -and-enrolling-in-the-real-world/.

27. Robert I. Lerman, "Expanding Apprenticeship: A Way to Enhance Skills and Careers," Urban Institute (October 2010), http://www .urban.org/uploadedpdf/901384-Expanding-Apprenticeship.pdf.

28. Eric Westervelt, "The Secret to Germany's Low Youth Unemployment," *Morning Edition,* NPR, April 4, 2012.

29. Ibid.

30. Robert I. Lerman, "Training Tomorrow's Workforce: Community College and Apprenticeship as Collaborative Routes to Rewarding Careers," Center for American Progress, December 2009.

31. Robert I. Lerman, "The Youth Unemployment Crisis: A Fix That Works and Pays for Itself," *PBS NewsHour,* February 7, 2013, http://www.pbs.org/newshour/making-sense/the-youth-unemployment-crisis/.

32. Author interviews with Kane Sarhan and Shaila Ittycheria; Nikhil Goyal, "Can This New Nonprofit Make Apprenticeships Cool Again?" *GOOD Magazine,* October 20, 2012, http://magazine.good.is/articles/can-this-new-nonprofit-make-apprenticeships-cool-again.

33. Lisa de Moraes, "President Obama and Michelle Obama Stop by 'The View,'" *Washington Post,* September 25, 2012, http://www.washingtonpost.com/blogs/tv-column/post/president-obama-and-michelle-obama-stop-by-the-view/2012/09/25/4672e060-0720-11e2-afff-d6c7f20a83bf_blog.html.

34. Lauren Weber, "Kaplan to Buy Software-Development School Dev Bootcamp," *Wall Street Journal,* June 24, 2014.

35. Adam Bryant, "In Head-Hunting, Big Data May Not Be Such a Big Deal," *New York Times,* June 19, 2013.

36. Thomas Friedman, "How to Get a Job at Google," *New York Times,* February 22, 2014.

37. Gerald Jonas, "Ray Bradbury, Who Brought Mars to Earth with a Lyrical Mastery, Dies at 91," *New York Times,* June 6, 2012.

38. Ray Bradbury, "Speech at the National Book Awards Ceremony," November 15, 2000, http://www.nationalbook.org/nbaacceptspeech_rbradbury.html.

39. Sam Weller, *The Bradbury Chronicles: The Life of Ray Bradbury* (New York: William Morrow, 2005), 27–30.

40. Ken Kelley, "Playboy Interview: Ray Bradbury," *Playboy,* May 1996.

41. Maria Popova, "Ray Bradbury on Facing Rejection . . . and Being Inspired by Snoopy," *The Atlantic,* May 21, 2012.

42. Ray Bradbury, "In His Words," *Ray Bradbury's Blog,* December 2001, http://www.raybradbury.com/inhiswords02.html.

43. Weller, *The Bradbury Chronicles,* 82.

44. Ibid, 82–83.

45. Ibid, 91.

46. Ibid, 88.

47. Jonathan R. Eller, *Becoming Ray Bradbury* (Champaign: University of Illinois Press, 2013), 64.

48. Ray Bradbury, *Bradbury Stories: 100 of His Most Celebrated Tales* (New York: William Morrow, 2003), 739.

49. Jennifer Steinhauer, "A Literary Legend Fights for a Local Library," *New York Times,* June 19, 2009.

50. "Taxpayer Return on Investment in Florida Public Libraries," Haas Center for Business Research and Economic Development (2013), via David A. Graham, "Libraries Face Increasing Budget Cutbacks," *Newsweek,* August 23, 2010.

51. "American Experience. The Richest Man in the World: Andrew Carnegie," PBS, http://www.pbs.org/wgbh/amex/carnegie/film more/transcript/.

52. Andrew Carnegie, *The Autobiography of Andrew Carnegie and the Gospel of Wealth* (New York: Signet Classics, 2006), 44–45.

53. Ibid, 44–45, 57–58.

54. "Libraries," Carnegie Corporation of New York, http://carnegie .org/about-us/foundation-history/about-andrew-carnegie/carnegie -for-kids/libraries.

55. Lars Willnat and David H. Weaver, "The American Journalist in the Digital Age," Indiana University School of Journalism (2014), via Kendzior, "College Is a Promise the Economy Does Not Keep."

56. Author interview with Sarah Harvard.

57. Henry Blodget, "The Andrew Ross Sorkin Story," *Business Insider,* May 23, 2011, http://www.businessinsider.com/andrew-ross-sorkin -interview-too-big-to-fail-hbo-2011-5.

58. Jonathan Faust, "Q&A with Andrew Ross Sorkin," *SHS Maroon,* May 24, 2013, http://www.shsmaroon.org/qa-with-andrew-ross -sorkin/; Gabriel Sherman, "The Information Broker," *New York,* November 8, 2009.

59. Shefali Luthra, "Q&A with Andrew Ross Sorkin," *Brown Daily Herald,* December 5, 2011, http://www.browndailyherald .com/2011/12/05/qa-with-andrew-ross-sorkin/.

60. Michelle Spektor, "Sorkin Recounts How He Got His Start at *The New York Times*—at Age 18," *Cornell Chronicle,* October 25, 2010, http://chronicle.cornell.edu/stories/2010/10/sorkin-recounts -how-he-got-his-start-ny-times.

61. Monica Chon, "Q&A: Jon Steinberg '99, COO and President of BuzzFeed," *Daily Princetonian,* September 24, 2013, http://

dailyprincetonian.com/news/2013/09/qa-jon-steinberg-99-coo-and
-president-of-buzzfeed/.

62. Katherine Goldstein, "I've Read 500 Cover Letters for Entry-Level
Media Jobs," *Slate*, August 29, 2013, http://www.slate.com/articles
/ business/moneybox/2013/08/cover_letter_writing_advice_how
_to _write_a_cover_letter_for_an_entry_level.html.

63. Author interview with Ryan Holiday.

64. Ryan Holiday, "How Dropping Out of College Can Save Your Life,"
December 2, 2013, http://www.ryanholiday.net/how-dropping
-out-of-college-can-save-your-life-2/.

65. Ibid.

66. Author interview with Molly Crabapple.

67. Molly Crabapple, "Shooter Boys and At-Risk Girls," *VICE*, February 1, 2013, http://www.vice.com/read/shooter-boys-and-at-risk
-girls.

68. Jeremy Mercer, "Jeremy Mercer's Top 10 Bookshops," *The Guardian*, December 6, 2005.

69. Catherine Rampell, "It Takes a B.A. to Find a Job as a File Clerk,"
New York Times, February 19, 2013.

70. Ivan Illich, *Deschooling Society* (New York: Harper & Row,
1971), 11.

CHAPTER 9

1. John Holt, *Instead of Education: Ways to Help People Do Things
Better* (New York: Dutton, 1976), 8.

2. Ivan Illich, *Deschooling Society* (New York: Harper & Row, 1971),
2, 78–79.

3. Matthew Green, "London Cafes: The Surprising History of London's Lost Coffeehouses," *The Daily Telegraph*, March 20, 2012.

4. Markman Ellis, *The Coffee House: A Cultural History* (London:
Orion Publishing Group, 2004), 61.

5. Green, "London Cafes."

6. Tom Standage, "Social Networking in the 1600s," *New York
Times*, June 22, 2013.

7. Laura Boyle, "A Proper Cup of Coffee," Jane Austen, June 17, 2011,
http://www.janeausten.co.uk/a-proper-cup-of-coffee/.

8. Emily Appelbaum, "One Hundred Days of Spring: As Mid-Market
Talks, Two Organizers Do," *San Francisco Bay Guardian*, June 29,
2011.

9. "An Experiment: Philadelphia's 'School Without Walls,'" *Life,* May 16, 1969.

10. "The Parkway Experiment," *Time,* March 23, 1970.

11. John Bremer and Michael Von Moschzisker, *The School Without Walls, Philadelphia's Parkway Program* (New York: Holt, Rinehart and Winston, 1971), 111.

12. Author interview with Beth Swanson.

13. Author interview with Megan Cole.

14. "Mayor Emanuel Announces City of Learning Initiative to Continue Year-Round Momentum of Summer of Learning," *Open Badges Blog,* December 21, 2013, http://openbadges.tumblr.com /post/70674243477/mayor-emanuel-announces-city-of-learning -initiative-to.

15. "CSOL and Beyond: Reflections on the Chicago Summer of Learning," *Open Badges Blog,* October 15, 2013, http://openbadges .tumblr.com/post/64106438071/csol-and-beyond-reflections-on -the-chicago-summer-of.

16. Author interview with Sybil Madison-Boyd.

17. Michael Katz, *Class, Bureaucracy, and Schools: The Illusion of Educational Change in America* (New York: Praeger, 1971), xvi.

18. Allen Graubard, *Free the Children: Radical Reform and the Free School Movement* (New York: Pantheon, 1972), 260.

CONCLUSION

1. Jiddu Krishnamurti, *Education and the Significance of Life* (New York: Harper & Row, 1953), 16.

SELECTED BIBLIOGRAPHY

Alexander, Thomas. *The Prussian Elementary Schools*. New York: Macmillan, 1919.

Anderson, Chris. *Makers: The New Industrial Revolution*. New York: Crown Business, 2012.

Bazelon, Emily. *Sticks and Stones: Defeating the Culture of Bullying and Rediscovering the Power of Character and Empathy*. New York: Random House, 2013.

Bowles, Samuel, and Herbert Gintis. *Schooling in Capitalist America: Educational Reform and the Contradictions of Economic Life*. New York: Basic Books, 1976.

Bremer, John, and Michael Von Moschzisker. *The School Without Walls, Philadelphia's Parkway Program*. New York: Holt, Rinehart and Winston, 1971.

Brown, Stuart. *Play: How It Shapes the Brain, Opens the Imagination, and Invigorates the Soul*. New York: Avery, 2009.

Cairns, Warwick. *How to Live Dangerously: Why We Should All Stop Worrying and Start Living*. New York: St. Martin's Griffin, 2009.

Callahan, Raymond E. *Education and the Cult of Efficiency: A Study of the Social Forces That Have Shaped the Administration of the Public Schools*. Chicago: University of Chicago Press, 1962.

Chudacoff, Howard P. *Children at Play: An American History*. New York: New York University Press, 2008.

Couture, Laurie A. *Instead of Medicating and Punishing: Healing the*

Causes of Our Children's Acting-Out Behavior by Parenting and Educating the Way Nature Intended. Deadwood, OR: Wyatt-MacKenzie Publishing, 2008.

Cremin, Lawrence A. *American Education: The Colonial Experience, 1607–1783*. New York: Harper & Row, 1970.

Csikszentmihalyi, Mihaly, and Barbara Schneider. *Becoming Adult: How Teenagers Prepare for the World of Work*. New York: Basic Books, 2000.

Cubberley, Ellwood P. *Public Education in the United States: A Study and Interpretation of American Educational History*. Boston: Houghton Mifflin, 1919.

———. *Public School Administration: A Statement of the Fundamental Principles Underlying the Organization and Administration of Public Education*. Boston: Houghton Mifflin, 1916.

Dennison, George. *The Lives of Children: The Story of the First Street School*. New York: Random House, 1969.

Epstein, Robert. *Teen 2.0: Saving Our Children and Families from the Torment of Adolescence*. Sanger, CA: Quill Driver Books, 2010.

———. *The Case Against Adolescence: Rediscovering the Adult in Every Teen*. Sanger, CA: Quill Driver Books/Word Dancer Press, 2007.

Farnish, Keith. *Underminers: A Guide to Subverting the Machine*. Gabriola Island, BC, Canada: New Society Publishers, 2013.

Freire, Paulo. *Pedagogy of the Oppressed*. New York: Herder & Herder, 1970.

Gatto, John Taylor. *Dumbing Us Down: The Hidden Curriculum of Compulsory Schooling*. Gabriola Island, BC, Canada: New Society Publishers, 2002.

———. *The Underground History of American Education: A Schoolteacher's Intimate Investigation into the Problem of Modern Schooling*. New York: Odysseus Group, 2000.

———. *Weapons of Mass Instruction: A Schoolteacher's Journey Through the Dark World of Compulsory Schooling*. Gabriola Island, BC, Canada: New Society Publishers, 2010.

Goodman, Paul. *Compulsory Mis-Education and the Community of Scholars*. New York: Random House, 1966.

———. *New Reformation: Notes of a Neolithic Conservative*. New York: Random House, 1970.

Gopnik, Alison. *The Philosophical Baby: What Children's Minds Tell Us About Truth, Love, and the Meaning of Life*. New York: Farrar, Straus and Giroux, 2009.

Gorbis, Marina. *The Nature of the Future: Dispatches from the Social-structed World*. New York: Free Press, 2013.

Graham, Patricia Albjerg. *Schooling America: How the Public Schools Meet the Nation's Changing Needs*. New York: Oxford University Press, 2005.

Graubard, Allen. *Free the Children: Radical Reform and the Free School Movement*. New York: Pantheon, 1972.

Gray, Peter. *Free to Learn: Why Unleashing the Instinct to Play Will Make Our Children Happier, More Self-Reliant, and Better Students for Life*. New York: Basic Books, 2013.

Greenberg, Daniel. *The Crisis in American Education: An Analysis and a Proposal*. Framingham, MA: Sudbury Valley School Press, 1970.

————. *Free at Last: The Sudbury Valley School*. Framingham, MA: Sudbury Valley School Press, 1995.

Greenberg, Daniel, Mimsy Sadofsky, and Jason Lempka. *The Pursuit of Happiness: The Lives of Sudbury Valley Alumni*. Framingham, MA: Sudbury Valley School Press, 2005.

Greenberg, Hanna, et al. *The Sudbury Valley Experience*. Framingham, MA: Sudbury Valley School Press, 1992.

Greene, Robert. *Mastery*. New York: Viking, 2012.

Harrington, Michael. *The Other America: Poverty in the United States*. New York: Macmillan, 1962.

Hecht, Yaacov. *Democratic Education: A Beginning of a Story*. Roslyn Heights, NY: Alternative Education Resource Organization, 2011.

Hern, Matt. *Field Day: Getting Society Out of School*. Vancouver: New Star Books, 2003.

Herndon, James. *How to Survive in Your Native Land*. New York: Simon & Schuster, 1971.

Holt, John. *Escape from Childhood: The Needs and Rights of Children*. New York: E. P. Dutton, 1974.

————. *How Children Fail*. New York: Pitman, 1964.

————. *How Children Learn*. New York: Pitman, 1967.

————. *Instead of Education: Ways to Help People Do Things Better*. New York: Dutton, 1976.

————. *Teach Your Own: A Hopeful Path for Education*. New York: Delacorte, 1981.

————. *The Underachieving School*. New York: Pitman, 1969.

Illich, Ivan. *Deschooling Society*. New York: Harper & Row, 1971.

Kaestle, Carl. *Pillars of the Republic: Common Schools and American Society, 1780–1860*. New York: Hill and Wang, 1983.

Kanigel, Robert. *The One Best Way: Frederick Winslow Taylor and the Enigma of Efficiency.* New York: Viking Penguin, 1997.

Katz, Michael. *Class, Bureaucracy, and Schools: The Illusion of Educational Change in America.* New York: Praeger, 1971.

———. *The Irony of Early School Reform: Educational Innovation in Mid-Nineteenth Century Massachusetts.* Cambridge, MA: Harvard University Press, 1968.

———. *In the Shadow of the Poorhouse: A Social History of Welfare in America.* New York: Basic Books, 1996.

Kett, Joseph. *Rites of Passage: Adolescence in America, 1790 to the Present.* New York: Basic Books, 1977.

Key, Ellen. *The Century of the Child.* New York: Putnam, 1909.

Klein, Naomi. *The Shock Doctrine: The Rise of Disaster Capitalism.* New York: Picador, 2008.

Kohn, Alfie. *Feel-Bad Education: And Other Contrarian Essays on Children and Schooling.* Boston: Beacon Press, 2011.

Kozol, Jonathan. *Free Schools.* Boston: Houghton Mifflin, 1972.

Krishnamurti, Jiddu. *Education and the Significance of Life.* New York: Harper & Row, 1953.

Labaree, David. *Someone Has to Fail: The Zero-Sum Game of Public Schooling.* Cambridge, MA: Harvard University Press, 2010.

Land, George, and Beth Jarman. *Breakpoint and Beyond: Mastering the Future Today.* New York: Harper Business, 1992.

Lasch, Christopher. *The World of Nations: Reflections on American History, Politics, and Culture.* New York: Knopf, 1973.

Mercogliano, Chris. *In Defense of Childhood: Protecting Kids' Inner Wildness.* Boston: Beacon Press, 2007.

Messerli, Jonathan. *Horace Mann: A Biography.* Knopf: New York, 1972.

Miller, Ron. *Free Schools, Free People: Education and Democracy After the 1960s.* Albany: State University of New York Press, 2002.

Montgomery, Zachariah. *Poison Drops in the Federal Senate: The School Question from a Parental and Non-Sectarian Stand-Point.* Washington, D.C.: Gibson Bros., 1885.

Neill, Alexander Sutherland. *Summerhill: A Radical Approach to Child Rearing.* New York: Hart Publishing, 1960.

Pope, Denise. *Doing School: How We Are Creating a Generation of Stressed-Out, Materialistic, and Miseducated Students.* New Haven, CT: Yale University Press, 2003.

Posner, Rick. *Lives of Passion, School of Hope: How One Public School*

Ignites a Lifelong Love of Learning. Boulder, CO: Sentient Publications, 2009.

Postman, Neil. *Technopoly: The Surrender of Culture to Technology*. New York: Vintage, 1993.

Postman, Neil, and Charles Weingartner. *Teaching as a Subversive Activity*. New York: Delacorte, 1969.

Priesnitz, Wendy. *Beyond School: Living as if School Doesn't Exist*. Toronto: Natural Life Books, 2012.

Ravitch, Diane. *Left Back: A Century of Failed School Reforms*. New York: Simon & Schuster, 2000.

———. *Reign of Error: The Hoax of the Privatization Movement and the Danger to America's Public Schools*. New York: Knopf, 2013.

Rogers, Carl. *Freedom to Learn*. Columbus, OH: Charles E. Merrill, 1969.

Silberman, Charles E. *Crisis in the Classroom: The Remaking of American Education*. New York: Random House, 1970.

Taylor, Frederick Winslow. *The Principles of Scientific Management*. New York: Harper & Brothers, 1911.

Tocqueville, Alexis de. *Democracy in America*. New York: Pratt, Woodford, 1848.

Tyack, David B. *The One Best System: A History of American Urban Education*. Cambridge, MA: Harvard University Press, 1974.

Violas, Paul. *The Training of the Urban Working Class: A History of Twentieth Century American Education*. Chicago: Rand McNally, 1978.

INDEX

ABOUT THE AUTHOR

Nikhil Goyal is a journalist. He has appeared on MSNBC and FOX and written for *The New York Times,* MSNBC, *The Nation,* and other publications. Goyal has also had speaking engagements with the Clinton Global Initiative University, Google, Stanford, Cambridge University, SXSW, and the LEGO Foundation, among others. In 2013, he was named to the *Forbes* 30 Under 30 list. He is also a recipient of the 2013 Freedom Flame Award. He lives in New York.